Easton /ccninformationstore
ccnlibraryblog.wordpress.com

Alan Tomlinson/Scott Fleming (eds.)

Ethics, Sport and Leisure
Crises and Critiques

Meyer & Meyer Sport

First published in 1995 by
CSRC
Chelsea School Research Centre
Chelsea School of Physical Education,
Sports Science, Dance and Leisure
University of Brighton
CSRC Topic Report 5
Ethics, Sport and Leisure: Crises and Critiques

British Library Cataloguing in Publication Data
A catalogue record for this book is available from the British Library

Ethics, Sport and Leisure :
Crises and Critiques / Alan Tomlinson/Scott Fleming (eds.).
2nd Ed. – Oxford : Meyer & Meyer (UK) Ltd., 2004
(Chelsea School Research Centre Edition ; Vol. 1)
ISBN 1-84126-060-6

© 1997 by Meyer & Meyer Sport (UK) Ltd.
Aachen, Adelaide, Auckland, Budapest, Graz, Johannesburg,
Miami, Olten (CH), Oxford, Singapore, Toronto
Member of the world
Sportpublishers' Association (WSPA)
Typesetting: Myrene L. McFee
Printed and bound in Germany by
Mennicken, Aachen
ISBN 1-84126-060-6
e-mail: verlag@m-m-sports.com
www.m-m-sports.com

Contents

Preface and Acknowledgements vii

Introduction
Ethics, Sport and Leisure: Prevalent Themes
Alan Tomlinson xi
Ethics and Sport: Some Reflections
Graham McFee xvii

I: **Ethical Issues and Ethics in Sport and Sports Practice**
Ethics, Deviance and Sports: A Critical Look at Crucial Issues
Jay Coakley 3
Running the Rule over Sport: A Sociologist's View of Ethics
Chas Critcher 25
Elite Sports Coaching in Practice: Ethical Reflections
— An Interview with Peter Keen
Alan Tomlinson and Scott Fleming 37
Value Foundations of Ethical Decisions in Children's Sport
Martin Lee 55
Ethics and Practice in Outdoor Adventure Education
Tony Westbury 79

II: **Ethical Issues in Research in Sports Science**
The Physiological Assessment of Athletes
J. Doust 95
Informed Consent? A Case Study from Environmental
Physiology
Graham McFee and Paul McNaught-Davis 111
Problems of Referral and Time in Applied Sport Psychology
Consultancy
Stephen J. Bull 127

III: Ethical Issues in Research in the Sociology of
Sport and Leisure 135

Qualitative Research Into Young People, Sport
and Schooling: The Ethics of Role-Conflict

Scott Fleming 137

Researching Sport and Sexual Harassment: The Ethics
of Covert Participant Observation and Open Methods

Ilkay Yorganci 151

Covert Ethnography and the Ethics of Research:
Studying Sports Subcultures

Belinda Wheaton 163

Private Parts: Ethical Issues in the Observation of Wrestlers

Roger Homan 173

Insider Dealing: Researching Your Own Private World

Ben Pink Dandelion 181

Questionnaires as Instruments of Intrusion

Pauline Cox 203

Field Workers Rush In (Where Theorists Fear to Tread):
The Perils of Ethnography

John Sugden 223

Flattery and Betrayal: Observations on Qualitative
and Oral Sources

Alan Tomlinson 245

Index 265

Preface and Acknowledgements

Thanks to:

—all the contributors for their cooperation and responses in the making of this volume;

—the former PCFC (Polytechnics and Colleges Funding Council) for research funding which primed the early stages of the production of the volume;

—the Faculty of Education, Sport and Leisure, The University of Brighton, for funding from its HEFCE (Higher Education Funding Council for England) research budget, which made possible Professor Robert Burgess' contribution to the Faculty's research seminar programme, and the later stages in the completion of this volume;

—Myrene McFee for her combination of literary and technological skills in the publication process;

—Dr Roger Homan, whose work, teaching and thinking on ethics and the research process has provoked and stimulated CSRC (Chelsea School Research Centre) researchers in many important ways in recent years;

—and to all those professional bodies which proffer such full but varying guidelines on principles of referencing and writing! Reflecting the multi-disciplinary pedigree of this volume, there is some variation across the contributions to the volume, in the minor detail of reference style and writing convention. But despite the social scientific, humanities and natural science backgrounds of the contributors, we have adopted a broadly consistent style throughout the book.

Professor Alan Tomlinson
Chelsea School Research Centre (CSRC)
September 1995

I am pleased to be able to write an extension to the above, a year on from the publication of this volume. The collection has been consistently in demand, and its re-issue is the third publication in the CSRC Editions launched by Meyer & Meyer in partnership with the Chelsea School Research Centre, The University of Brighton.

Professor Alan Tomlinson
CSRC
January 1997

INTRODUCTION

ETHICS, SPORT AND LEISURE — PREVALENT THEMES

Alan Tomlinson
University of Brighton

This volume originated in a sense of common interests around the theme of ethics in sport/leisure research, a sense transcending disciplinary boundaries. Discussion in Chelsea School Research Centre (CSRC) work-in-progress seminars has often focused upon issues of method and methodology in different research projects. The particular techniques chosen in different studies, and the justification for the choice of such techniques, has been a major emphasis in the multi-disciplinary research seminar programme. In particular, I recall an exchange between an interpretive sociologist and a sport psychologist, at one of the CSRC seminars, in which the ethnographic work of the sociologist was seen as ethically problematic (even dubious) from the point of view of the psychologist for whom codes of informed consent appeared to be pretty straightforward, yet who unambiguously and explicitly misinformed — or, at the least, under-informed — some subjects as to the precise nature of the projects in which they were becoming implicated.

Common interests — around ethical procedures, the ethics of research protocol, and the specifics of sport and leisure practices in generating ethical questions and issues — sparked some lively debate and reflection, and on the basis of this I proposed that CSRC members' work across the sport sciences and leisure studies be drawn upon in a volume dedicated to ethics, sport and leisure. This proposal met with enthusiastic support among colleagues, and original material for the collection began to be generated in the early Summer of 1993.

On looking more closely at the available sources it became even clearer that a reflective, multi-disciplinary (and in some appropriate cases, inter-disciplinary) volume of complementary articles would be a valuable contribution to the fields. Also, the specificity of social life and practice in which ethical issues loom large became increasingly clear. In the light of this, further contributions were sought on the wider question of the ethics of sport, and the ethics and values characteristic of sport at its different levels of operation, practice and participation.

On the basis of these guiding principles, the volume has been ordered into an introduction and three sections.

In his piece within the introductory section to the volume, Graham McFee identifies some core philosophical themes, pointing out that there is an "essential connection between sport itself and issues of the contravention of rules", also linked to "the possibility of harm to other persons". This core question is examined in various ways in the articles in Part One. McFee also cites two other "reasons for sport's raising ethical questions": moral issues around the spectating of sport; and, in the context of research into sport, the rights of subjects, and concerns about academic freedom and the public right to know. These latter two concerns pervade the methodologically reflective discussions in the contributions to Parts Two and Three.

In Part One Jay Coakley proposes that much of the crisis in contemporary sport derives from the overconformity of athletes and participants to the sport ethic. He proposes that athletes be encouraged to "question the normative structures of sports and sport organizations, and raise questions about *why* they are participating in sports and how participation is and should be related to the rest of their lives". Chas Critcher covers similar themes, summarising sociological approaches to deviance and also stressing that "the organisation of sport actually contributes to disorder, deviance and unethical behaviour by its emphasis on success, the ambiguity of its rules and its occasional institutionalisation of corruption".

In an interview with Olympic cycling consultant (and adviser to Chris Boardman) Peter Keen, Alan Tomlinson and Scott Fleming raise issues about practical ethics, and elicit from Keen the views that applied sports science is as intuitive as it is analytical; and that, at the end of the day, "you are left with little choice but to formulate your own set of ethical or moral tools with which to deal with ... problems".

Martin Lee reviews philosophical and social-psychological sources on ethics, fair play and the nature of values as expressed in children's participation in sport, before reporting from a data-base on young people's participation. His main argument is that "in order to understand better the nature of fair play and sportsmanship ... it is necessary to understand the value structure that sustains the participation of each individual".

In the final contribution to Part One, Tony Westbury applies some mainstream thinking on ethics to his own practice as a tutor in outdoor-education settings, and to situations typical of risk-sports in those settings, asserting that "confronting and resolving ethical issues is an everyday concern of the practitioner".

Part Two of the volume comprises commentaries upon ethical practice in sports science and applied sports science. J. Doust provides an overview of areas of ethical concern in the physiological assessment of athletes, observing that in an area of work which can be either laboratory or field-based, "the practice of science cannot be removed from the social context in which it is performed". Graham McFee and Paul McNaught Davis, in a case-study on the principle of informed consent in environmental physiology, show the complexity of the principle in its application in a real-life situation — so exemplifying Doust's general point.

Stephen J. Bull concentrates upon two issues — referral and time-allocation — in applied sport psychology consultancy. He cites codes of conduct of professional bodies, but recognises that whatever the nature of formal guidelines, it is important "that sport psychologists are able to adopt a flexible style.... This would seem to be particularly relevant for individuals acting as on-site consultants during competitions".

Part Three comprises contributions from social researchers and sociologists on the nature of the research process, the researcher-researched relationship, the role of the researcher (covert or overt?) in qualitative work, and the assumptions and moral principles underlying the use of particular research strategies and techniques. Most contributors are researchers working explicitly in the sociology of sport and leisure, though two articles have been included from researchers in the sociology of religion and the sociology of education.

Scott Fleming recalls some of the conflicts which he experienced in carrying out participant observation in a secondary school, concluding that "in many of the issues ... there are no 'rights' and 'wrongs', just realistic and pragmatic solutions". Ilkay Yorganci looks back at her multi-method study of sexual harassment in sport, identifying different sorts of ethical problems raised by the particular research technique employed. She also maintains that, whatever technique is employed, "where research reveals that the behaviour of some people has a deleterious effect on other people, then the researcher should be concerned for those being harmed and not for those perpetrating the harm". Belinda Wheaton, drawing upon her ethnographic work on windsurfing subculture, discusses ethical issues concerning the covert research role, and the complexities of the dual role of covert researcher and journalist. "In every situation", she concludes, "the researcher must find a compromise between purist ethics and pragmatic judgement, based on an awareness of how the 'real world' operates". Roger Homan's observation of wrestlers allows him to pose ethical questions concerning the principle of privacy. He recommends "the cultivation of a research *morality* in which the values are made explicit and the means of achieving them left to the researcher"; achievable, he argues, "by means of an educative code" rather "than through the implementation of regulatory codes".

Ben Pink Dandelion draws upon his research in the sociology of religion, in which the role of researcher was often in tension with his personal and professional identity as Quaker. He provides a typology of insider research and an account of his own problems of role-identity. Adhering to the view that informants have the right to be informed about the research that is going on into their lives, he nevertheless concludes that "the principle of informed consent ... is ethically problematic", and that "ethical systems based on principles are practically inappropriate to human society". Much of Pink Dandelion's discussion is relevant to the closed world of sport and leisure (sub)cultures. Pauline Cox, drawing upon examples from educational research and reaffirming her central points by critiquing studies in applied leisure studies, demonstrates the inherent intrusiveness — and slyness — of the approach to social research embodied in conventional questionnaires. She argues that there "must be trust and confidence between the professional researcher and the client; between the profession as a whole and the public", and shows that questionnaire-based research often fails to meet this ethical criterion.

John Sugden draws upon fieldwork experiences in the USA, Cuba and Belfast to demonstrate the physical as well as ethical perils that are involved in ethnographic work, in this case into boxing and its subculture(s). He also reminds us that "we need to develop empathy with our subjects without getting emotionally tied to them". Alan Tomlinson considers the generation, interpretation and use of qualitative — primarily oral — sources, rooting his discussion in examples from journalism, broadcasting, autobiography and oral history. "Pragmatism rather than purist ethics", he claims, should be "the guiding principle" in the use and interpretation of oral sources.

It is not claimed in this volume that all matters of an ethical kind in the world of sports practice, sports science and sport and leisure research have been raised and given due consideration. But too often ethical issues and their relationship to the pragmatics and realities of the fieldwork situation and the research process are given too little consideration, or given mere lip-service. One suspects, for instance, as a number of contributors also point out, that classic arguments for the benefits of informed consent for the subject are in actuality projected professional defences for the researcher should anything go wrong in the experimental situation. The themes raised in this volume are a reminder that ethically reflective work on and in the context of the sport ethic should be more honestly reflective than any tokenistic nod towards a rigid code of professional practice. Honest researchers — as well as practising elite and professional sportspersons — know the truth of this.

There are further ethical themes that could have been raised. For instance, the researcher-sponsor relationship is one with which many researchers in the field have difficulties or potential problems. What is the status of research when it is funded by, say, an industry or an agency with vested interests in a particular outcome or set of findings? Such questions have been raised very provocatively by Robert Burgess in a presentation on ethical issues arising from sponsored and contract research[1]. He argued that the researcher should always ensure that the contractor role is not reduced to that of mere technician; that the *research* agenda should be set by the researcher at the point of the research design; and that the academic research contractor (in his own case, CEDAR, the Centre for Educational Development and Research at the University of Warwick) should seek to retain ownership of the data generated by any contracted project. Burgess' arguments have great relevance to sport and leisure researchers working on projects funded by external clients. He stressed too the importance of partnership in the client-contractor relationship, and of forms of reporting and dissemination.

If such matters are not clarified in such a relationship, expectations and outcomes could well be disputed.

Only one of the contributions to this volume derives from funded research of a client-contractor kind; several others are based upon more independently-pitched forms of funding, such as personal research grants or post-graduate research awards. This balance is perhaps indicative of an openness and reflexivity within independent research which permits candid and frank consideration of ethical issues in sport and leisure and of the research dynamics and processes around sport and leisure. Much rhetoric is expressed about the crisis in contemporary sport and the morality — or a-morality — of contemporary leisure. This volume is conceived as a contribution to open debate about crises and critiques concerning ethics, sport and leisure, and how such areas are investigated, researched and understood.

Note

[1] Robert Burgess made this presentation at a Faculty of Education, Sport and Leisure Research Seminar at the University of Brighton on February 19 1993.

ETHICS AND SPORT: SOME REFLECTIONS

Graham McFee
University of Brighton

In their everyday lives, people regularly appraise the behaviour and attitudes of others from an ethical or moral point of view. For instance, they urge that Jones *should have* returned the wallet that he found in the road: that, in failing to do so, he acted *wrongly*. Or that Smith did *the right thing* in donating to famine relief. Again, we think that Williams would be a *better person* if she paid more attention to the feelings of others.

In contrast, philosophers writing about ethics have typically been puzzled about **the nature of ethical judgement** (how, if at all, does saying that one ought not to do action X, where this is a moral "ought", differ from saying that one ought not to do X for prudential reasons?); about **the bases of moral obligation**[1] (is the moral rightness of an action determined by the agent's intentions or by what he accomplishes?); about **the objectivity**, or otherwise, **of ethical judgements**[2] (can it be *true* that one ought to do X, or that doing Y is wrong?); and about **the possibility** of (validly) **drawing value-laden conclusions from descriptive premises**[3] (the is/ought or fact/value debate). These, sometimes called "meta-ethical issues", provide a background to standard ethical discussion. However such issues are ultimately resolved, it is clear that ethical questions — questions about what it is right or wrong to do, or what one ought or ought not to do, or about what actions are right or wrong — typically arise when humans interact: when they look towards or hope for respect from others, in virtue of a shared humanity.

It will follow, of course, that sporting situations will provide areas where ethical issues might well arise. Sport, though, is not *just* one such human practice among many; and for two (or three) reasons.

The **first reason** is that ethical questions arise naturally from sport itself, from the inherent characteristics of typical sports: sports are typically culturally-valued[4]; they typically have explicit rules (and therefore the contravention of those rules is possible); there is often the possibility of harm to participants (especially if rules are not followed); and the rhetoric of sport is replete with metaphors employed in general ethical discussion — the idea of 'fair play' or of 'a level playing field', for example. So that discussion of, say, the place of performance-enhancing drugs might turn on the issue of whether or not there was a centrally moral question here (or whether it is merely a medical one); but that too is an ethical discussion. Thus ethical issues arise, we might say, from the nature of sport. Of course, calling sport "ethical" in this fashion is recording that it is a suitable site for ethical investigation, not suggesting that it is always (or even typically) conducted ethically. The wags who, drawing on issues in professional/Premier League soccer in the UK in the 1994-95 season, suggested a 'Spot the Bungs' competition (from photographs of soccer managers with their hands out awaiting [possible] bribes) may be exaggerating; but they highlight (arguably) another moral scandal for sport.

Further, discussion of the ethical questions here is essentially (and not just accidentally) a discussion of sport itself. For ethical or moral questions are (*pace* Hume[5]) those where the specifics of the activity are most relevant. As Arthur Danto (1979) puts it:

> It is through their factual content and presuppositions that moral terms and propositions have some purchase on the world ... (p. 22)

> ... [S]uch morally charged terms as honesty, thrift, chastity, courage, obedience, and the like, require ...the elaboration of conditions that must be understood in purely factual terms. (p. 21)

Another way to make this point (or a related point) employs a contrast[6] between:

> ... two very different sorts of ethical concepts: abstract ethical concepts (Williams calls them "thin" ethical concepts), such as *good* and *right*, and more descriptive, less abstract concepts (Williams calls them "thick" ethical concepts), such as *cruel, pert, inconsiderate, chaste*.

So that employing, or even understanding, one of the "thick" ethical concepts requires that one be aware of the 'evaluative interests' with which that term is connected. And so studies of the "thick" ethical concepts used in respect of sport must look in detail at *sport*, to consider these 'evaluative interests'. For example, a discussion of the concept *fair play* might need to address any differences between, say, basketball (where there is the expectation of fouling) and sports where intentional fouls get the player sent off. No doubt there will be parallels with non-sporting concerns, but studying fair play *just is* investigating such sporting contexts. Then a study of ethical matters here will be centrally a study of sport — the philosophical issues will be ineliminably linked to sport.

Assuming that these ideas are roughly correct, they suggest that differences in the activities themselves (that is, differences in the "factual terms") will pose issues about the precise application of the (general) ideas to the specific activities: for instance, if we had a broad understanding of the notion of fairness, say, we might still ask what it amounted to for this or that sporting context[7].

One might even think, in some moods, that *moral* evaluation is somehow 'proper' to sport (viewed as action). Perhaps one only thinks this after reading some "athleticist" literature, emphasising the [supposed] moral benefits of participation in sport — for example:

> It was in the Public Schools during the second half of the [19th] century that two basic new theories were developed. The first was that competitive sport, and especially team games, had an ethical basis, and the second was that training in moral behaviour on the playing field was transferable to the world beyond. (McIntosh, 1979: p. 27)

As John Hargreaves (1986: p. 41) puts it:

> In the 1830s the notion of *'mens sana'* was almost unknown, but by 1860 it was everywhere.

And at the heart of that conception was the essentially moral or ethical base of sport — if true, such a view might partially explain sport's having an ethical character.

Our first reason for sport's raising ethical questions, therefore, has turned on the essential connection between sport itself and the issues of the contravention of rules, and of the possibility of harm to persons. The other two reasons can be dealt with more summarily.

For the spectating of sport (as a culturally-valued practice) might well inherit characteristics from sport itself; for instance, through a comparison of competition within the sport and partisanship in respect of teams. So that one might extend the essentially moral nature of sport onto the spectating of sport — our potential **second** way in which sports activities generate ethical questions. And even those who do not accept this line of argument will acknowledge that sporting events, as opportunities for inter-personal interaction on a largish scale, will be occasions for ethical issues to arise.

Finally, as a **third reason** for the engagement of the ethical, sport is increasingly a topic for research; and such research inevitably brings with it questions concerning the rights of subjects as well as the concerns of academic freedom, and of the public right to know (if any). So that one crucial set of concerns here — shared with other areas where humans might find themselves as subjects — are those relating to the ethics of experimentation.

In mapping this framework for ethical discussion, the thought has been both to identify, in an abstract way, the substantive issues of ethical concern and to mention briefly their meta-ethical presuppositions. A substantive study of the 'ethics of sport', as a variety of applied philosophy, requires clarity in the formulation of its problems and developed cases for analysis. These should come from the theory and practice of those engaged both in trying to understand sport and in trying to research it.

Notes

[1] In particular, the relative merits of consequentialist and deontological pictures: see, for example, Norman (1971), Ch 4; Danto (1989), pp. 67-75.

[2] See, for example, Bambrough (1979) Ch 2.

[3] See, for example, McNaughton (1988) p. 17.

[4] See the discussion of the culturally-valued status of sport in John Alderson and David Crutchley (1990) pp. 37-62.

[5] David Hume, the defender of the fact/value distinction. See his [1739] 1978 p. 469:

In every system of morality, which I have hitherto met with, I have always remark'd, that the author proceeds for some time in the ordinary way of reasoning, and establishes the being of God, or makes observations concerning human affairs; when of a sudden I am surpriz'd to find, that instead of the usual copulations of propositions, is, and is not, I meet with no proposition that is not connected with an ought, *or an* ought not. *This change is imperceptible; but is, however, of the last consequence. For as this* ought, *or* ought not, *expresses some new relation or affirmation, 'tis necessary that it should be observ'd and explain'd; and at the same time that reason should be given, for what seems altogether inconceivable, how this new relation can be a deduction from others, which are entirely different from it.*

For discussion, see Stroud (1977) pp. 186-188; especially note 7 [p. 265]. Also Hampshire (1989) pp. 88-93.

6   Putnam (1992) p. 86; and (in almost the same words) in Putnam (1990) p. 166: as Putnam notes, one of the first English-speaking philosophers to emphasise this difference was Iris Murdoch (1970), esp. pp. 41-42; and the citation is to Williams (1985) p. 140.

7   A contrast with philosophical aesthetics is revealing here for, as Arthur Danto (1993: p. 206) points out, a book in aesthetics:

... being philosophical, entails no stylistic agenda whatever.... [It] cannot and should not discriminate among artworks. Philosophy's task is to say something true ... of artworks as a class, however stylistically they may vary.

So, one might urge, while aesthetic discussions treat art works as examples, ethical discussions have a more direct purchase on substantial practical detail: in that sense, such discussions in respect of sport are generated by a distinctiveness of sport.

References

Alderson, J. and Crutchley, D. (1990) 'Physical education and the National Curriculum', in Neil Armstrong (ed) *New directions in Physical Education Vol 1.* Rawdon: Human Kinetics Publishers, pp. 37-62.

Bambrough, R. (1979) *Moral scepticism and moral knowledge.* London: Routledge.

Danto, A. (1972) *Mysticism and morality.* Harmondsworth: Penguin.

———— (1989) *Connections to the world.* New York: Harper & Row.

———— (1993) 'Responses and replies', in Mark Rollins (ed) *Danto and his critics.* Oxford: Blackwell, pp. 193-216.

Hampshire, S. (1989) *Innocence and experience.* Harmondsworth: Penguin.

Hargreaves, J. (1986) *Sport, power and culture.* Cambridge: Polity Press.

Hume, D. [1739] (1978) *A treatise of human nature* [1739]. Oxford: Oxford University Press.

McIntosh, P. (1979) *Fair play: Ethics in sport and education.* London: Heinemann.

McNaughton, D. (1988) *Moral vision.* Oxford: Blackwell.

Murdoch, I. (1970) *The sovereignty of good.* London: Routledge, Kegan Paul.

Norman, R. (1971) *Reasons for actions.* Oxford: Blackwell.

Putnam, H. (1990) *Realism with a human face.* Cambridge, Mass: Harvard University Press.

Putnam, H. (1992) *Renewing philosophy.* Cambridge, Mass: Harvard University Press.

Stroud, B. (1985) *Hume.* London: Routledge & Kegan Paul, 1977

Williams, B. (1985) *Ethics and the limits of philosophy.* London: Fontana.

I:

ETHICAL ISSUES AND ETHICS
IN SPORT AND SPORTS PRACTICE

ETHICS, DEVIANCE AND SPORTS: A CRITICAL LOOK AT CRUCIAL ISSUES[1]

Jay Coakley
University of Colorado at Colorado Springs, USA

Introduction

This paper was written after listening to journalists, policy makers, and other connected with sports and sport organizations as they express extreme disappointment about what they see as the erosion of values and the decline of ethics in contemporary sports. In the eyes of these men, today's sports lack the moral and ethical purity that characterized sports in times past, and today's athletes lack the moral character possessed by athletes in times past[2]. These men recount stories of a time when sports, as they remember them to be, were governed by a commitment to sportsmanship, and athletes played purely for love of the game. And as they recount these stories, they grieve what they see as the loss of this ethical purity and commitment to fair play.

As they grieve, these men often use their power and influence in an effort to recover the past. Usually, this involves calling for more rules and regulations in sports, for tougher policing of athletes, for more agents of social control, more testing, more surveillance, stricter sanctions — anything that will rid sports of the "bad apples" who are spoiling things for everyone.

Of course, the assumption often underlying the analyses made by these men is that "sport" has an essential nature that is somehow above or separate from the realities of social and cultural life. Furthermore, their analyses conveniently overlook the fact that sports in the past were characterized by systematic racism, sexism, and the use of class to exclude from participation those who did not come from privileged backgrounds. Also overlooked is that dominant sports in the past often depended on an economic system in which the labor of the less privileged was used to supply leisure time and the "proper" clothing and equipment used by gentleman and a few lady athletes. But for a variety of reasons, they do not see these as ethically problematic when they reminisce about the past.

This general "loss of values and ethics" analysis put forward by some people connected with sports also have counterparts in segments of the academic literature where ethical problems and deviance in sports are explained by using a range of models including the following:

- The *defective personality model* in which deviance and ethical problems are attributed to faulty socialization or defective characters among athletes unable to constrain their own behaviour or assess its consequences for others.

- The *basic behaviourist model* in which all the behaviour of athletes, especially deviant or unethical behaviour, is attributed to the pursuit of individual self-interest in the form of external rewards.

- The *money-and-TV-have-corrupted-sport-and-athletes model* in which deviance among athletes and other ethical problems are seen as products of television coverage and "excessive" material rewards now available in certain sports.

- The *oppression and exploitation model* in which athletes are cast as naive victims of management and team owners, and the deviance and unethical behaviour of those athletes is attributed to powerlessness and processes of victimization.

- The *moral fundamentalism (or "just say no") model* in which ultra conforming behaviour is held up as the ethical ideal for all athletes to emulate, and any digression from this ideal is identified as a form of deviance.

The purpose of this paper is twofold: first, I will offer an explanation for why so many people are concerned with ethics, deviance, and what they perceive as an erosion of values in sports today. Second, I will make the case that understanding the ethical problems and many forms of deviance in sports requires a critical analysis of the normative structures of the sport organizations and sport cultures that serve as the context for the behaviour of athletes, coaches, and others involved in sports.

Why are ethics and deviance in sports such hot topics today?

As I respond to this question my point is *not* to argue that ethical issues and deviance in sports today are not deserving of serious attention. Instead, I want to highlight the major reasons why concerns about ethics and deviance seem to dominate the thinking of so many people who comment on the contemporary sport scene. In general, there are 5 factors that have led ethics and deviance in sports to be especially popular topics today:

(1) *Since the mid-1970s heavily publicized accounts of deviance and ethical problems in sports have panicked those believing that "sport" is inherently pure and that participation in sport automatically builds character.*

People who hold these "essentialist" views of sport have seldom recognized that what they think of as "sport" has never been free of deviance or ethical problems, and that the development of "character" has never been an automatic outcome of sport participation. Now that their unquestioned beliefs have been challenged by highly publicized media accounts of deviance in sports, they've panicked. These people are disappointed that their expectations for athletes to serve as models for what they think the world *should be like* have not been met. And their disappointment and occasional panic are both factors that fuel contemporary concerns about ethics and deviance in sports.

In light of this fact there is a need to be cautious about expecting athletes to be models for every child who has ever kicked a football or run around a track. This is not to say that athletes in any country should be judged by a watered down set of standards, but condemning the character of every athlete who fails to reaffirm the naive belief that sport is inherently pure and character building is misdirected.

(2) *Sports are more rigidly organized than they have ever been in the past; sports and sport organizations today have more rules, and there are more ways to break rules than ever before.*

The perception that there are more ethical problems and cases of deviance in sports today has been fuelled by the fact that sports are more formally organized and rule centered than they've ever been. There are simply more rules governing athlete behaviour and more ways for today's athletes to violate rules than in the past. In fact, rule books in many sport organizations are often 100s of pages long! In the face of this dramatic increase in formal rules, rule violations are bound to be more frequent today than in the past, regardless of the so-called "character" of athletes.

The implications of this increase in rules have been illustrated a number of times as I've observed world class amateur athletes who train and compete at the United States Olympic Training Center (USOTC) in Colorado Springs. I live in Colorado Springs and, occasionally, small groups of athletes stay in my home when the USOTC is short of housing for special events. Many of the conversations of these athletes revolve around the myriad of rules and regulations that set the conditions of their participation. Many of the athletes are exceptionally fearful they will inadvertently fail to conform to the rules of their coaches, of their events, of their federations, of the USOC, of the IOC, or of the other organizations that regulate their sport lives. These athletes don't even eat food in my home unless they are reassured that the things they ingest won't show up as banned substances on a drug test; they read ingredients labels closely! They're overwhelmed by all the rules they're expected to follow and, not surprisingly, rule violations are relatively common.

Therefore, policy makers in sports should be careful to limit the proliferation of rules controlling the lives of athletes, especially their lives off the field. And they also need to involve athletes in rule making and rule enforcement processes. Unless care is taken to limit the proliferation of rules, every athlete will need to retain personal paralegal assistants in order to be eligible to compete.

(3) *The behaviour of athletes is more heavily monitored, scrutinized, and publicized than ever before.*

This point can be illustrated by using a quote from an article written by an editor for *Sports Illustrated* after he interviewed a sport reporter who wrote for a major newspaper in the 1920s and 1930s:

> It is 1928 and the baseball writers covering the NY Yankees (baseball team) on this rail trip are sitting in the train's club car, playing nickel-ante poker. Suddenly the door to the club car bursts open and Babe Ruth sprints down the aisle, followed closely by an attractive young woman wielding a knife. "I'll kill you, you son of a bitch!" the woman screams as she disappears after Ruth into the next car.
>
> The writers observe the action, then turn and look at each other. "That'd make a helluva story," one of them says. The others chuckle and nod, and the poker game resumes.
>
> Of course, no one reported the incident.... (Telander, 1984)

This process of hero building, quite common in the media coverage of sports and athletes in the past, had a significant effect on how people perceived athletes and issues related to ethics in sports. Questions about whether ethical problems or deviance was getting out of control, or whether the moral foundation of sports was being eroded away, were seldom asked. But today things are different. Relationships between athletes and reporters have changed, the media are more efficient and invasive now, and they put a greater premium on entertainment than they did in the past. These changes have not only led to the "discovery" of deviance and violations of ethical standards in the lives of athletes (and other public figures as well), but to forms of disclosure that emphasize the spectacular. These disclosures have certainly affected popular perceptions of ethics and deviance in sports and perceptions of the moral character of today's athletes. This is not to say that athletes today are without fault, but I'm not so sure they're much different than many of their counterparts from the past. The important sociological issue to consider is how deviance is defined, who defines and applies those definitions, and whose interests are served in the process; similar consideration need to be given to ethics.

Furthermore, media people should be more careful about invading and disclosing information about the private lives of athletes. As one respected sportswriter in the United States has recommended, a journalist should never hurt anyone unintentionally; when someone is hurt, it should be done intentionally, and for good reasons (Koppett, 1981). Without good reasons, the disclosures are simply cheap, self-serving, forms of sensationalism that accomplish nothing related to the social good or the promotion of ethical behaviour.

(4) *Today's athletes come from more diversified racial, ethnic, and class backgrounds than athletes in times past.*

When any amount of racism or class-based antagonism co-exists with a situation where members of low income or minority groups are athletes and where privileged non-minority people make, interpret, and enforce the rules of sports, report and publicize rule violations, and hold all the major positions of power within sports, there are bound to be differences in definitions and perceptions of rules and rule violations. These differences are likely to increase as athletes from minority and less privileged class backgrounds enter sports in greater numbers.

The growth of racial, ethnic, and class diversity within any sphere of life often leads to new expressions of concern over ethics, values, and deviance. And, usually, those concerns are voiced by people who have strong vested interests in the past rather than those new to the scene who focus on the present and future. Unfortunately, those who look to the past often forget that "the good ole days" were characterized by systematic exclusion of minority participation. This exclusion subverted any notion of ethics or "fair play" in sports of times past; however, those who have overly romantic memories of the past do not see it that way. Ignorance may remain blissful for people remembering the "good ole days," but past systems of exclusion based on race, ethnicity, gender, and class were clearly pervasive forms of deviance that raise questions about memories of the ethical purity of sports in days gone by.

The matter of equal access to participation at all levels of sports must be addressed if one is concerned about ethics. Too often, sport organizations have a place for minorities only to the extent that minorities can do the work of winning contests and medals. But when the involvement of minorities goes no further than this, and there are no concerted attempts to develop supportive and nurturing environments for minorities at management levels, sport becomes a modern day plantation system. Ethical problems grounded in racism do exist in sports today, and people in sport organizations spend too much time and energy denying them rather than facing them head on and doing something about them in the form of assertive fairness and equity programs.

(5) *In today's sports there are more "non-athletes" with financial and political stakes in sports than ever before.*

The commercial and political value of sports is closely tied to popular acceptance of myths about the ethical purity and character molding nature of "sport". People who want to make money, build reputations, or establish corporate or nationalist positions of power and privilege can capitalize on these myths. It's not only easier to market and sell an activity defined as "clean and wholesome" by the general public, but being associated with such an activity can be very valuable. This is why sponsors pay large fees to connect themselves with selected sports, and why they are often concerned with issues of ethics and the control of deviance in sports and among the athletes who endorse their products or ideologies. The power of these sponsors has frequently been used to promote this concern about ethics to the point that it has become a highly visible issue today.

Caution is needed before letting marketing issues masquerade as concerns about "ethics." Keeping something clean to make it easier to sell is okay, but when the issues of fairness, equal access to participation, and human rights take a back seat to marketing, then ethical concerns become closely akin to pandering for capitalist interests.

After listing the five factors fuelling contemporary concerns about ethics and deviance in sports, a qualification is in order: highlighting these factors does not mean that we should ignore ethical issues and forms of deviance in sports today. However, I think it is important to keep our concerns in perspective so we can avoid an "epidemic mentality" when assessing what is occurring in sports. There *are* problems in contemporary sports, and we need to carefully determine how serious they are, and why they exist.

Data on deviance in sports and among athletes

When discussing ethical issues and deviance in sports today it is important that we consider the following questions:

- Are there proportionately more ethical problems and cases of deviance associated with sports today than there were in the past?

- Are rule violations in sports today getting out of control to the point that they are eroding the moral foundations of sports?

- What are the origins of ethical problems and forms of deviance in sports, and are they related to the character of the people in sports or to factors related how sports are organized and how they are connected to social forces and conditions?

From what we've read, heard and seen in recent media reports, there seems to be a nearly unending list of rule violations in sports, especially among those from less privileged and minority backgrounds. However, simply listing cases of player misconduct is not very helpful when trying to get a sense of ethical problems and current rates of deviance, and a sense of whether those problems and rates have increased over time. At present, I've come across no study reporting that cheating, dirty play, shaving points, or any form of deviance in sport, except the use of performance-enhancing drugs, is more common today than it was in the past. Some historical reviews even make a strong case that there is less deviance and fewer ethical problems today, and provide convincing data showing that the behaviour of athletes in recent years is more "civilized" and rule governed than athlete behaviour in the past (Elias and Dunning, 1986; Guttmann, 1978, 1986; Maguire, 1986). Of course, these data do not make it so, but they give reason to be cautious when talking about the so-called erosion of values in today's sports.

Cases of off-the-field deviance among athletes and other sport participants now receive widespread public attention. When athletes are arrested, involved in fights, caught using "street drugs," or linked to shady business deals, it makes headlines. But there has been little systematic research on how athletes, coaches and others connected with sports behave off the field, and how their behaviours compare with behaviours of people from comparable backgrounds who are not involved in sports. Without such research it is difficult to talk about the so-called erosion of values in sports today.

There are a few studies on delinquency and sport participation among high school students, mostly in the United States. These studies generally have serious methodological weaknesses, but their findings generally contradict attention-grabbing headlines about athletes: high school athletes in varsity sports have never been found to have higher rates of delinquency than their counterparts who don't participate in varsity sports. Of course, students with histories of deviant behaviour don't often participate in adult organized and controlled sports, and coaches may cut them when they try out or protect them when they get into trouble, but until we know more about rates of off-the-field behaviour among athletes compared to their counterparts outside sports, we can't draw any definite conclusions.

So, at this point, research doesn't answer many of our questions about the extent of ethical problems and deviance in today's sports. However, ethical problems and forms of deviant behaviours do exist, and it is important to understand the contexts in which they emerge. This brings me to the second topic of this paper.

Ethics and deviance in social context: behaviour and the normative structure of sports

Unethical or deviant behaviour in sports, as in any sphere of social life, is related to multiple factors, but I will focus on three that I think are especially crucial to consider, partly due to their importance and partly due to the fact that other analyses have generally ignored them. These factors are:

(1) *Athletes at many levels of participation, especially elite levels, have less control over the conditions of their sport participation than in the past.*

Whenever people lose control over the conditions of their own participation in an activity, they are less likely to conform to formal rules or traditional informal expectations for their behaviour. When people actually participate in the creation and control of their own activities, they are much more likely to be sensitive to ethical issues, to respect formal rules, and to be committed to following informal expectations that emerge in their interactions with fellow participants. After all, when participants create their own activities, the rules are their own. This is true for athletes as well as the rest of us.

Today's athletes might be wealthier and more popular than athletes in times past, but in many sports, especially those in which people think rates of ethical problems and deviance are highest, athletes have very little control over the conditions of their sport participation. Control often rests in the hands of team owners, federation directors, coaches and managers, corporate sponsors, advertisers, media personnel, marketing and publicity staff, accountants, and agents. This absence of control among athletes not only leads them to give less attention to the formal rules of the game, but it separates them from their opponents to such an extent that social order during games and matches comes to be seen as something enforced by outsiders rather than an outgrowth of a spirit, or an "ethic" if you will, maintained for the sake of fellow participants or the contest itself.

This decline of the spirit underlying the social order of sports and sport events may account for some ethical problems and forms of deviance during training and competition. But, these are not grounded in athletes' lack of character; instead, they are at least partially grounded in the fact that athletes have so little control over the conditions of their own participation in sport.

For example, in my own research on youth sports I've found that when children participate in organized, adult controlled games, they think little about issues of fairness. They simply assume that fairness will be guaranteed by the referees. Their goal as players is to determine how referees will interpret and apply the rules in a contest. In their minds, the control of the contest is out of their hands, so they don't feel they must attend to issues of fair play. This certainly opens the door for certain ethical problems and forms of deviance, especially as players get older and the stakes associated with participation get higher.

My point here is that when athletes lose control over the conditions of their own participation in sport, and have nothing to say about rules, rules are perceived as constraints rather than the guidelines needed for an organized activity to exist. When this happens, the negotiation underpinning the formation of ethical sensitivities is missing and rules are less likely to be followed voluntarily.

Dealing with this source of ethical problems and deviance in sports requires critical restructuring of power relations in sports and sport organizations. Athletes must become more involved in the process of dealing with issues of rules and rule enforcement in their sports, as well as dealing with other matters that affect their sport lives. Doing this is a challenge since the tide seems to be going the other way. Some people have suggested that athletes may need some kind of "responsibility training" to clean up sports. This may be true, but research clearly tells us that people don't become responsible moral actors without being empowered to make choices and to take action on the basis of their choices. However, in most sport settings athletes seem to have fewer and fewer opportunities to make choices and take action related to the conditions of their participation. Effectively dealing with deviance requires a reversal of this trend.

(2) *More than ever before, the rewards associated with sport participation are dependent on athletes' abilities to entertain mass audiences — large portions of which do not have much knowledge about the technical skills and strategies used in the sports they watch.*

Whenever sports are converted into forms of commercial entertainment, success depends on entertaining masses of people who lack detailed technical knowledge about the skills of athletes and the strategies used during contests. This generally shapes the orientations of athletes, coaches and others in sports, as well as those who report sports in print and electronic media. When the goal is entertaining a naive audience there is a tendency to emphasize what might be called the "heroic" dimensions of sport participation. This means that as the need to entertain naive audiences increases, so does an emphasis on the following:

- the danger and excitement of movement;
- "style" and the mastery of dramatic expression;
- a willingness to exceed personal physical limits; and
- a commitment to seek success in terms defined by commercial sponsors.

This change encourages athletes to be responsive to issues important to spectators and sponsors. Although they do not ignore issues important to fellow sport participants, this change may dull the sense of "give and take" between competitors that is at the foundation of social order in sports. To the extent that this occurs, athletes may even become cynical about their own sport participation. Such cynicism would further subvert a commitment to following rules and increase concerns with how to boost one's heroic appeal to spectators.

In the face of such a prospect there needs to be more attention paid to the impact of commercial marketing and media "hype" on what spectators expect and what athletes provide in sport events. Instead of developing "hype" into an art form, attention should be devoted to controlling physical danger in sport. Turning athletes into gladiators may make money, but it doesn't foster a commitment to following formal and informal rules on or off the field of play. Athletes need to be encouraged to avoid exceeding the limits of their endurance, and spectators should be given opportunities to learn about the subtle dimensions of skills and strategies that would give them something other than "blood and guts" to hold their interest in an event.

I am being careful not to say that money and commercialization by them-selves are the roots of all ethical problems in sport. But it seems clear that a shifting relative emphasis on heroic values in many spectator sports does encourage some forms of athlete behaviour that differ, at least in frequency, from the behaviours of athletes in times past. My third point will address the dynamics and group processes through which heroic actions may take deviant forms and lead to ethical problems.

(3) *Athletes are systematically encouraged to over-conform to a unique set of norms embodied in what might be called a "sport ethic"; therefore, certain deviant behaviours among athletes are grounded in an unquestioned acceptance of what it means to be an athlete within the normative structure of many sports.*

It is seldom recognized that many ethical problems and forms of deviance in sports are not due to athletes denying or rejecting social values or norms. Instead, they are due to athletes accepting and committing themselves without question or reservation to the normative guidelines that constitute what might be called the "ethic" of many sport cultures today (and some sport cultures from the past — a topic for another paper).

What I will refer to as the "sport ethic" refers to what many people in dominant sports have come to use as the collective criteria for defining what it means to be an athlete, to be recognized as an athlete, and to actually take on the identity of *athlete*. In my work with athletes and coaches, four normative guidelines seem to frame this sport ethic (for empirical support for the existence of the sport ethic and its consequences for deviance among athletes, see Curry, 1993; Ewald and Jiobu, 1985; Hilliard and Hilliard, 1990; Johns, 1992; Wasielewski, 1991). These are the following:

(a) *Being an athlete involves making sacrifices for "the game".*
The idea underlying this normative guideline of the sport ethic is that "true athletes" must love "the game," above all else, and prove it by subordinating other interests for the sake of an exclusive commitment to their sport. To prove their dedication and have their identity as an athlete socially reaffirmed, participants must have the proper attitude, make a deep commitment to involvement, meet the demands of fellow athletes, and make personal sacrifices to stay involved (Donnelly and Young, 1988). In this sense, being an athlete means that a person will consistently do what is necessary to meet the demands of a team, or the demands of competition. This is the spirit underlying the notion that athletes must makes sacrifices, that they must be willing to "pay the price" to stay involved in sport. Pep talks and locker room slogans are full of references to this normative guideline.

(b) *Being an athlete involves striving for distinction.*

The Olympic motto of *"Citius, altius, fortius"* (swifter, higher, stronger) captures the meaning of this normative guideline of the sport ethic. In other words, "true athletes" seek to improve, to get better, to always strive to come closer to perfection. Winning symbolizes improvement and establishes distinction; losing is tolerated to the extent that it's part of the experience of learning how to win. Breaking records is the ultimate standard of achievement among "true athletes" since they are a special group dedicated to climbing the pyramid, reaching for the top, pushing limits, excelling, and exceeding or dominating others. It is worth noting here that many sport scientists have intervened in sports in ways that certainly reinforce this guideline and promote over-conformity to it; the often unquestioned application of new performance-enhancing technologies is widely accepted in the process of striving for distinction (Hoberman, 1992).

(c) *Being an athlete involves accepting risks and playing through pain.* According to this normative guideline of the sport ethic, a "true athlete" does not give in to pressure, pain, or fear. Many sport activities pose inherent risks of injury, but voluntarily accepting the possibility of injury is a sign of courage and dedication in dominant sport cultures (among both men and women athletes). Moral courage is also encompassed by this guideline. This is reflected in golf and tennis, for example, where success is linked to the ability to sustain physical performance under extreme psychological pressure. The idea is that someone who is a "true athlete" never backs down from a challenge, that standing up to a challenge involves moral courage and, in many sports, a willingness to take physical risks as well. Thus, being accepted by other athletes as an athlete demands that a person willingly confronts and overcomes the fear and the challenge of competition, and accepts the increasing risk of failure, pain, and injury. And if an athlete's willingness to over-conform to this aspect of the sport ethic wanes, some sport scientists will help them play past and through risks, pain, and fears.

(d) *Being an athlete involves refusing to accept limits in the pursuit of possibilities.*

In line with the normative guidelines of the sport ethic, "true athletes" (along with their coaches and managers) stress the openness of possibilities for achievement in sports, and the imperative to wholeheartedly pursue them. They promote the idea that an athlete doesn't accept a situation without trying to change it, to overcome it, to turn the scales. It is believed that sport is a sphere of life in which anything is possible, *if* a person lives the sport ethic. Those recognized within sport cultures as athletes are obligated to pursue dreams without reservation. External limits are not recognized as valid. In other words, "true athletes" are obliged to believe in *the attempt to achieve success*. And when perceived limits impede achievement, there are many sport scientists (too many?) who will provide pep talks, therapy, or technology to alter those perceptions.

Now back to the major point: how is the sport ethic related to deviance and the perception of ethical problems in sports? When people talk about deviance, they usually assume it involves a rejection of norms, or allegiance to different norms than those accepted by the majority of people in a culture. So deviance is seen as negative, and is morally condemned and punished. But what I'm suggesting here is that significant forms of deviance among athletes do *not* involve a rejection of norms, or conformity to a set of norms not endorsed in the rest of society. Instead, much deviance in sports occurs when athletes care too much for, accept too completely, and over-conform to what has become the basic value system in many sports and sport groups across a wide range of participation levels. If athletes never question that value system grounded in the sport ethic, even though the sport ethic consists of what most people would consider to be positive values, problems of deviance are likely. This is especially true for high performance athletes, although it's certainly not limited to them.

A new look at ethical issues and deviance in sports

This analysis puts ethical issues and deviance in sports in a sociological light: on the one hand, some athletes are indeed scorned (by people in and out of sport) for their sometimes bizarre behaviours as they over-conform to the sport ethic; but, on the other hand, many of the behaviours eliciting this scorn are different only in degree, *not in kind*, from behaviours positively valued in the rest of society and in sport as a whole. This creates problems for those concerned with deviance in sports, especially if they do not understand that the most dangerous forms of deviance in many sports actually involve extreme over-conformity among athletes rather than a rejection of norms. Drafting new rules and enforcing them more closely will only exacerbate problems when much deviance involves over-conformity and unquestioned acceptance of norms in the first place.

We now have a situation in which a portion of the deviance and the ethical problems in sports is actually grounded in the way athletes use the normative guidelines of the sport ethic to assess and evaluate their own behaviours and the behaviours of fellow sport participants. For example, in the United States, my colleague Bob Hughes and I have found many "serious" athletes who zealously pursue and over-conform to the ideals of the sport ethic to such an extent that their sport participation is disruptive to everything from their family relationships and work responsibilities, to their physical health and personal comfort (Hughes and Coakley, 1991). Other people sometimes perceive these athletes as "different" or "weird" but the actual behaviours of the athletes clearly reflect commonly held values. In fact, I have found similar forms of over-conformity and unqualified acceptance of the norms constituting the sport ethic time and time again in my interviews, conversations, and experiences with elite athletes.

There are two reasons why deviance grounded in over-conformity to the sport ethic occurs so frequently in sports. First, athletes find their experiences in sport so exhilarating and thrilling that they want to continue participating as long as possible. And second, the likelihood of being chosen or sponsored for continued participation is increased if athletes over-conform to the sport ethic. These athletes realize that most coaches praise and use as role models those who over-conform; furthermore, coaches often accuse athletes of lacking "hustle" and "effort," of not "caring" enough. And what better way for athletes to prove their own hustle, effort, and caring than through over-conformity to and unquestioned acceptance of the sport ethic?

This is how over-conformity to the sport ethic comes to pervade, if not actually define, the sport experience in many sport groups and for many athletes. This is the case even when over-conformity causes them trauma and pain, disrupts important relationships in their lives, interferes with other responsibilities and roles, jeopardizes physical health, or even shortens life itself. Bob Hughes and I have identified these forms of behaviour as "positive deviance," not because of their consequences, but because of their origins in an over-acceptance of norms rather than a rejection of norms (Hughes and Coakley, 1991).

It is important to note that athletes themselves seldom define their over-conformity to the sport ethic as deviant or ethically problematic; they see it as confirming and reconfirming their identities as "athletes" and as members of select sport groups (in terms of the way "athlete" has been socially constructed in those groups). Following the guidelines of the sport ethic to an extreme degree is simply what you do as a "true athlete," especially when continued participation and success in sports take on significant personal and social meaning.

Of course, not all athletes are equally likely to engage in over-conformity to the normative guidelines of the sport ethic. In fact, Bob Hughes and I (1991) have hypothesized that forms of "positive deviance" in sports would be most common among:

(1) those athletes who have doubts about self worth, and who, for other reasons, are vulnerable to group demands and less able to withstand pressures to sacrifice themselves for the group;

(2) those athletes who for some reason see their sport as an exclusive mobility route in their lives, and for whom mobility goals are so strong that they are willing to make great personal sacrifices in the process of striving for achievement.

In other words, athletes whose identities or future chances for material success are exclusively tied to sports are most likely to engage in deviance grounded in over-conformity to the sport ethic.

It would also be expected that over-conformity to the sport ethic would be more characteristic among men than women since men are more likely to use sport as an exclusive identity and/or mobility source, among low income minority athletes in revenue producing sports (for similar reasons), and among those whose relationships with significant others have been based exclusively on continued involvement and success in sport. However, neither women nor men from privileged backgrounds would be exempt from pressures to engage in deviance grounded in over-conformity to the sport ethic.

What we might refer to as the "corruption of sport" at least partially involves a process by which ethical guidelines and self-imposed restraints on behaviour give way to encouragement to engage in potentially self-destructive behaviours in an effort to demonstrate worthiness for continued group membership and status within a specific sport group. Therefore, it is the athlete's vulnerability to group demands, combined with the desire to gain or reaffirm group membership through over-conforming to these demands, that is a critical factor in the incidence of positive deviance.

Along these lines, it has been suggested that one of the "qualities" of "great" coaches is their ability to create environments that keep athletes in a perpetual state of adolescence. This leads athletes to continually strive to confirm their identities and eliminate self-doubts by engaging in behaviours that please their coaches and teammate-peers. When this dependency-based commitment occurs, over-conformity to the sport ethic becomes increasingly common, and many young people become willing to sacrifice their bodies and play with reckless abandon in the pursuit of affirmation and approval as "true athletes." Coaches often encourage this, intentionally or naively; after all, it helps to win games and matches and enhance their reputations as "great motivators."

Collective commitment to the sport ethic, especially under conditions of extreme stress, also tends to create special bonds between athletes. These bonds not only reaffirm their *unqualified acceptance of and commitment to* the sport ethic on a day to day basis, but they also create special feelings of fraternity, especially in groups of athletes in the same sports. These special feelings separate athletes from other people when it comes to what athletes see as a "true" understanding of the sport experience. Most athletes think that "outsiders" really do not know what it is like to be a "true athlete." When this sense of separateness and uniqueness is combined with the fact that athletes are often held in awe by "outsiders" (who are, by definition, naive), athletes feel and exhibit hubris, a sense of superiority combined with a disdain for those "normal" members of the community who live their lives without sacrificing for a team, seeking distinction, taking risks, or pushing limits.

The consequences of this hubris, especially when it is exhibited in a disdain for "non-athletes," has not been studied. However, I think it leads some athletes to assume they're somehow beyond the law, and that people outside "the athletic fraternity" don't deserve their respect. Another possibility is that this disdain can become such a part of an athlete's view of the non-sport world that it may even be turned inward and transformed into self-disdain when athletes fail to over-conform to the guidelines of the sport ethic in their own behaviour, or when they must retire from active participation in their elite sport. This is why some elite athletes try so hard to extend their playing careers, and why they may even mourn the passing of those careers. Losing membership in the special and elite athletic fraternity presents difficulties in itself, but the threat of entering the disdained category of "non-athlete" or "outsider" is especially upsetting to those who have regularly over-conformed to the norms of the sport ethic. Becoming separated from those few others who truly understand what it means to be an athlete can be a frightening experience, especially for those whose identities and feelings of significance and superiority are exclusively tied to sport.

This is probably why some athletes decide to have knee surgery after knee surgery so they can play for "just one more year." This is also why others inject unbelievable amounts of hormones into their bodies on a regular basis without even thinking twice. The motivation is *not* just to win, or to make money, or to please a TV audience; more importantly, *it is simply to play, to be a "true athlete," and to maintain their identity and membership in a special and elite athletic fraternity.*

This type of deviance creates unique social control problems in sports, and unique ethical dilemmas. Owners, managers, sponsors, and coaches — all of whom are agents of social control in sports — often benefit when athletes over-accept and over-conform to the sport ethic. Having athletes who over-zealously live their lives over-conforming to and accepting without question the ideals framed by the ethic is seen by most of these people as a blessing. The fact that athletes have learned to use over-conformity to the sport ethic as a gauge of personal commitment and "courage" for themselves and fellow athletes works to the advantage of those concerned with victories or entertainment. The issue of social control is even further complicated by the tendency to promote extreme over-conformers into positions of power and influence in sport — after all, they've already proven they're willing to "pay the price" and to live the sport ethic in an unqualified way; they often become coaches!

So athletes often get strong encouragement to over-conform to the guidelines of the sport ethic. This means that a powerful source of deviance among athletes is the normative structure of sport itself, at least in the way sport has been socially constructed in many situations. Furthermore, these forms of deviance are encouraged through athletes' relationships with one another and with their coaches and managers. Paradoxically, the "sport ethic," when taken to an extreme and accepted without question, actually promotes forms of deviance that corrupt the foundation of social order in sports. And dealing with this paradox is the biggest challenge facing those concerned with ethics and deviance in sports today.

For example, I've found that this over-conformity model is the only explanation of deviance in sport that helps me understand why athletes use performance enhancing substances, especially the potentially dangerous ones. The use of these substances is not the result of defective characters among athletes, or the existence of too many material rewards in sports, or television coverage, or exploitation by coaches and managers, or moral weaknesses among athletes (see the models listed in the opening section of this paper). After all, users are often the most dedicated and committed people in sports! Instead, I would argue that most substance use and abuse is clearly tied to an over-commitment to the sport ethic itself; it is grounded in over-conformity — the same type of over-conformity that leads injured distance runners to continue training even when training may cause serious physical problems, and American football players to risk their bodies through excessively violent physical contact week after painful week in the NFL, and figure skaters to risk leg injuries by doing triple after triple after quadruple jumps in their quests for "perfection" (despite the Nancy Kerrigan incident, figure skaters destroy their knees, ankles, and feet on the ice, voluntarily; and this is much more of a danger than being clubbed after training!).

Conclusion

This paper grew out of my opposition to those whose explanations of ethical problems and deviance in sports are based on models that lead to sweeping condemnations of the character and moral worth of athletes, that blame money and television coverage for behaviour that does not measure up to their standards, that attribute deviance to the systematic oppression and exploitation of all athletes, or that use absolute conformity to norms as the measure of ideal behaviour in sports. My purpose in the paper has been to argue that there are a number of factors, apart from the lack of ethics and problematic forms of deviance, that have led many people, especially those with essentialist conceptions of sport and sport participation, to perceive and become concerned with the "moral state of sports" today. Since their concerns often lead to calls for more rules, more surveillance, and more rigid systems of social control over athletes, who already face more rules, more surveillance, and more rigid controls than ever before, my goal has been to highlight an approach to understanding deviance that recognizes social context and social relations as factors influencing behaviour in sports. Those who simply condemn athletes and argue that a quest for victory or the existence of human greed causes deviance in sports are creating a partial smokescreen subverting potentially successful efforts to deal with some serious problems.

My purpose has not been to argue that deviance in sports does not exist or should be ignored, or that its frequency and origins have not changed over the years. Nor has it been to argue that ethical problems are absent in today's sports. Instead it has been to call attention to the fact that many athletes who clearly realize they will never win championships, or make money from their athletic accomplishments, still engage in forms of deviance including violence and the use of performance-enhancing substances. This is not to say that a desire to win or make money is irrelevant to athletes; both are important parts of the overall context in which many forms of deviance and many ethical problems occur. But my argument is that many of the ethical problems and the cases of deviance among athletes today clearly rests in the social organization and normative structure of sports and sport cultures themselves, including the very values embodied in what I have described as "the sport ethic."

To the extent that ethical problems and deviance in sports is grounded in an unquestioned acceptance of and over-conformity to the norms of the sport ethic, effective behavioural controls require the development of processes through which athletes and others in sports critically question the normative structures of sports and sport organizations, and raise questions about *why* they are participating in sports and how participation is and should be related to the rest of their lives. As in other settings, recognized limits on commitment and conformity must be made more explicit in sports so that athletes who engage in over-conforming deviance will not be defined as heroes and models for the society as a whole by people in sports or by people who cover sports for the media.

Questioning and qualifying the sport ethic also needs to be combined with processes of creating new norms related to the use of "sport science" and technology in sports. This is not a unique challenge; it is faced in many spheres of social life, although the widespread uncritical acceptance of the sport ethic does pose problems in sports. But unless critical self-reflection occurs within sports and among athletes themselves, deviance grounded in over-conformity will continue to occur. Only when athletes and coaches themselves develop new guidelines that strike a balance between acceptance and critical reflection will over-conformity to the sport ethic be discouraged. Hopefully, those guidelines will also create concerns about health and development as well as performance and competitive outcomes.

As it is now, we face a future without clearly defined ideas about the meaning of achievement in sports, especially elite competitive sports. Meanings have been blurred by changes in the rewards for participation, by the new importance of participation in the lives of many young athletes, and by the availability of new performance-enhancing technologies, including drugs and soon to be available genetic manipulation (Hoberman, 1992). We need new guidelines rather than simply trying to "get back to basics" or returning to "the values of the past." We are facing new issues today, and they call for new responses, new processes, and new forms of critical self-reflection and empowerment.

Notes

[1] This paper is a revised and updated version of a paper presented at a National Conference on Ethics and Sport, Leeds, England (February, 1991). The latter section of the paper draws on material in Hughes and Coakley (1991) and Coakley (1994); a similar version of this paper is included in the readings used for the M.Sc degree program at the University of Leicester.

[2] My use of 'men' in this opening section is intentional. Although some women may make a similar case, I have never heard it.

References

Coakley, J. (1994) *Sport in society: Issues and controversies.* St. Louis: Mosby.

Curry, T. J. (1993) 'A little pain never hurt anyone: Athletic career socialization and the normalization of sports injury', *Symbolic Interaction* 16(3), pp. 273–290.

Donnelly, P. and K. Young (1988) 'The construction and confirmation of identity in sport subcultures', *Sociology of Sport Journal* 5(3), pp. 223–240.

Elias, N. and E. Dunning (1986) *Quest for excitement.* New York: Basil Blackwell.

Ewald, K. and R. M. Jiobu (1985) 'Explaining positive deviance: Becker's model and the case of runners and bodybuilders', *Sociology of Sport Journal* 2(2), pp. 144–156.

Guttmann, A. (1978) *From ritual to record: The nature of modern sports.* New York: Columbia University Press.

Guttmann, A. (1986) *Sport spectators.* New York: Columbia University Press.

Hilliard, D. and J. M. Hilliard (1990) 'Positive deviance and participant sport', paper presented at the meetings of The Association for the Study of Play, Las Vegas, April.

Hoberman, J. (1992) *Mortal engines: The science of performance and the dehumanization of sports.* New York: The Free Press.

Hughes, R. H. and J. Coakley (1991) 'Positive deviance among athletes: The implications of overconformity to the sport ethic', *Sociology of Sport Journal* 8(4), pp. 307–325.

Johns, D. (1992) 'Starving for gold: A case study in overconformity in high performance sport'. Paper presented at the meetings of the North American Society for the Sociology of Sport, Toledo, November.

Koppett, L. (1991) *Sports illusion, sports reality.* Boston: Houghton Mifflin Co.

Maguire, J. (1986) 'The emergence of football spectating as a social problem, 1880–1985: a figurational perspective', *Sociology of Sport Journal* 3(3), pp. 217–244.

Telander, R. (1984) 'The written word: Player-press relationships in American sports', *Sociology of Sport Journal* 1(1), pp. 3–14.

Theberge, N. (1993) 'Injury, pain and "playing rough" in women's ice hockey'. Paper presented at the meetings of the North American Society for the Sociology of Sport, Ottawa, November.

Wasielewski, P. L. (1991) 'Not quite normal, but not really deviant: Some notes on the comparison of elite athletes and women political activists', *Deviant Behaviour: An Interdisciplinary Journal* 12, pp. 81–95.

RUNNING THE RULE OVER SPORT: A SOCIOLOGIST'S VIEW OF ETHICS [1]

Chas Critcher
Sheffield Hallam University

Introduction: sociology, deviance and sport

This paper will consider the potential contribution of sociology to analysing and responding to the state of ethics in sport. In principle, such a contribution should be substantial, since *the basic concern of sociology is with the maintenance of order in any society or human activity.* The classic question of sociology is: 'How does society work?': how is it that all these individuals pursuing their own private interests does not lead to chaos and anarchy? The answer, for the sociologist, can never be simple as 'It's human nature'; indeed, you could make the opposite argument, that human beings are inherently selfish. The social order can and does break down into civil war, as has been seen in Lebanon, Northern Ireland or the former Yugoslavia.

The same question can in principle be asked of sport: 'How is order most effectively attained?'. Thus sociology ought to have much to say to those concerned with ethical or unethical behaviour in sport. Unfortunately such efforts are frequently undermined by the jargon-ridden and abstract philosophising to which sociologists are prone.

Nevertheless there is much of use which can be salvaged. In particular, sociology has produced voluminous work on the topic of deviant behaviour. The approach of the sociologist is different from that of the psychologist. The psychologist tries to answer the question: 'Why is this person deviant?'. Consequently, s/he will explain deviance primarily in terms of the individual: personality factors, such as aggression or the need to win at all costs, or situational factors, such as the models of conduct they are offered by those closest to them. The sociologist, while not denying the existence of such factors, asks and tries to answer a different question: 'How is the occurrence of deviance related to the way society is organised?'. In the case of sport, that question becomes: *'What is the relationship between deviance in sport and the way sport is organised?'*.

The question is clear-cut but the answers given by sociologists rarely are. But they can still be pirated for some potentially constructive ideas about why and how ethical codes of conduct are or are not implemented in sport. However, 'ethics' is not a term sociologists use. They prefer, for good reasons, to talk about rules, norms and values.

Now these considerations must affect our understanding of what deviance is. For *it is not enough to say that deviance is any conduct which breaks the rules.* This is only one of the levels at which deviance can take place. We can in principle have:

- deviance from the rules, clearly observable (in principle at least);

- deviance from the norms, behaviour which is not expressly forbidden by the rules but which breaches established expectations;

- deviance from values, in which the whole purpose of the activity is denied.

Thus, there are at the very least different kinds of deviance (though as we shall see, the whole definition of deviance is itself problematic). This time let's take a sporting example. I've taken cricket, though you can choose your own. The following different kinds of deviance can be applied to cricket:

- a no-ball is deviance from the rules;

- short-pitched bowling is a deviance from the norms (despite attempts to outlaw it);

- spurious appealing is deviance from the values of cricket, since it attempts to intimidate umpires and invalidates the whole point of the game to win by outappealing rather than outplaying the opposition.

It can be seen how a sociological approach can illuminate problems of deviance and conformity — or, to put it another way, ethical and unethical behaviour in sport. The sociologist will insist that cheating and fair play are two sides of the same coin. If we can explain why someone breaks the rules, breaches the norms or denies the values, this may help to explain why others do not.

- *Rules* are simply the laws of any group, frequently written down.

- *Norms* are a much looser set of expectations about how people ought to behave: they are prescriptions which stop short of being formal rules.

- *Values* are the key moral principles on which rules and norms are based.

This last may be the nearest term to ethics but there are good reasons why sociologists make this three-fold distinction. It enables us to understand different kinds and levels of normal and abnormal behaviour.

Before exploring that further, I want to make one qualification, one distinction and one observation.

The *qualification* is that, in society and in sport, deviance occurs more often than the authorities ever notice. It is as mistaken to believe that sports people constantly obey the rules as it is to believe that citizens habitually obey the law.

The *distinction* is that between different kinds of deviant behaviour: *instrumental behaviour*, designed to achieve a tangible end; and *expressive behaviour* which gives vent to the actor's feelings. Both may be defined as deviant but are different in their intent and thus in their cause and potential remedy.

The *observation* is that, in society and in sport, the male of the species is more prone to deviant behaviour than the female. There may be as many explanations of that fact as there are readers of this piece but I shall suggest later that gender identity is an important factor influencing conformity and deviance, ethical and unethical behaviour in sport.

In what follows, I consider the relationship between deviance in sport and the way sport is organised by looking first at three propositions about deviance in sport, derived from major schools of sociological theory about deviance in general. Then I shall examine the way sociologists think about how people are persuaded to behave conventionally, to see if sport somehow fails to inculcate ethics as effectively as it might.

Three propositions about factors affecting deviance in sport

The intention here is to offer some specific examples of the ways in which sociologists have argued that the organisation of any human activity can provoke or even encourage deviance. (Each of these comes from a particular school of sociological thought but this will be of marginal interest here, since we are concerned with their practical implications rather than their philosophical integrity.) An example of the occurrence of each proposition will be given for contemporary sport. The possible remedial action will be outlined and its viability assessed.

Proposition 1   (Overemphasis on success) (Functionalism)

Deviance is likely to occur where there is an imbalance between the ends or rewards of an activity and the means of achieving them.

This most often occurs where there is a disproportionate emphasis on success, so that any viable means, legitimate or not, may be used to achieve it.

Examples: The deliberate breaking of rules in order to gain an advantage over an opponent (e.g. physical blocking of an opponent, use of performance-enhancing drugs, attempts to demoralise opponents etc.).

Remedies: Restoring the importance of means at the expense of ends through more rigorous rule enforcement but equally de-emphasising success as the main or only reward.

Comment: In many ways, this states the obvious since it appears to say no more than that there is too much emphasis on winning in sport. What is important however is that this is not merely a matter of changing attitudes. The very structure of sport which distributes prestige and money according to the level of competitive perform-ance seems bound to increase the probability that deviant means will be used to achieve success.

Proposition 2   (Labelling Theory)

Deviant acts of one kind or another are committed all the time but only some are identified or labelled as such.

In society and sport, whether an act is recognised as deviant often depends upon the perceived motive.

Some individuals become labelled as habitually deviant and are more likely to have their actions treated as such; conversely, some individuals of high status are less likely to be labelled as deviant even when their actions invite it.

Examples: Most sports' rules distinguish between accidental and deliberate foul play but referees and umpires are left to make quite fine judgements (e.g. jostling in track races, seeking to gain an advantage from an offside position, a tackle intentional in its violence, time wasting, ungentlemanly conduct).

Sport is also beset by the problem that there are individuals of such high status that the authorities are unable or unwilling to take action against them, a problem particularly acute in professional tennis and, increasingly, in motor racing.

Remedies: The intention of an act must be deduced from its actual or likely outcome.

Umpires and referees must operate a consistent set of criteria in making such judgements.

No individual should be seen to be above the rules.

Comment: Again, a familiar idea, put in a slightly different way. In whatever sports we play or watch, the need for more consistency amongst umpires and referees will be a familiar lament. But we must recognise how much this is built into sport. In particular, rule structures which must always allow for some discretion are often vague where they need to be precise about how to identify a deviant act, which category it comes into and what is the appropriate penalty. In society and in sport, badly drafted laws may trap the innocent and fail to trap the guilty.

Consideration of those who appear to be above the law brings us to the third proposition.

Proposition 3   (Radical Criminology)

It is possible for a whole area of human activity or for an organised group to become institutionally corrupt, committed to the systematic breaking of rules.

The key factor here is that those who ought to be upholding the laws are themselves colluding in deviant behaviour (e.g. in society, the police).

Example: The most obvious is that of the use of drugs and other dubious methods inherent in the 'old' East European athletics system. However, it is arguable that the management of soccer teams at all levels shows signs of such institutionalised corruption.

It is also possible for several agencies to collude in condoning deviance. Inaction against deviant behaviour amongst male professional tennis players often results from the desire of sponsors and television to keep in the tournament players whose deviant behaviour draws the crowds. Thus all are implicated in this moral corruption, underwritten by commercial considerations. (The same may be true of motor racing.)

Remedy: The detection and punishment of those responsible for deviant strategies. This is of course especially difficult where they are represented at the top level of the sport.

Comment: It may be that such institutionalised corruption can only be rooted out by blanket bans or even by abandoning those sports where corruption is endemic (e.g. power field events).

When taken together, the three propositions so far outlined suggest that *the way sport is organised invites high levels of deviant behaviour.*

The sociologist would not be too surprised to find high levels of deviance and hence concern about ethics in any activity where there is:

* an excessive emphasis on success;

* an ambiguity of rules;

* a corruption of some management.

It is, I have suggested, the distinctive contribution of sociology to identify how deviance can be seen as a matter of organisation as much as attitude or personality. I can add a fourth proposition, to explain what I earlier defined as expressive deviance. This might explain why the nature of sport as exploring *the limits of psychological as well as physical endurance should have a tendency to produce states of extreme tension which find outlets in verbal and physical aggression towards opponents and officials.* While in part a function of particular personalities, such acts are again inherent in the way we design and experience our sports. It is less easy to identify how those involved can be encouraged to keep a sense of proportion.

However, measures of control are only part of the equation. For conventional or ethical behaviour to be upheld, it must be learned and reinforced, so that fear of punishment is not the main incentive to behave 'properly'. Sociologists have examined these processes too.

Propping up the social order

Ask any sociologist to explain in brief what enables social order and you are likely to get a variation on three themes: socialisation, social control and ritual.

Socialisation is but a posh word for the process of moral learning. The rules governing human interaction are established for the new member in a process which is very complex, as any harassed parent will attest. It is not simply a question of crime and punishment: example is as important as edict, reward as important as punishment, internal acceptance as important as external enforcement.

Highly structured activities, like schooling or sport, may place much emphasis on formal rules but can only work if children have been adequately socialised in the first place. Only the armed forces and prisons can seek to ensure order through sheer force (and then, as prison riots show, not always effectively). Thus a key question is how young people are socialised into sport. If they understand only about winning, then the rules are likely to be regarded as an obstacle to their success. I'm not suggesting that this is the case. Most people are not wholly conformist or wholly deviant but rather an inconsistent mixture of the two. Nevertheless we do eventually get the sports people we deserve: we, after all, have brought them up.

Social control is the means by which deviant behaviour is discouraged. A range of sanctions are involved, from the withdrawal of approval through shame and stigma to incarceration. It is often and mistakenly thought that physical punishment is the most effective immediate form of control but in fact forms of social ostracism are much more effective. The ability to shame deviants is the first line of defence of a community, punishment following only when the sense of shame is incommensurate with the magnitude of the deed. It is here that sport is weak: it tends to leave deviance lightly admonished or move quickly into coercive social control. What is absent is a sense of shame: either you got away with it or you didn't. That you ought to be ashamed of having got away with it, is not how sports people at all levels think about ethics or morals. This is one of the few areas where the media can perform sport a service. By recording those instances where someone got away with it and by attempting to mobilise a sense of outrage, the media can sometimes do something other than ignore or punish deviance — they can *shame* it. Sometimes authorities will issue pronouncements on developments they disapprove of, or charge someone with bringing the game into disrepute, yet generally the sense of shame is absent.

The balance between and the nature of socialisation and social control is thus crucial. Each of these complements the other. It's no good bringing up children with a sense of right and wrong if they then perceive that the righteous are not rewarded on this earth and the sinful go unpunished. It's no good (as our penal system demonstrates) seeking to inculcate morals by manipulating rewards and punishments if the seeds of moral behaviour were never planted in the first place; nor is it any good appealing to a common sense of values if those values are not continually reaffirmed on those occasions when the community seeks to express its own identity. This brings us to the third element in the maintenance of social order: all societies, and organisations within it, depend upon ritual reinforcement of the social order.

Rituals are ceremonial recognition of the common symbols and interests of the group.

The symbols involved include national flags, royal families, uniforms and anthems. They are displayed in such ritual occasions as weddings, openings of parliament, state visits, even criminal trials. They give a sense of the sacred to otherwise secular activities. For rules to be seen as genuinely collective, they have to be embodied in symbolic behaviour: the judge in wig and gown, the priest before the cross, the national flag and emblem, the umpire in distinctive clothing — these express the communality of the ideals behind the rules.

Sport is apparently strong on such rituals, as embodied in the Cup Final or the opening and closing ceremonies of the Olympic Games. Unfortunately what follows is often profane rather than sacred. Nevertheless, there is strong argument for extending the prevalence of ritual, for it expresses a general commitment to the social order which helps those involved to recognise their common participation in a wider set of interests than theirs alone.

Conclusion: of morals, men and manifold discontents

Thus far I have dealt with two contradictory tendencies in sport. In the first, I suggested ways in which the organisation of sport actually contributes to disorder, deviance and unethical behaviour by its emphasis on success, the ambiguity of its rules and its occasional institutionalisation of corruption. In the second, I indicated the ways in which sport can or could be organised to ensure high levels of conformity or ethical behaviour through mechanisms of socialisation, social control and ritual.

In these closing remarks, I want to address some of the complexities of sport which make understanding these contradictory tendencies quite difficult.

The first is that we are all hypocrites, at least men in sport are. There is part of me which doesn't actually care if the football team I support wins by a goal which is palpably offside or the opposing batsman is given out caught behind when he never touched it. I can of course rationalise this attitude by suggesting that it will all even itself out in the end: the other team will score a dubious goal, I will be the victim of a bad umpiring decision. But I shall then be outraged and appeal to a sense of justice conveniently suspended when the decision went in my favour. I don't think that this is an unusual attitude. We have to recognise that sport brings out the worst as well as the best in us. All we can do is to recognise it, try to feel ashamed and remind ourselves of what sport is supposed to be about.

The ideal at least is clear: to enable all to compete at their own level under conditions of formal equality. And yet there is a problem. In order for this sporting ideal to be realised, there has to be a collective commitment to something above and beyond the activity itself, to its rules but also its spirit: what some define as ethics but what could equally and perhaps more accurately be caught by calling it *the ethos of sport*.

That is what I take to be at stake when we appeal to 'the spirit of the game'. We do not just mean adherence to the rules. For what we are often objecting to as a violation of the spirit of the game may not be expressly forbidden by the rules ('It's not cricket'). What we object to is a violation of the code we believe should govern the game. The term ethics really does seem to me too narrow and unsubtle to encompass such a set of expectations which govern not only behaviour but attitude; not only what we do but how we see the whole activity.

Earlier I made a distinction between rules, norms and values. What I am now suggesting is that it is not enough, though it may be an essential starting point, to ensure mere compliance with the rules. Order cannot rest on fear of punishment alone. It must also involve commitment to what the game stands for. We cannot, in life or in sport, return to Victorian values — which in any case were often not what they have since been cracked up to be. What we have to find are values appropriate to our time, not the largely mythical past.

There are no easy answers here. How do we construct a code of behaviour which encompasses rules, norms and values? We obviously have to look very hard at all the areas I've indicated:

— the emphasis on winning;

— the ambiguity of rules;

— the corruption of management;

— the mechanisms of socialisation, social control and ritual.

Questions

There are also some sports and sports people who have retained some notion of code which we need to understand and exploit. To do this we need to examine four areas.

a.   Differences between the sexes

Q. *Why are women, in sport and in society, more conventional than men?*

A. For me, there is no biological answer to this. The reasons are social, to do with female socialisation. This may suggest that the problem we have is one of misplaced masculinity, in which 'being a man' has come to mean deviating from the rules when your sense of male self is at stake. Look not only at the behaviours exhibited by men but also at the solutions offered by women.

b. Differences between sports

Q. *How do some sports retain a strong sense of order, such as golf or the martial arts?*

A. Significantly, both of these are kinds of sport which are strong on ritual, sometimes mistakenly called etiquette. The emphasis on winning is contained within a sense of the wider meaning of the game.

c. Differences between levels of the same sport

Q. *Why is it that some sports which experience problems at the highest level are orderly at more humble levels, such as tennis?*

A. One answer would be that for the average player neither their identity nor their income depends upon sport. Perhaps the reward structure of professional sport should be examined. If it is not the winning but the taking part which is important, why should winners get all the money and the glory?

d. Differences between kinds of deviance

Q. *Why do some sports suffer from 'instrumental' behaviour (e.g. violence) but are able to contain 'expressive' behaviour (e.g. dissent), the sport in mind here being both rugby codes?*

A. In some ways this is the hardest question, potential answers to which may lie in the combination of penalties for dissent and attitudes towards authority.

I would argue, though I can in no way prove this to be so, that answering these questions does support some aspects of the sociological case. That is so, because the kinds of answers I have given refer precisely to the elements I have argued to be central to the sociological approach: socialisation, social control and ritual, rule and reward structures. In the way we organise such elements of our sports lie some basic explanations of ethical and unethical behaviour, conformity and deviance, order in sport and its threatened disintegration.

Note

1   This chapter is based upon an oral presentation to a National Conference on Ethics and Sport, Leeds, England (February, 1991).

ELITE SPORTS COACHING IN PRACTICE: ETHICAL REFLECTIONS — AN INTERVIEW WITH PETER KEEN*

Alan Tomlinson
University of Brighton

Scott Fleming
Cardiff Institute of Higher Education

* *At the time of the interview, conducted 21st September, 1993, all participants — Peter Keen [P.K.], Alan Tomlinson [A.T.] and Scott Fleming [S.F.] — were members of the Chelsea School Research Centre. Scott Fleming has since moved to the Cardiff Institute of Higher Education.*

A.T. *Peter, throughout your coaching experience have you had any grounding in or discussion about the question of ethics?*

P.K. The simple answer is no as a coach, but yes as a Sports Scientist. There is little attention given to discussions of ethics in the training and education of coaches. I know BISC (British Institute of Sports Coaches) worked on producing an ethical code for coaches, but it is not widely circulated.

A.T. *Are you a member of BISC?*

P.K. No. It no longer exists as a separate organisation. It is now a division of the National Coaching Foundation (NCF).

A.T. *Are you a member of any professional coaching association?*

P.K. The British Cycle Coaching Scheme, and the British Association for Sport and Exercise Sciences (BASES). I think it is worth pointing out that I am perhaps not a typical coach — more of a sports science technician. I don't coach large groups of cyclists or sports people; I work with a small number of individuals competing at the highest level in sport.

A.T.   *So you are not the kind of coach who looks out for young talent?*

P.K.   I have not had a great deal of experience of coaching young or developing athletes. I am very aware of some of the issues that concern coaching across all age groups but principally from a physiologist's point of view rather than that of the practitioner.

A.T.   *Were you tempted to join BISC?*

P.K.   No. I am a bit embarrassed by this because I was awarded 'Coach of the Year' by BISC and I wasn't a member. But I think this reflects how little of my time I actually spend in what I perceive as a straight coaching role. I see coaching as just one part of my work in exercise physiology and sports science. It is the best way of checking the real practical value of a lot of the work done in these fields. You have to face down-to-earth issues and test the practical value of research findings in coaching.

A.T.   *You describe yourself as a technician. Are you saying that your coaching practice is a matter of applied science?*

P.K.   Only one aspect of it is, but it is the one that people seem to want to focus on. Journalists always try to get stories out of me about this area of my work; they like to portray my coaching as scientific. I constantly make the point to them that very little of what I actually do in coaching is based upon scientific evidence. I have used scientific knowledge, where it is appropriate, to address issues I face as a coach, but virtually all coaching is still entirely pragmatic — based on personal experience and in the case of myself some background knowledge of science. But coaching is not a science — far from it.

S.F.   *What is the angle journalists have used when they have approached you wanting to find out about your work?*

P.K.   They seem to start with an initial perception of me — a white-coated scientist, and want to build an image around that. Chris Boardman (a leading professional cyclist I have coached for some time) has been nicknamed 'RoboChris', presumably because he is perceived as taking a very mechanistic approach to his sport.

Journalists seem attracted to this very clinical view — that sports scientists or coaches who have a science background are just focused on what it is about an athlete's body that is going to make it go faster; that they do not see the whole person. I constantly fight against this when I talk to the press, but usually end up having confusing discussions about the definition and nature of science. Most journalists appear to think that all my work is scientific, and that I must therefore be the polar opposite of a "humanistic" coach.

It seems you must be labelled as one or the other at the moment. If you are a scientist your approach is utterly clinical; everything is measured and quantified — there is no place for the human. You are preparing a machine for competition. At the other extreme is the romanticised view of the old style coach or athlete — a person who just acts on feel and emotion. This is exactly how the clashes between Chris Boardman and the Scot Graham Obree have been portrayed by the media. Obree is shown as a romantic who built his own bike out of a washing machine and trains in a haphazard fashion. He is reputed to be anti sports science and yet, in my opinion, his training methods and particularly his bicycle designs are the products of classic deductive science. He has looked at available data, he has an open-minded view of things and rejects a lot of the mythology surrounding the sport of cycling, and has refined a way of propelling himself on a bicycle which is very fast.

A.T.   *So Obree is portrayed as a rugged romantic individualist?*

P.K.   Oh yes. But this need to categorise people concerns me. I think it is potentially dangerous to allow people to continually portray me and perhaps other people from my background as clinical scientific practitioners because the reality of human performance in sport is that there is a vast amount of information that we do not have and do not understand. Even what definitely fatigues somebody in the events that I coach remains poorly understood, let alone what can ultimately limit somebody's performance on a day be it emotional or physical. Actually coaching somebody on a day-to-day, month-to-month basis is far from scientific in the way I would define science.

A.T.   *That is really quite important. The French term "RoboChris" implies a relationship between coach and athlete which is little more than a scientific experiment. This raises a number of ethical issues we may return to later.*

S.F.   *Where do you place yourself on the continuum between the extremes you describe — the clinical scientist and the romantic humanist? If there was a scale of 1 to 9, with 9 being the scientist where would you place yourself?*

P.K.   I would like to place myself right in the middle because I think both perspectives have very important things to contribute to developing human performance. If I think about coaching the cycling team for the Barcelona Olympics, one of the most important things we as a team did was to sit with our sports psychologist in the hotel learning to talk to each other — practising what we had learnt in terms of how to communicate our feelings and thoughts to each other in a way that was constructive and not inflammatory. I had a team of individuals who appeared willing to kill each other at times because of the day-to-day disputes that occur in the weeks before a major competition. I am pretty certain that the techniques we were taught and used were not scientific, and the individual helping us is far from a scientist. Yet I firmly believe that the psychologists assistance made the difference between the fourth the team achieved, and not even qualifying for the quarter finals.

S.F.   *It would be interesting to discuss the ethics of such interventions in people's lifestyles. How much of that goes on? And how much of it is directly sport-related?*

P.K.   The further you go up the performance ladder the more critical everything becomes. If you are simply not getting on with somebody in a team you have to deal with that, and if that means digging fairly deep into where you are coming from, then that is necessary. Our team psychologist was a qualified pyschotherapist and the techniques he often used with us were derived from classic therapeutic methods. They were very effective, particularly when we were under severe pressure.

A.T.   *Have you hit a point ever where you think "I'm going too far here, I'm intervening in areas which really are too private"?*

P.K.   I think you always walk that line at high levels of performance in sport. The reality of sport as I understand it is that so many things could make the difference between gold and failure that you are forever trying to find the factor that is impeding progress. It could be the training programme or diet, but it could equally be somebody's general lifestyle, the relationship with their wife or girlfriend. You are forever trying to work out where you draw the line and whether it is worth it or not, for the individual, to initiate a discussion about a particular concern.

A.T.   *Have you ever had one of your performers say 'you have gone too far'? Or 'I can't go that far with you'?*

P.K.   No it is actually the reverse. I have been with individuals who want to do things that I am not comfortable with and I have had to withdraw from the working relationship.

A.T.   *Can you give us an example of that?*

P.K.   Yes. I worked with an individual who decided to explore the possibility of using a physiological intervention known to improve performance which, although undetectable, is banned by the International Olympic Committee (IOC), and is thought to be potentially very hazardous if not performed correctly.

A.T.   *How did you learn about this?*

P.K.   It was discussed.

A.T.   *With the subject?*

P.K.   Yes.

A.T.   *Openly discussed?*

P.K.   Oh yes. I was aware of what was going on. Over a period of time I had to work out where I stood on it, was I prepared to assist in this, or should I pull out. It was a fine line.

S.F.   *You sound as though you are silently condoning it?*

P.K.   It was not a simple situation. This particular individual was a professional athlete, sport was his living and I didn't have sufficient influence to affect many of the decisions made. I continued for some time to advise the person because I felt my limited influence might be a positive one in terms of providing balanced information about the risks. This athlete appeared to have a "win at all costs" philosophy on sport. It is a very challenging thing to work with somebody who takes that view of things!

A.T.   *They say it is worth it whatever the price?*

P.K.   That's inferred but it is not stated because somebody that takes that stance has to convince themselves that what they are doing is basically safe or worthwhile. You hear a lot of reports that sportspeople make statements like "I will take a drug that will kill me in 10 years in order to win today". I think that is rhetoric — or at least a conditioned response to an ill-conceived question. I don't think this individual, who did do things that were potentially very hazardous, would honestly agree with this statement. I actually tried to initiate a discussion along these lines with this individual and the other support personnel after failure in a major competition.

A.T.   *You were raising quite strong ethical concerns?*

P.K.   I was. I tried to make clear my feelings before withdrawing my support. As it happened I think they were misinterpreted and that was unfortunate, but I had to walk away from this scenario — I didn't feel I was actually contributing positively and that was why I got out.

S.F.   *Could you please explain again why you got out. Was it because of concern about the athlete?*

P.K.   Mostly. I felt that the athlete was making the wrong decisions, and was not prepared to listen to reasoned arguments about the matter. The only way left for me to express my concern was to withdraw from my role as coach/ advisor.

A.T.   *What do you mean by getting out? How do you get out?*

P.K.   I basically said "I can't work with you any more".

A.T.   *You didn't have a contract?*

P.K.   No!

A.T. *It's not like being coach to a top Italian Football side?*

P.K: No, there was no formal arrangement at all. In fact I am not aware of any formal contracts in individual coaching relationships in this country. The athlete came to me for training advice early in my coaching career, felt the information was useful and kept coming back for more. A closer working relationship thus developed. I learnt a great deal from this. A particularly important lesson was to be clear why somebody is seeking my help. Do they see me as a physiologist/Sports Coach, someone who provides guidance on training theory and practice, or someone who can provide psychological support by providing a service they feel they must have because the East Germans, for example, had Sports Scientists working with them?

A.T. *The manager of the British Women's Athletics Team has been in the news in the last week because of the Chinese women's running achievements in their own stadium in Beijing — I wonder if the clocks are working accurately there?*

P.K. I'd measure the track first I think, go for the simple things!

A.T. *A top female athlete claimed she withdrew from the sport in the late 70s because she felt she could not attain the level of the East Europeans and Soviet competitors and she didn't want to be involved with the training regime based upon performance-enhancing interventions (drugs). Britain has rather a pure line on this, led by the Sports Council. Are you suggesting that despite Britain's lead on this there is a rather schizophrenic situation?*

P.K. I just don't know. Given the extent of discussion on the subject it is difficult to avoid the conclusion that more people are involved in performance-enhancement through the use of drugs etc., than the numbers caught suggest. One must therefore assume there are ways to avoid detection or prosecution. But, what I find curious, is that I have no idea how such a "system" works. One of the many reasons why I would not administer anabolic steroids to an athlete is that I would have no idea how to protect the individual from detection.

A.T.   *Do you mean accessing information on masking substances?*

P.K.   No. I suspect that it would be relatively easy to access information on the
       use of, for example, masking agents. What concerns me is the frequently
       discussed suggestion that it may be possible to prevent a person being
       tested or if that person does get tested, preventing that test either being
       analysed so the right sample gets out or if it gets analysed avoiding the
       inevitable outcome of that test. There are all sorts of conspiracy theories
       that abound in sport about the corruption of dope control administration.
       It is annoying that there appears to be no way of investigating such a taboo
       subject.

A.T.   *Well I think it is probably linked to what you are identifying.*

P.K.   I think the saddest thing about the situation of the Chinese women runners
       is that we just don't know, and we aren't going to know for sure that their
       performances are not drug-dependent. They will always be suspected
       because of the cloud of suspicion that now surrounds all great athletic
       achievements. It could well be that it is simply the huge daily volume of
       training they claim to do.

A.T.   *Close to marathon level?*

P.K.   Close to marathon level. Just supposing that is the case — that is terribly,
       terribly sad.

A.T.   *Why is it sad?*

P.K.   Because the whole world thinks that they are not just doing that.

S.F.   *The effect of drugs might be minor in terms of their contribution to an
       overall performance but it might be enough to take somebody from being
       very mediocre to being the best.*

P.K.   No, I wouldn't agree with that. In the case of cycling the majority of
       substances used will not have a measurable effect physiologically. That is
       what the available research suggests. However, I believe it is the poten-
       tially massive placebo effect of drug use in sport which needs to be consi-
       dered. Medical science has to employ complex experimental designs to
       avoid or to account for placebo mechanisms. Some medics not only accept

that positive placebo responses occur, but argue that we should be researching them more thoroughly as adjuncts to conventional treatments.

Outside of medicine I can think of very few situations other than sport where you are likely to get such a potentially powerful placebo effect. People really want to get better when they are ill, and they really want to win in sport. At high levels of competition a huge array of interventions, both illegal and legal, are used in an attempt to improve performance. Many have no direct physiological effect but could be having a dramatic effect on performance via psychological mechanisms that we don't yet fully understand.

A.T. *On the level of the mind?*

P.K. On the level of the mind ultimately affecting or enabling us to untap more of the straightforward physical potential that we have.

A.T. *How would you define or recognise the point at which you draw the line in the application or use of performance-enhancing interventions? Do you rely on an outside body or on your own perceptions?*

P.K. Given the picture I have painted of people not being able to discuss openly what they see or know happens in sport I think you are left with little choice but to formulate your own set of ethical or moral tools with which to deal with these problems. My approach is to play it safe, for both the athlete and myself. You look at what somebody is proposing to do or asking you to consider and say "is this safe?" in the broadest sense of the word either for the person in terms of their health either immediate or long term, and their social standing in terms of whether they will get caught if they did something which was illegal. Athletes competing at the highest level cannot be objective, the stakes are too high, the pressure on them too great. They often make decisions about these things when they are close to major competitions. They are therefore dependent on others to a certain extent for clear guidance.

There are methods of performance-enhancement that are either not detectable or are not banned, but are potentially very risky. These can appear very attractive to athletes on the verge of major success.

A. T   *Would an example be blood doping?*

P.K.   Yes. Still not detectable and rumoured to still be widespread. I don't have answers to these problems, all I can do as an individual is consider what is safe in the broadest possible sense.

A.T.   *Do you think the blood doping case with the Finns was an utterly acceptable form of preparation?*

P.K.   It depends entirely on what they did.

A.T.   *We don't fully know what they did.*

P.K.   If you were to draw an individual's own blood and freeze-store it and re-infuse later, all under close medical supervision, you would be performing a relatively safe routine medical procedure. Contrast that with this scenario: you find a suitably matched donor from which you withdraw two units of blood in an Hotel suite, drain off some of the plasma and then infuse this straight into your recipient athlete with two days to go before competition. The first situation is medically quite safe, well proven, well researched but not as practical or potent for enhancing performance as the second scenario which is fraught with risks. So even one particular method of performance-enhancement isn't easy to address from an ethical point of view. However, on a practical level when you go to the Olympics you can't take a transfusion service with you, so you are left with only the donor approach. I cannot approve of that but it has been done and will probably continue to be. Ironically, athletes may under-perform because of transfusion shock — mild rejection.

A.T.   *Well, you describe a muddy world.*

P.K.   No. I describe a world that in places is muddy. But you have to contrast this side with the real human joy and experience of people succeeding in sport through what I know to be safe and legitimate ways.

A.T.   *Well we could move on to talk about ethical dimensions of that clean world unmuddied by these sort of considerations. Would you like to pick some up, Scott?*

S.F.   *One of the things I am interested in is the ethical considerations that you have as a coach in relation to children and children's performance, though I know you say you haven't done much work with children. Can you say anything on that in general terms then, rather than your own particular experience?*

P.K.   I would start by saying that this topic is not discussed enough in coach education programmes. From my own personal experience as a teenager involved in competitive sport, my coach was probably the most significant person in my life other than my mother. He was a powerful influence on my intellectual and emotional development.

A.T.   *What sport was that in?*

P.K.   That was in cycling. It was a very positive experience being coached by a person who thought very carefully about what we did and encouraged me to study at school as well as to train. I often credit him with the reason I am where I am now. He taught me to think, to question what I did and to strive for excellence. I am convinced that coaching a young person is a very responsible task.

S.F.   *When you have got someone in their mid-teens do you have problems in getting informed consent and getting their approval for what you, as a coach, want them to do? How much obligation do you think there is on the coach to make it very explicit to an athlete of that age exactly what they are doing and why they are doing it?*

P.K.   The style of coaching I advocate for any level is one based on co-operation, education and facilitation. You do not tell the athlete what to do, but discuss issues and agree on plans. It depends on the level you are working at to a certain extent, but I can never see a situation in which I would just tell an athlete what to do. I feel compelled to explain and to discuss things, so even with a child of 12 I would try to explain the rationale behind what I was asking him/her to do right from the start. I would try and encourage them to question me, and the things we were doing. Coaching is not just about obtaining a performance, it is about a person's development as an athlete — their understanding about what they are doing. I am totally uncomfortable with autocratic styles of coaching.

S.F.   *It is interesting that you mention the age 12. Does that mean that there is*
        an age cut-off point? For example an athlete aged 8 or 10 would be less
        inclined to give the information or you would be less inclined to coach
        them at that age?

P.K.   That is very difficult to say because I only have experience of some sports.
        Cycling is a sport where people typically achieve peaks at international
        level in their mid-twenties. If you are a gymnast then you have to start
        young if you are going to compete in sport as it is currently defined and
        judged. The younger an athlete is the harder it will be to discuss and debate
        things. I really don't know how, for example, you explain to a 7 year
        gymnast why you are asking them to do lots of stretching.

S.F.   *What would be the normal rate of progress of an elite-level cyclist who*
        would make the very top by their mid-twenties? When would they have to
        start?

P.K.   For the peak of success at the very highest level you are probably looking
        on average at a 6 year progression.

S.F.   *Starting from what point?*

P.K.   Starting from joining a club. An East German publication suggests it takes
        eight years to produce an elite athlete, but the claim is not explained.

A.T.   *With a cyclist you wouldn't need to start at 12 , would you?*

P.K.   We cannot say for certain.

A.T.   *You could start someone off at 16?*

P.K.   People have done, but that does not mean it is necessarily optimal. I am
        very interested in the impact of heavy exercise training in pre-pubescent
        and pubescent children, and in particular, what impact it has on athletic
        development in later life.

        As a cyclist I trained hard from the age of 13, sometimes cycling 120 miles
        a day, or racing 50 times a year before the age of 16. I enjoyed it! Now I
        am curious as to what impact that has had on my adult physiological
        status. My fitness level, even after prolonged periods of inactivity, is much

higher than the population average. Is this simply reflecting any innate properties I had before I started cycling, or is it partly a consequence of relatively extreme conditioning at an early age? I suspect some research on this was done in the former Eastern bloc where they trained children from an early age, and experimented with different types of training in a relatively controlled way. I am not aware of research in North America or Western Europe that sheds light on this, but if there is a significant effect of training intervention on development into elite athletes then it has implications for how we approach conditioning of young children.

S.F.　*It has implications for the role of the coach and its effects on children's behaviour.*

P.K.　And the role of the coach in general.

S.F.　*It sounds as though coaching could become a mechanism of social control and the rhetoric could become very evocative?*

P.K.　I think there is a big problem here. The more we look at it the more we realise what a responsible occupation coaching is. Then we look at the status that coaches have, not just within sport but within the society — and we see it is very low. The potential to earn a moderate living from coaching is almost non-existent in most sports, and this is reflected in the quality of training that most coaches get. There is not enough awareness of the responsibilities involved in coaching a developing person.

A.T.　*Have you coached female cyclists?*

P.K.　Yes.

A.T.　*Do you find differences between coaching females and coaching males?*

P.K.　I have found females to be more co-operative as individuals but I am not quite sure why that is. They have less firmly held opinions about how they should train or compete. Coaching women has often been a more productive experience because they are more open minded. One of the important lessons I have learned is women can and do train and compete as hard as men. In the case of some women cyclists I advocate lower volumes of training but that is because at the moment their races are shorter. I see no evidence though that they can't tolerate the kind of training structure that I would advocate for any elite male athlete.

A.T.   *Going back to a question we asked at the very beginning, have you ever encountered any problems of intervening too much in lifestyle aspects or sensitive physical areas?*

P.K.   I think it may be slightly different for me than for many coaches. My initial encounters with the women that I coach have taken place in the laboratory setting when they undergo an initial physiological assessment. I suspect that in this physician/patient scenario many female athletes are more willing to discuss sensitive physical issues

A.T.   *The description of coaching you have just given us is very clinical isn't it?*

P.K.   In some respects.

A.T.   *Professionally clinical and diagnostic in a way.*

P.K.   The trust many athletes place in me right from the outset is probably due to my background and where I work, which is different from most coaching scenarios.

A.T.   *Do you think coaches ought to avoid ever becoming emotionally involved in their subjects on the level of, say, a full sexual relationship?*

P.K.   I find it difficult to answer that question from purely a coaching perspective.

A.T.   *Do you think there might be an ethical dilemma about a relationship developing?*

P.K.   Possibly. There are parallels here with other professional scenarios, for example teacher/pupil, clinician/patient.

S.F.   *A teacher/pupil sexual relationship would be said to be unprofessional behaviour. I don't get the sense of the same feeling in the athletic world, that that would be unprofessional behaviour by a coach.*

P.K.   It depends on your perspective as a coach. I advocate a coach/athlete relationship which is essentially a partnership, or a co-operative in the case of a team. You work together towards the common goal. In this situation there is no imbalance of power and therefore little risk of exploitation. If you see coaching more as educating or treating a person then you are faced with the same ethical dilemmas as teachers and healthcare professionals. I coach people of a similar age to myself in a very pro-active manner, and thus do not see any specific reason professionally to disapprove of coach-athlete relationships.

S.F.   *It is also an unusual coaching situation isn't it?*

P.K.   It is and this is why I'm probably not a typical coach.

S.F.   *You have expressed curiosity about the effects of training regimes on the young, and have stated that there was no evidence for training women less intensively than men. Would you be interested in work that explores these issues further, or are you concerned about the ethical issues this could raise?*

P.K.   That is difficult to answer because I have such a thirst for knowledge. I don't think there is a single subject relevant to human performance in which research topics have been exhausted. I thought the question you were going to ask was if I would wish to access knowledge that may have been gathered through morally or ethically questionable experiments.

A.T.   *Well that is a version of it.*

P.K.   It is a really difficult question. Am I prepared to examine anything that could relate to human performance?

A.T.   *The question is — do you want the knowledge if it is other people's hands that are dirty?*

P.K.   That's right. Whether knowledge derived by morally questionable means exists in my field of interest is unclear to me. I suspect a significant human cost was incurred in gathering the knowledge available from the former Eastern bloc sporting system, and possibly others. If there is information there then I would want access to it. However, I would like to think that my own research would strive to achieve high ethical standards.

S.F.   *Let me put it another way then. If you were working with an athlete and you heard of a radically different intervention that would improve the person's performance would you go ahead and do it?*

P.K.   I would have to consider the implications with respect to my own ethical standards.

A.T.   *And you would discuss the issue with the athlete?*

P.K.   Absolutely!

S.F.   *It is worth stressing that, isn't it?*

P.K.   I think it is very important. In the scenario we discussed earlier, the individual who decided to employ risky procedures was frustrating to work with because there was never true open dialogue about such issues.

A.T.   *Can I move to a different situation. You are exercise testing or training someone and they say "look this is going too far it's hurting" what do you say?*

P.K.   Stop.

A.T.   *Always?*

P.K.   Yes.

A.T.   *That is definitive.*

P.K.   I cannot push or ask somebody to do something they don't want to do. I struggle with athletes who simply want me to push them without explanation or discussion about what I was instructing them to do.

A.T.   *In the coaching community isn't there a dominant view which states 'no pain, no gain' — hurting is beneficial?*

P.K.   I think there are two different things here. There is the nature of the training process. All forms of effective conditioning for sports performance involve some degree of discomfort — some can be quite unpleasant. I try to explain to athletes why this is the case and what the benefits might be. They can then make informed decisions about how they train. This is a different issue to imposing your will on somebody psychologically — an authoritarian style of coaching. To me it is all about co-operation: working together to achieve a goal. It might be different in a situation where people are under a certain obligation to train, for example in a penal institution or the Armed Forces, but to me that is not coaching. It is conditioning for a purpose but it is completely different to sports coaching.

S.F.   *You know sports psychologists who work on adherence to training schedules. How far are you prepared to go to ensure that people do what they agreed they will do in training? How prepared are you to intervene to make sure they do as they have agreed to do?*

P.K.   I can't recall a situation where that has actually happened. One of the key features of my approach is the need to be flexible within a structured training framework. I may well have produced a weekly training programme that has purpose, rationale, and logic behind it, but if the athlete is completely exhausted after the first session, you cannot just continue with the programme, you have to modify it. You don't just push on regardless of the state of the athlete just because you wrote out a plan. Coaches and athletes tend to believe that once a programme is committed to paper it is right and cannot be questioned, so when people get injured or ill they continue to train and their performance drops. I commit ideas to paper all the time, but I try to build in flexibility and encourage athletes to listen to their bodies, to evaluate and make decisions for themselves, and where relevant, come back to me on it.

An interactive coaching method builds trust rapidly and also enables me to learn faster because I am evaluating along with the individual what we are trying to do. It also means that they are much more likely to tell you what they have really done. One of the real problems about learning in coaching is actually being able to trust that what you set was done. For example, if you ask an athlete to do twelve sets of lifts, and they can only manage eight but tell you they did twelve, then you never learn — the empirical process fails because you end up ascribing effects to the wrong cause. Coaching has to be a very interactive process. There is a component of science in it — but I do not believe that coaching is a science.

A.T. *The way you describe the process it would be equally difficult to try and write down some moral and ethical guidelines in tablets of stone, you have to keep some kind flexibility.*

P.K. Yes, I guess that is the nature of ethics. It is very difficult to give clear guidelines. We need to educate coaches far better in all respects, and we need high calibre people in coaching. It is a very demanding and responsible occupation. Poor coaching produces a lot of casualties: the burnt-out, the injured, the disenchanted.

A.T. *I think that is a nice endpoint, a reminder of the critical nature of ethics and the importance of ethical issues for the sports practitioner.*

VALUE FOUNDATIONS OF ETHICAL DECISIONS IN CHILDREN'S SPORT [1]

Martin Lee
University of Brighton

Introduction

Questions about the ethical basis of sports behaviour have become increasingly salient in recent years. Issues which have received widespread publicity have not been restricted to behaviour on the field but also extended to the conduct of players and administrators off the field. For example there have been serious accusations made concerning the conduct of football managers in the transfer of players, and of accusations of slanderous conduct by the promotions manager of the British Amateur Athletic Federation about a coach/journalist which are said by some to have contributed to the suicide of that coach. When these examples are added to the numerous examples of drug taking among athletes, e.g. Ben Johnson, Katrin Krabbe, and, at a less exalted level, the case of the golfer being taken to court for cheating by his competitors in a local tournament (*The Times*, 28 April, 1994) it is clear that ethical issues are important at all levels of sport. While these examples are derived from adult sport concerns are frequently expressed about conduct in children's sport. Indeed it has often been claimed that sport is an appropriate way to foster desirable moral character, though the veracity of the claim is open to question and it has been the subject of careful examination in a recent book by Shields and Bredemeier (1994).

This chapter will examine the topic of moral behaviour in children's sport from the perspective of underlying values and value systems.

Ethics

The term ethics has been used to denote different processes. Examination of the term "ethics" reveals two major categories of activity: (a) the scientific study, and (b) the philosophical study of morality. The first category is termed Descriptive Ethics and the second can be subdivided into two further categories, Normative Ethics and Analytic Ethics (Taylor, 1975). According to Taylor descriptive ethics refers to the "…description and explanation of actual morality" (p. 5). Such a description of moral processes and judgements provides the data for the critical analysis and reflection of moral philosophers. The data may, of course, be the product of investigation by psychologists, sociologists, and anthropologists among others. Normative ethics refers to the process of constructing and justifying a system of standards and rules which provide a framework for evaluating moral behaviour. When we indulge in this form of reflection we are conducting a philosophical exercise. Finally, analytical ethics is the philosophical process of clarifying the semantic, logical, and epistemological structure of moral discourse.

Briefly, then, the distinction is made between ethics as the study of systems of moral behaviour and ethics as the study of moral philosophy. Since this chapter is concerned with the psychological processes which underlie moral decisions which participants are called upon to make in sport, it is an exercise in descriptive ethics. Specifically it deals with cognitive priorities which provide the basis of moral decision-making among young athletes.

Ethical issues in sport

Warren Fraleigh (1984) explored the ethical basis for sports behaviour at some length in an attempt to provide moral guidelines for it and began by describing a number of common examples of behaviour which raise ethical questions. These included faking injury, intentional fouls, accommodating a linesman's error in tennis, the case of performance-enhancing drugs, and, finally, of specifying appropriate behaviour in the case of an uneven contest. Each of these cases poses a different problem and suggests to the contestants solutions based upon either convention (normative behaviour) or self-interest. However, Fraleigh argues that such solutions are inadequate on the grounds that, firstly, convention does not guarantee the rightness of an action and, secondly, self-interest, by definition, leads to conflict which cannot be resolved by reference to guidelines which are themselves a product of self-interest. He concluded that there must be an appeal to moral principles as a guide for the selection of correct behaviour in sporting situations. Having said this, competitive sport is an inherently self-interested activity, the purpose of which is to demonstrate superiority over others according to an agreed set of rules. Thoughtful coaches and players are moved to examine carefully the prescriptive rules of the activity in order to find out how best to exploit them. Indeed such preparation is often considered to be a mark of skill and thoroughness.

In an effort to identify the essence of fair play and sportsmanship Keating (1964/1988) drew a distinction between sport and athletics. He considered that the purpose of sport is to derive pleasure from the actions involved in the pursuit of achievement while also affording pleasure to fellow participants. He also believes that sport is characterised by competition primarily for the experience itself, rather than the outcome. The purpose of athletics, on the other hand, is to demonstrate excellence and superiority in a contest which is bound by rules. By applying a principle that it is desirable to conduct oneself in a manner which increases rather than decreases the pleasure of all participants he concluded that the essential features of sportsmanship were generosity and magnanimity. Given the conditions of athletic competition, which demand the demonstration of superiority, he argues that it is especially difficult for athletes to adopt such a manner.

This dichotomous view of sport and athletics may, however, be limited. The experience of many athletes is such that they are able to reconcile the demands of being "sportspersons" and "athletes" (see Freezell, 1988; Hemery, 1988). Indeed, as I write there has been an excellent example of sportsmanship in the World Championship snooker final. At a critical stage of the competition, while trailing 17–16 in a best-of-35 frame match the challenger, Jimmy White, made an error. The referee awarded a foul to the defending champion, Stephen Hendry, and the opportunity to play a "free ball". This would have allowed Hendry an excellent opportunity to clear the table and claim the championship. However, he examined the position and asked the referee to reconsider. When he did so the "free ball" was withdrawn making it more difficult for Hendry who eventually lost the frame and was forced into a final frame which he could also have lost. In the interests of justice Hendry had refused an advantage to which he did not believe he was entitled despite the decision putting in jeopardy his chance of retaining the title and gaining an extra £70,000 in prize money. This provides excellent evidence of generosity and magnanimity at a crucial stage in an intensely competitive event. It appears that commitment to competitive success need not necessarily eliminate benevolent behaviour between contestants and the principles of fair play can exist at the highest level. Rather than accepting Keating's dichotomy uncritically, therefore, it may be more fruitful to conceive of a continuum of sport and athletic commitment in which the pressures on participants to gain a competitive victory increase as the contest becomes more serious. Furthermore, while it may be difficult to refuse to accept an unfair advantage, which may occur by good fortune during a critical period of an important contest, such a course of action is not a necessary consequence of the situation. Moreover the decision to do so is qualitatively different from the conscious decision to behave in such a way as to gain an advantage where none exists, i.e. to cheat. Because the concerns about sportsmanship are expressed when its principles are violated it is important to record the expression of fair play, so central to the debate over the state of ethical behaviour in sport.

Approaches to the examination of ethical behaviour

Although Keating's analysis has sparked philosophical debate in pursuit of a clearer conceptual analysis, research into sportsmanship and fair play has been hampered by lack of conceptual clarity and agreement on acceptable operational definitions of these concepts. For many, the terms are close enough to be almost synonymous. However, perhaps it is helpful to consider that the notion of fair play appears to refer more to the specific exhibition of morally desirable acts, while sportsmanship appears to imply a personal characteristic of a performer which is demonstrated by the frequent exhibition of fair play. These patterns of behaviour may be characterised by an underlying concern for justice, equity, benevolence, and good manners. Sportsmanship, therefore, may be better understood through the examination of motivational priorities which underpin observed behaviour. In essence this is a search for the relative importance of the values which sustain participation in sport.

Moral decisions in sport, therefore, may be viewed from both behavioural and cognitive perspectives. A behavioural perspective requires the gathering of data on the nature and frequency of observable events. However, since the simple observation of a morally questionable action does not necessarily indicate any morally reprehensible motivation, an approach which relies on behavioural evidence alone is flawed. Though cognitive and behavioural variables are related they do not demonstrate perfect covariance; people do not always act in accordance with their professed attitudes (Wicker, 1969). Moral decisions are necessarily functions of the mind and, hence, cognitive approaches to the study of moral decision-making in sport seek to establish the cognitive processes behind behaviour. Hitherto the problem has been approached as one of attitudes, motivation, moral judgement, moral behaviour, and, particularly where children are concerned, moral development. If, however, moral dilemmas are recognised as requiring a choice on the part of the actor between competing demands, then it is essential to examine carefully the criteria which are employed in resolving them. There is also a need for conceptual clarification as a prerequisite of a comprehensive understanding of the issues involved. Clearly it is helpful to explore the relationships between behaviour and underlying psychological constructs.

Behaviour

Behavioural measures in response to moral dilemmas may be clearly defined and observed either informally or by the use of carefully structured observation instruments in accordance with established protocols. However, the behaviour exhibited in response to a given situation depends on the precise conditions operating at the time. Those conditions may be varied, for example, by the presence of others, by the rewards or penalties associated with the behaviour, or by emotional variations in the individual. Since behaviour is specific to the demands of the situation prevailing at the time, then the inference of underlying cognitions which affect it depends upon relative behavioural consistencies across a variety of similar, but not identical, situations.

Two weaknesses may be identified with a behavioural approach to describing moral judgements. First, while in some sports aggressive behaviour may be recorded, subject to satisfactory operational definitions of the category "aggressive", the occurrence of the more benevolent aspects of behaviour which may be regarded as representing fair play may be both less easy to define and even less frequent in occurrence. Second, the observation of an event which appears to be unethical does not necessarily imply any immoral intent. Thus a soccer player who makes a tackle which results in injury to an opponent may do so through lack of skill, not necessarily through any desire to cause harm. Hence, although the rightness or wrongness of an action can be shown to reside in the nature of its underlying motive, this is not, itself, addressed.

Cognitions

Fair play and sportsmanship are terms which arose in the English language and are commonly used throughout the world. They provide cognitive representations of the meaning of patterns of interpersonal behaviour. Despite Keating's (1964/1988) analysis, which did a great deal to express the qualities normally associated with those terms, it has not always been clear what they mean to sports participants themselves nor what their relationship is to other psychological constructs and the behaviours which they are thought to represent. Hence there is little agreement on the procedures to be adopted in order to identify and measure the constructs. Yet there are established fields of enquiry in psychology which can inform the study of fair play. They deal with beliefs, attitudes and, most particularly, values, and their relationships to human behaviour.

Beliefs can be considered to be a general category of cognitive structures which provide a framework from within which people view the world. In elaborating on the nature of beliefs Rokeach (1968) has described (a) descriptive beliefs which are capable of being verified and may be said to represent an individual's perceptions of reality and truth, (b) evaluative beliefs whereby an object is judged to be good or bad, i.e. attitudes, and (c) prescriptive or proscriptive beliefs by which actions or goals are considered to be desirable or undesirable, i.e. values.

Descriptive beliefs The descriptive beliefs which a person holds may be conditioned by the social context to which that person is subjected. For example, the belief that a particular opposing team plays in a particular manner, fairly or unfairly, may be the result of a prevailing social perception or stereotype. In accordance with the other stereotypical responses that belief may lead to patterns of over-generalised behaviour. Thus the British Lions rugby team which toured New Zealand in 1971 were subjected to violent play and believed that all future opponents would be aggressive; they consequently developed a strategy of "Get your retaliation in first!" (Dawes, 1971).

Attitudes An attitude is usually defined as a predisposition to respond in a positive or negative way to some specific stimulus, or attitude object. Attitudes have a number of components: cognitive (what one knows about the object), affective (how one feels towards the object), and behavioural (the tendency to behave in certain ways towards the object) (Stalhberg and Frey, 1988). However, the relationship between an attitude and consequent behaviour is notoriously unstable (e.g. Wicker, 1969) and one's actual behaviour might depend in the final analysis on a very precise determination of the situational variables in question and on one's attitudes towards competing objects or events. Since attitudes have an evaluative element, they are frequently measured by use of scales in which respondents are required to record their approval or disapproval of a particular attitude object, e.g. a Likert scale. These scales have the advantages of being easily administered, reliable, and easy to construct. They are however directed towards specific attitude objects and do not necessarily represent consistent underlying cognitions.

Values The notion that sport is an effective medium for the development of desirable social and moral values has long been advanced, and has recently come to the fore in the United Kingdom as a result of public and political debate over the role of team sports in physical education. Values are another form of belief, related to, but distinct from, attitudes. Probably the most influential conceptualisation has come from Milton Rokeach (Rokeach, 1973) who considered them to be central cognitive constructs by which people organise their lives. According to Rokeach a value is defined as:

> ...an enduring belief that a specific mode of conduct or end-state of existence is preferable to an opposite or converse mode of conduct or end state of existence. (Rokeach, 1973: p. 5)

Since people possess a range of values they are organised into systems which reflect their relative importance. A value system is defined as:

> ...an enduring organisation of beliefs concerning preferable modes of conduct or end-states of existence along a continuum of relative importance. (Rokeach, 1973: p. 5)

Building upon the work of Rokeach, Schwartz (1992) has specified five characteristics of values. He considers that they "... (1) are concepts or beliefs, (2) pertain to desirable end-states or behaviours, (3) transcend specific situations, (4) guide selection or evaluation of events, and (5) are ordered by importance" (p. 4). In particular, Schwartz emphasises the distinction of values from attitudes

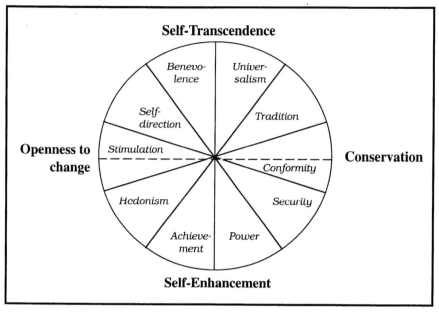

Figure 1   Theoretical model of structural relations among motivational types of values (adapted from Schwartz, 1992)

by their generality and hierarchical ordering, i.e. ranking in order of importance. This critical distinction has not always been recognised in the literature of sport psychology in this area (e.g. Hastad et al., 1986). In the same paper Schwartz goes beyond the description of single values which are implicitly independent and describes a model of types of values which represent different motivational domains. The types are structurally organised in relation to two orthogonal core dimensions which reflect (a) openness and conservatism, and (b) self-enhancement and self-transcendence (see Figure 1). The model has received empirical support in an extensive series of studies using 40 samples in 20 different countries. On the basis of the model Schwartz has suggested a number of conflicts between sets of value types. One such conflict, confirmed in the cross-cultural samples, was between Universalism/Benevolence and Power/ Achievement (p. 35). In the present context that conflict may be expressed in terms of the competing demands of fair play and sportsmanship and of competitive success (winning), or in Keating's (1964/1988) language it represents the conflicting demands of sport and athletics.

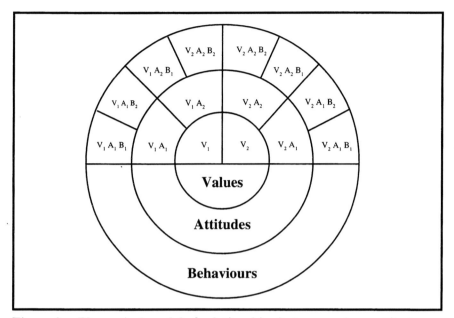

Figure 2   Theoretical model of relationships between values, attitudes and behaviour

The views advanced by Rokeach (1973), Schwartz (1992) and others represent a perspective of values as criteria for the evaluation of actions and objectives rather than as inherent qualities of objects (see Schwartz, 1992: p. 1). This conception of values as a system of central organising constructs suggests that a limited number of values may underpin a wide range of both attitudes and behaviour. Hence the construct of values permits the development of a strategy to examine the nature of fair play which depends on the application of general principles of conduct which supersede the immediate demands of the situation. These principles guide the decision-making process and hence influence the expression of attitudes and behaviour in specific situations. Thus a three-tiered structure of (a) value system, (b) expressed attitudes, and (c) behaviour which is activated in a specific situation can be proposed (see Figure 2). It follows that, in order to understand fair play and sportsmanship, it is important to examine the role of conflict between specific values in the social context in determining resultant attitudes and behaviour. Therefore it is proposed that the investigation of the values which are activated provides a more coherent approach to the study of moral decision-making in sport than an approach which deals only with attitudes or, worse, lacks any clear theoretical or methodological formulation.

Research into fair play in youth sports

Attitudes

Much of the research into aspects of fair play in sports has taken the form of attitudinal studies, possibly because of the relative ease of collecting data. The following general conclusions may be made from attitudinal research. A strong commitment to winning above playing well and playing fairly is associated with increases in age (e.g. Webb, 1969; Blair, 1985; Johns and Eldridge, 1992); instrumental and aggressive behaviour is more acceptable with increasing age (Lee and Williams, 1989; Bolland, 1981, Waters, 1982); perceptions of acceptable aggression decrease with levels of moral reasoning (Bredemeier, Weiss, Shields, and Cooper, 1987); winning is more important for competitive participants than for recreational participants (Knoppers, Schuiteman and Love, 1986; Mantel and Van der Velden, 1974; Maloney and Petrie, 1972; Nicholson, 1979); professional attitudes are stronger among boys than girls (Webb, 1969; Maloney and Petrie, 1972; McElroy and Kirkendall, 1980; Blair, 1985), and that mature athletes distinguish between sport and life settings when making moral judgements (Bredemeier and Shields, 1984). Unfortunately, Bredemeier (1994) could not replicate the last result with a sample of pre-adolescent children in a summer sport camp. This may have been due either to the age of subjects or to the essentially recreational nature of their sport involvement.

Several of the studies dealing with the attitudes of participants have been carried out with juvenile samples and many have used the Professionalization of Attitudes Scale (PAS) devised by Webb (1969). This instrument, however, by requiring respondents to express preferences between available options, is more accurately described as a value measure, albeit with little theoretical basis. The implications of the response format have not generally been recognised by researchers using the instrument though there have been criticisms of the assumption of uni-dimensionality and contextual specificity (Greer and Lacy, 1989; Greer and Stewart, 1989; Knoppers, 1985; Knoppers, Schuitemen and Love, 1986).

Values

Studies of values in sport, apart from those which use the PAS, have been very few though Wandzilack (1985) has argued for the implementation of an instructional model for value development through physical education. The proposed model draws upon Rokeach's (1973) conception of values and Kohlberg's (1969, 1976) structural-developmental theory of moral development. Simmons and Dickinson (1986) developed an instrument to measure values in athletic populations. While they drew upon Rokeach's work to provide a rationale there is no indication that the values they include in the instrument are derived either from a clear theoretical basis or from the populations of interest. Despite Rokeach's influence in mainstream psychology little work using his approach has been conducted in sport. Lee (1977), using the Rokeach Value Survey (RVS) in a cross-sectional study, found that college athletes valued competence values rather more than moral values and, not surprisingly, were concerned predominantly with competitive success, though this does not imply any causal relationship between sport participation and value structure. However, no research using this instrument with children has been identified, although other studies have suggested that the values of children in sport may differ from those of adults. There is evidence that many children place a greater emphasis on fun, developing skills, affiliation, fitness, and fair play, in preference to winning (Dubois, 1986a, 1986b; Whitehead, 1987). Some studies have recently been reported which derive from the international programme of which this research formed the basis (e.g. Cruz *et al.*, 1991; Telama *et al.*, 1993) and others are in preparation. The results essentially support the limited number of values in sport presented below.

Rationale

I have argued that the identification of values among young athletes is of prime importance to understand better the processes by which they make decisions about their behaviour in sporting situations. Further, in accordance with a requirement for ecological validity any such research should examine those values which are salient to the situation under investigation (Braithwaite and Laws, 1985; Schwartz and Bilsky, 1987). Consequently a series of interviews was conducted among young football and tennis players with the objective of identifying values which appeared to underpin moral decision-making during a contest.

Method

Subjects   Subjects were (a) male football players and (b) male and female tennis players randomly selected from a pool of 305 athletes (see Table 1). All

Table 1   Distribution of subjects by sex, sport and age

Age group		12	13	14	15	16	Total
Gender:	Sport:						
Male	Football	12	11	14	12	11	60
	Tennis	1	2	5	1	0	9
Female	Tennis	6	2	2	6	2	18
Total		19	15	21	19	13	87

were between 12 and 16 years of age and were participants in competitive sport as defined by representing teams in school or club leagues. The level of performance in football included school, club, district, regional and international. In the tennis sample players competed at club, county, and regional level.

Instrument   Data were collected by interviews which consisted of a semi-structured discussion of hypothetical dilemmas which might occur in the subject's sport. Subjects were presented with two dilemmas, each of which was designed to provoke one of three different types of behaviour: (a) instrumental, (b) aggressive, and (c) altruistic. The dilemmas, drawn from a pool of six football and seven tennis situations, were randomly assigned to subjects from each of those sports. This procedure ensured that all dilemmas were used in the study and, hence, elicited the widest range of values available.

Procedures   Interviews were conducted in quiet rooms, recorded using micro-cassette recorders and later transcribed to facilitate content analysis. After a short introduction and explanation subjects were asked to read the first dilemma; the interviewer then checked subjects' comprehension of the situation described before proceeding with the discussion. Subjects were encouraged to clarify their reasoning for advocating particular forms of action. This gave access to underlying motives and hence to the values which underpinned their stated behavioural decisions.

Response coding   The initial response categories were developed from a small sample of pilot interviews but additional categories were added as responses were found which did not fit existing ones and appeared to represent the expression of values. Interestingly, no new categories were found after the nineteenth interview. This gave confidence that young players activate only a relatively small number of values in their sports experience. In order to get a preliminary indication of the importance of the values within the population, following content analysis, the frequency of occurrence of each value was recorded.

Results

The content analysis resulted in the identification of 18 value categories. A full account of the process of category identification may be found in Lee and Cockman (in press) and Table 2 gives a description of the nature of those categories.

Table 2: **Spontaneously expressed values identified from football and tennis players aged 12-16 yrs**

Value	Descriptor
Achievement:	Being personally or collectively successful in play.
Caring:	Showing concern for other people
Companionship:	Being with friends with a similar interest in the game
Conformity:	Conforming to the expectations of others in the team
Conscientious:	Doing one's best at all times, not letting others down
Contract Maintenance:	Supporting the essence of agreeing to play the game, to play in the spirit of the game
Enjoyment:	Experiencing feelings of satisfaction and pleasure
Fairness:	Not allowing an unfair advantage in the contest/judgement
Good Game:	Enjoying the contest regardless of outcome, usually embodying a balance between the contestants
Health and Fitness:	Becoming healthy as a result of the activity, and in becoming fit to enhance performance
Obedience:	Avoid punishment, being dropped, sent off, suspended
Public image:	Gaining approval of others
Sportsmanship:	Being of good disposition, accepting bad luck with the good, demonstrating positive behaviours toward opponents, and accepting defeats
Self-Actualization:	Experiencing the activity for its own sake and accompanying transcendent feelings
Showing skill:	Being able to perform the skills of the game well
Team Cohesion:	Doing something for someone else, for its own sake, doing it for the team performance
Tolerance:	Being able to get along with others despite differences between each other
Winning:	Demonstrating superiority in the contest

Of course, both the value labels and descriptors are presented here in adult language; before they can be meaningfully used to investigate *value systems* among young athletes they must be transformed into a language which is meaningful to the population of interest. Having said that, they display a variety of interests and concerns which suggests that the children who took part represented a wide range of opinion.

Value Frequency

The number of subjects who expressed a particular value statement indicates the relative importance of the value in the population and is given in Figure 3. This does not, however, indicate the importance of any value to a particular individual, which is a function of the structure of that individual's value system as a whole. The most commonly occurring values were *Winning* (95.4%), *Enjoyment* (89.7%), and *Sportsmanship* (83.9%). However, the frequency of occurrence of a given value in the population may be more accurately described as representing a collective attitude. The value accorded to the concepts only becomes clear when subjects are required to state their preferences when values conflict. Thus, the hierarchy is only accurately revealed when subjects are forced to prioritise. The apparent occurrence of *Winning* as the prime value is, therefore, misleading since when subjects were asked to indicate which were the most important things for them in playing; *Enjoyment* was most frequently given as the most important. This doubt over the primacy of the pursuit of victory as a key value in sport has been demonstrated elsewhere (e.g. Johns and Eldridge, 1992).

The values which received least support were *Tolerance* (2.3%), *Health and Fitness* (10.3%), *Conformity* (19.5%) and, less noticeably, *Showing Skill* (25.3%). *Tolerance* may be a rather mature concept which had not yet developed in many of the subjects chosen. In an age when health is being promoted as a major objective of physical education it is, perhaps, instructive that it does not hold a place of priority in the minds of the young people who took part in this study. The value *Conformity* appears to be related to *Obedience* and *Team Cohesion* and was more evident among football players than among the tennis players. The relatively low frequency of *Showing Skill* is surprising in view of the research based upon the PAS and of the bulk of recent research in motivation which draws attention to the different motivational categories identified among children and defines a group who seek mastery goals as a priority (see Duda, 1993; Roberts, 1993).

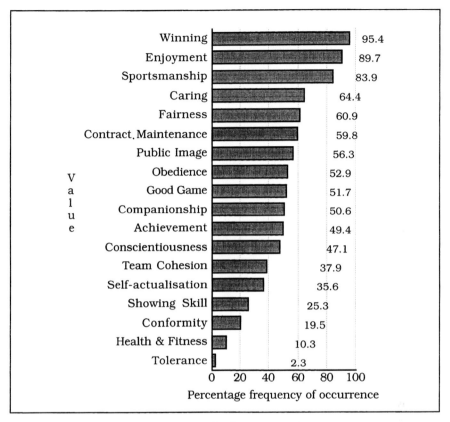

Figure 3: Percentage frequency of value expression

Conclusion

In this paper I have argued that in order to understand better the nature of fair play and sportsmanship, and hence to promote them among youth sport partici- pants, it is necessary to understand the value structure that sustains the partici- pation of each individual. A model has been proposed that links values, attitudes, and behaviour and hence places the responsibility for control into the hands of the actors to a greater extent than is implicit in moral development models. For example, stage theories (e.g. Kohlberg, 1969, 1976; Haan, 1978) suggest that there is an invariant sequence in which moral maturity is reached and that the stage is not subject to regression although research has shown that regression can be demonstrated in response to moral dilemmas in sport (Bredemeier and Shields, 1984). This view leads to a rather deterministic view of moral judgement which reduces individual responsibility for weighing moral dilemmas, i.e. judgements are limited by levels of moral development and not influenced by social forces. A model which relies on the process of value conflict between competing "goods" places responsibility more firmly in the hands of the actor and permits an analysis in which cultural influences can be accorded greater significance.

If this analysis can be upheld with a larger sample and a pattern of relation-ships between value types in sport similar to that proposed by Schwartz (1992) can be established, it would highlight the difficulty in modern sport of recon-ciling demands for competitive success with prosocial values of sportsmanship and fair play. This strategy does lend credence to the contention that a worth-while way of exploring concepts of fairness in children's sport is through the identification of value systems.

Value frequency

Let me turn to the frequency of expression of values in the sample and pay particular attention to social and moral values. The most frequently occurring value was that of winning. This, of course is hardly surprising given that all subjects were engaged in competitive sport. Another value which implies a similar orientation was *Achievement* of sporting success. Hence there were two expressions which recognise that sport is indeed a competitive setting in which the explicit purpose of the contest is to demonstrate superiority.

A great many subjects considered *Sportsmanship* to be important and, when pressed to make a choice, many considered it to be more important than competitive success. Indeed a significant majority expressed the importance of playing within the spirit of the laws (*Contract Maintenance*) and to ensure that each contestant had no unfair advantage over the other (*Fairness*). Further evidence for the levels of altruism existing within this sample can be found in a clear concern for the welfare of others, both physically and psychologically, shown by the value *Caring*, and possibly *Tolerance*; though since the latter appeared only infrequently it may not form an separate element in a collective value structure.

Perhaps the most consistent value of participating in sport is the personal pleasure to be gained from it. While most young people may experience some difficulty in articulating what it is that they enjoy about sport, they certainly feel it very strongly (see Wankel and Krieisel, 1985). Thus the value *Enjoyment* is supported by others expressing a variety of pleasures to be gained from participating, e.g. *Companionship, Good Game,* and *Self-Actualisation.* Recent research indicates that children have different achievement goals which relate to sports participation (see Duda, 1987; Whitehead, 1990) in the light of which it is reasonable to suggest that the attainment of these goals is a prime constituent of enjoyment. For example, children who gain satisfaction from showing skill may be expected to have an enjoyable experience when they play well, irrespective of the competitive outcome; others, who receive adult approval for participating, may enjoy the praise of their parents after a game even if the level of skill displayed is low.

Value domains

At first glance the data appear to demonstrate that there are values which are specific to sport, e.g. *Good Game, Sportsmanship.* However, even if this is the case, closer examination suggests that the values obtained here can be grouped at a higher order level which represents more general categories. Thus these two values may simply be manifestations of more general principles which are particularly salient to sport. In accordance with Schwartz and Bilsky's (1987) advice that values research should use indices based on value domains rather than single items, Lee and Cockman (in press) have proposed five groups of values which appear to have common features and are conceptually distinct from other groups. They are as follows: Competence values, Self-expressive values, Group maintenance values, Moral values, and Social values. Two values (*Health and Fitness* and *Public Image*) do not readily fit into the categories. However, the value types and the secondary categories revealed in this study developed here do appear to fit Schwartz' (1992) typology of motivational types which can also embrace the two unclassified values. A possible relationship between these two analyses is presented in Table 3 (following page). One point of contention may lie in the placement of *Self-actualisation* in a group characterised by enjoyment where Schwartz (1992) distinguishes between hedonism and self-direction (Figure 1).

Table 3: Correspondence between expressed values in children's sport, proposed value domains and Schwartz' (1992) primary motivational types

Values	Value Domain	Schwartz' Motivational Type
Caring, Companionship, Tolerance	Social	Benevolence
Contract maintenance, Fairness, Sportsmanship	Moral	Universalism
Conformity, Obedience, Team Cohesion	Group maintenance	Conformity
Health and fitness	Unclassified	Security
Public Image	Unclassified	Power
Achievement, Conscientious, Showing Skill, Winning	Competence	Achievement
Self-actualisation, Enjoyment, Good Game	Self-expressive	Hedonism

The major motivational types in Schwartz' model can account for the value conflict inherent in the moral dilemmas facing competitive athletes (see Figure 1). Given the analysis above, certain of the values fit the pattern required to exemplify the conflict between Benevolence/Universalism and Achievement/Power. Furthermore, if the value *Health and Fitness* is included in Schwartz' Security motivational type as in the original model this, too, is closely aligned with the Achievement/Power groups on the dimension of Self-enhancement to Self-Transcendence. In the terminology commonly in current use in sports psychology this conflict represents that between desirable social and moral values, and competence — whether it is more important to be fair and display sportsmanship or to win the contest at whatever cost.

This model holds considerable hope for a fuller understanding of the moral problems faced by competitive athletes and by youngsters as they begin to face the consequences of their own aspirations and abilities. However, while it puts these dilemmas into sharp perspective it does not deny that highly successful competitors can pursue achievement goals while also maintaining a spirit of sportsmanship and concern for the essential qualities identified by Keating (1964/1988) and which have been seen recently in professional sport. If it can be demonstrated consistently that the values and value domains identified here do represent the principles by which young athletes organise their experiences, make moral decisions, and judge their satisfaction in sport then it will be important to investigate the ways in which they develop those values. Hence, future research in this area should (a) investigate whether the values identified here are more widely applicable in youth sports, (b) examine the value systems of populations of young athletes in different sports, and (c) investigate the relationships between athletes' value systems and the value systems, both expressed and perceived, of significant others and sports institutions with which they are associated[2].

Notes

[1] The qualitative analysis which preceded the data presented herein has been published in "Ethical Problems in Sport", a special issue of the *International Review for the Sociology of Sport* (in press).

[2] The author gratefully acknowledges the assistance of the Sports Council (London) in funding the research on which this article is based.

References

Blair, S. (1985) 'Professionalisation of attitude towards play in children and adults', *Research Quarterly*, 56, 1: pp. 82-3.

Bolland, C. (1981) An examination of attitudes of young football players to the professional foul. Unpublished dissertation, Trinity and All Saints College, Leeds, England.

Braithwaite, V. A. and Laws, H. G. (1985) 'Structure of human values: Testing the adequacy of the Rokeach Value Survey', *Journal of Personality and Social Psychology*, 49, 1: pp. 250-263.

Bredemeier, B. J. L. (1994) 'Children's moral reasoning and their assertive, aggressive, and submissive tendencies in sport and daily life', *Journal of Sport and Exercise Psychology*, 16, 1: pp. 1-14.

Bredemeier, B. J. and Shields, D. L. (1984) 'Divergence of moral reasoning about sport and everyday life', *Sociology of Sport Journal*, 1: pp. 348-357.

Bredemeier, B. J., Weiss, M. R., Shields, D. L., and Cooper, B. A. B. (1987) 'The relationship between children's legitimacy judgements and their moral reasoning, aggression tendencies, and sport involvement', *Sociology of Sport Journal*, 4, pp. 48-60.

Cruz, J., Boixadós, M., Valiente, L., Ruíz, A., Arbona, P., Molons, Z., Call, J., Berbel, G. I., Capdevila, L. (1991) 'Identificación de valores relevantes en jugadores jóvenes de futbol' [Identification of relevant values in young soccer players]. *Revista de Investigación y Documentación sobre las Ciencias de la Educación Fisica y del Deporte*, 19: pp. 81-99.

Dawes, J. (1971) Personal communication.

Dubois, P. E. (1986a) 'The effect of participation in sport on the value orientations of young athletes', *Sociology of Sport Journal*, 3, 1, pp. 29-42.

——— (1986b) 'Gender differences in value orientation toward sports: A longitudinal analysis', Paper presented at the 7th Annual Meeting of the North American Society for the Sociology of Sport, Las Vegas, Nevada, Oct. 29–Nov. 1.

Duda, J. L. (1987) 'Toward a developmental theory of children's motivation in sport', *Journal of Sport Psychology*, 9, 2, pp. 130-145.

Duda, J. L. (1993) 'Goals: A social cognitive approach of the study achievement motivation in sport', in R.N. Singer, M. Murphey, and L. K. Tennant (eds) *Handbook of research on sports psychology*. New York: Macmillan, pp. 421-436.

Fraleigh, W. (1984) *Right action in sport*. Champaign, Ill.: Human Kinetics.

Freezell, M. (1988) 'Sportsmanship', in W. J. Morgan and K. V. Meier (eds) *Philosophic inquiry in sport*. Champaign, Ill.: Human Kinetics, pp. 251-260.

Greer, D. L. and Lacy, M. G. (1989) 'On the conceptualisation and measurement of attitudes towards play: The Webb Scale and the GOS', *Sociology of Sport Journal*, 6, pp. 380-390.

Greer, D. L. and Stewart, M. J. (1989) 'Children's attitudes towards play: An investigation into their context specificity and relationship to organized sport experiences', *Journal of Sport and Exercise Psychology*, 11, pp. 336-342.

Haan, N. (1978) 'Two moralities in action contexts: Relationships to thought, ego regulation, and development', *Journal of Personality and Social Psychology*, 36, 3, pp. 286-305.

Hastad, D., Segrave, J. O., Pangrazi, R., and Peterson, G. (1986) 'Causal factors of deviant behaviour among youth sport participants', in L. Vander Velden and Humphreys, J. H. (Eds), *Psychology and sociology of sport: Current selected research*. Vol. 1, pp. 149-166. New York: AMS Press.

Hemery, D. (1986) *In pursuit of sporting excellence*. London: Willow Books.

Johns, D. P. and Eldridge, G. (1992) 'Fairplay and the organization of sport', in T. Williams, L. Almond, and A. Sparkes (eds) *Sport and physical activity*. London: E. and F. N. Spon. pp. 504-511.

Keating, J. W. (1964/1988) 'Sportsmanship as a moral category', in W. J. Morgan and K. V. Meier (eds) *Philosophic inquiry in sport*. Champaign, Ill.: Human Kinetics, pp. 241-250.

Knoppers, A. (1985) 'Professionalization of attitudes: A review and critique', *Quest*, 37, 1, 92-102.

Knoppers, A., Schuiteman, J. and Love, B. (1986) 'Winning is not the only thing', *Sociology of Sport Journal*, 3, 1, 43.

Kohlberg, L. (1969) 'Stage and sequence: The cognitive developmental approach to socialization', in D. Goslin (ed) *Handbook of socialization theory and research*. Chicago: Rand-McNally.

————(1976) 'Moral stages and moralization: The cognitive-developmental approach', in T. Lickona (ed) *Moral development and behaviour: Theory, research, and social issues*. New York: Holt, Rinehart, and Winston.

Lee, M. J. (1977) *Expressed values of football players, intramural football players, and non-football players*. Eugene, OR: Microform Publications.

Lee, M. J. and Cockman, M. (in press) 'Values in children's sport: Spontaneously expressed values among young athletes', *International Review for the Sociology of Sport: Special edition Ethical problems in sport*.

Lee, M. J. and Williams, V. (1989) 'Over the top', *Sport and Leisure*, March-April, pp. 27-28.

Maloney, T. L. and Petrie, B. M. (1972) 'Professionalisation of attitudes toward play among Canadian school pupils as a function of sex, grade, and participation', *Journal of Leisure Research*, 4, 3, pp. 184-195.

Mantel, R. C. and Vander Velden, L. (1974) 'The relationship between professionalisation of attitude toward play of preadolescent boys and participation in organised sport', in G. H. Sage (ed), *Sport and American society: Selected readings*. Reading, Mass.: Addison-Wesley.

McElroy, M. and Kirkendall, D. (1980) 'Significant others and professionalized sport attitudes', *Research Quarterly for Exercise and Sport*, 51, pp. 645-653.

Nicholson, C. (1979) 'Some attitudes associated with sports participation among junior high school females', *Research Quarterly for Exercise and Sport*, 50, pp. 661-667.

Roberts, G. C. (1993) 'Motivation in sport: Understanding and enhancing the motivation and achievement of children', in R. N. Singer, M. Murphey, and L. K Tennant (eds) *Handbook of research on sports psychology*. New York: Macmillan, pp. 405-420.

Rokeach, M. (1968) *Beliefs, attitudes, and values*. San Francisco: Jossey-Bass.

——— (1973) *The nature of human values*. New York: The Free Press.

Schwartz, S. H. (1992) 'Universals in the content and structure of values: Theoretical advances and empirical tests in 20 countries', in M. P. Zanna (ed) *Advances in experimental social psychology*, Vol. 25. New York: Academic Press.

Schwartz, S. H. and Bilsky, W. (1987) 'Toward a universal psychological structure of human values', *Journal of Personality and Social Psychology*, 53, pp. 350-362.

Shields, D. L. and Bredemeier, B. J. L. (1994) *Character development through physical activity*. Champaign, Ill.: Human Kinetics.

Simmons, D. D. and Dickinson, R. V, (1986) 'Measurement of values expression in sports and athletics', *Perceptual and Motor Skills*, 62, 651-658.

Stahlberg, D. and Frey, D. (1988) 'Attitudes I: Structure, measurement, and function', in M. Hewstone, W. Stroebe, J-P. Codol, and G. M. Stephenson (eds) *Introduction to Social Psychology*. Oxford: Blackwell.

Taylor, P. W. (1975) *Principles of ethics: An introduction*. Encino, Calif.: Dickenson.

Telama, R., Heikkala, J., and Laasko, L. (1993) 'Conceptions about fair play and morals in sport among young Finnish athletes'. Paper presented at the AISEP meeting of experts, Ballarat, Australia, Nov. 8-12.

The Times (28th April, 1994) 'Driving ambition that took miner onto the fairways'.

Wandzilack, T. (1985) 'Values development through physical education and athletics', *Quest*, 37, 2: pp. 176-185.

Wankel, L. M. and Kreisel, P. S. J. (1985) 'Factors underlying enjoyment of youth sports: Sport and age group comparisons', *Journal of Sport Psychology*, 7, pp. 51-64.

Waters, C. (1982) Attitudes towards instrumental behaviour in youth football among players and non-players. Unpublished dissertation, Trinity and All Saints' College, Leeds, England.

Webb, H. (1969) 'Professionalization of attitudes towards play among adolescents', in G. S. Kenyon (ed) *Aspects of contemporary sport sociology.* Chicago: The Athletic Institute.

Whitehead, J. (1987) 'Why children take part', *ISCiS Journal*, 1, 1: pp. 23-31.

————(1990) *Motivation and sport persistence in children and adolescents.* Research report to the National Coaching Foundation, Leeds, England.

Wicker, A. W. (1969) 'Attitudes versus actions: The relationship of verbal and overt behaviour responses to attitude objects', *Journal of Social Issues,* 25 (Autumn): pp. 41-78.

ETHICS AND PRACTICE IN OUTDOOR ADVENTURE EDUCATION

Tony Westbury
Nene College, Northampton

Introduction

Thinking about ethics is difficult. It is fraught with theoretical complexity, which is not helped by a tendency by writers to define similar terms in different ways. Although difficult, there is a practical value for teachers to have an understanding of ethical issues. To this end much has been written about the general educational context, (e.g. Peters, 1972; Wood and Barrow, 1977) and, to a lesser extent, the physical education context (e.g. McIntosh, 1979; Kretchmar, 1994). Outdoor and adventurous activities are a prominent area of the curriculum which has been somewhat neglected in this literature. The theme of this short paper is to outline some of the theoretical questions involved in ethical issues and to highlight some typical areas of ethical consideration in the area of outdoor adventure education.

Mortlock (1987) is one of the many writers to have noted the inevitable tension in working with people in the outdoors: that between providing people with challenge and striving to ensure their safety. Many of the activities used in outdoor education are designed to be adventurous, their value lying in their novelty and their impact. Educational benefits which may take a long time to become evident in more traditional classroom-based teaching, such as the development of self-esteem and the ability to comfortably adopt different team roles, can be dramatically facilitated by using the natural environment to provide a surmountable challenge. In delivering an effective outdoor programme, teachers and instructors are frequently confronted with decisions which directly affect the safety and well being of their students: should we try the difficult route, or take the easier alternative?; should I persist in encouraging an anxious

79

participant to abseil?; should I highlight a participant's attention-seeking behaviour in the debrief? In contrast to other areas of ethical deliberation, those working with groups in the outdoors often do not have time for reflection and decision making. Decisions often have to be made rapidly and their consequences can be very serious. Errors of judgment by the party leader can result in the death or serious injury of group members. Because of the gravity of the decision making, debates surrounding ethical issues relating to the safety of groups using the outdoors are often highly emotive, particularly when they focus on the safety of children and young people.

The tension between offering challenge and ensuring safety is often discussed in terms of risk. Defined in its simplest form, risk involves the calculation of a statistical probability that an event with a negative consequence will occur. Human reasoning about risk is an interesting topic in itself; many biases operate on our thinking about what is risky and what is not. There is also often an incompatibility between our attitudes about a risky situation and our actual behaviour when confronted with it. There is a fatalistic line of thinking which suggests that the natural environment is highly challenging and changeable and human decision making is fallible and irrational, therefore it is inevitable that accidents will occur. This is an extreme view. However with the possibility of physical or psychological harm, difficult questions arise about the acceptability or unacceptability of a 'risky' activity. Is it possible to quantify risk, and then state that beyond a certain point the risks are too great and the educational benefits too small? If it is possible, who should decide where a line is drawn? If these questions are too difficult to answer, they may be resolved, as some people have argued, by banning the use of the outdoors as a medium for education. This conclusion reveals irrational and biased thinking; it is like banning the use of the motor vehicle because a number of people are killed or injured in road traffic accidents. Objective and unbiased thinking recognises the importance of balance between cost and benefit, although this 'utilitarian' approach is not without its own problems, which are discussed later.

So far, this introduction has focused specifically on the question of risk. The risk-benefit question is a very significant one in outdoor adventure education, but the ethical issues extend beyond this. This paper will also examine the nature of informed consent, secrecy and deception in outdoor education and practical ethics related to the use of the natural environment. It is not my intention in this paper to prescribe solutions to ethical questions, neither is it to present a 'cookbook' of methods of resolution. I do not claim to have a monopoly in thinking about ethical questions pertinent to outdoor education. My main aim is to provoke thought and discussion and to encourage practitioners to look at ethical decisions they may have made in the past, think about how they arrived at these decisions and — newly-armed with (it is to be hoped) an increased awareness of their own thinking — ask, "would I do the same again?"

Theoretical approaches to ethical issues

This section will briefly review the philosophical approaches to ethical questions. This is not simply an academic exercise. Every ethical decision necessitates the adoption of a philosophical stance. This section will highlight the fact that we are frequently inconsistent in the way in which we arrive at ethical decisions. It is important for practitioners to understand the logic of how a decision has been arrived at and therefore clarify their own thinking and decision making. Peters (1966) summarised the study of ethics as the study of why one situation or action is better or more desirable than another situation or action. One of the problems confronting practitioners is that 'better' may be interpreted as meaning many things: better able to achieve the desired educational aims; better able to maintain safety; or better able to maintain the financial viability of a centre. Scruton (1995) picks up this issue, highlighting that the 'good/better' discourse is inherently problematic. He cites three particular problems: firstly in terms of measuring good — is it possible to reliably measure the 'goodness' of a decision?; secondly, the problem of deciding whose good we are giving precedence to — mine, yours, theirs?; finally, a practical point — can we sacrifice what is 'good' for one person in favour of an overall collective 'good'? This final point is returned to later when group and individual ethics are discussed.

Hunt (1990) has written extensively on the subject of ethics in adventure-based experiential education. He argues that if the outdoor educator aims to provide good actions or situations, he or she needs to understand the differing conceptualisations of 'good' and where 'good' comes from. Hunt summarises the vast philosophical literature in this area into four theoretical approaches:

1. ethical subjectivism
2. ethical objectivism
3. consequentialist theories of ethics
4. nonconsequentialist theories of ethics.

Ethical subjectivism

The ethical subjectivist reasons that the only condition that needs to be satisfied for an action or decision to be acknowledged as good is that a person believes it to be so. This view, based on the work of the philosopher David Hume, is very common in many areas of decision-making. Essentially, ethical subjectivism can be divided into three types: hedonism ("I chose this option because it gives ME pleasure"); egoism ("I chose this option because it services MY interests best"); and intuitionism ("I chose this option because it feels right to ME"). General questions of right and wrong can be addressed but will be answered in terms of what the individual believes to be most pleasing, or in his or her interest, or feeling right. This type of reasoning is evident when party leaders decide on a particular route or challenge without reference to the nature of the party they are leading. This type of decision making, which is discussed further when we come on to consider paternalism, is not uncommon. However there are considerable logical and practical problems with subjectivism. Most significantly, since the sole criterion for deciding whether an act is a good one is a subjective judgment, it makes any discussion of resolving the issue of what is good and bad totally redundant.

Ethical objectivism

Ethical objectivity is based on the premise that for an act to be seen as good it must satisfy some source of 'good' which goes beyond the present situation. Objective ethical decisions are not based on what an individual believes to be right or wrong, rather they are based on some external set of 'moral rules'. This type of approach was described in its most extreme form by Plato, who suggested that ethical rules are as objective and universal as mathematical rules. An example of this type of ethical reasoning in Outdoor Education is that all decisions about what represents a good or bad course of action should be answered by the Department for Education and Science or Local Education Authority guide-lines. If it says you can do it, then it is a good action or decision. If not, it is a bad action or decision. This type of decision-making is also not uncommon; many practitioners feel more confident when they are following a clear guideline. However it does have a significant drawback, in that it leads to dogmatic and inflexible adherence to rules. Problems can and often do arise where the DES or LEA has failed to legislate for a particular situation.

Consequentialist theories of ethics

One of the most common methods of deciding between two courses of action is to determine which one satisfies the criterion of serving the greater good. To the ethicist this search for the greater good is called normative ethics. This approach is most clearly seen in the work of the nineteenth century philosopher John Stuart Mill, who advocated the 'Utilitarian' view that an action is good if its consequences bring the greatest good to the greatest number of people. This returns us to the earlier discourse about defining good.

However not all consequentialist theories are necessarily utilitarian. The search for the greater good may involve teachers at Outdoor Centres running courses which they know to be of a lower quality than they could deliver simply to maintain the cash flow, and therefore keep the Centre open. In this case the greater good is not good for the greater good in the immediate scenario, but for the greater good in the longer term.

Nonconsequentialist theories of ethics

The nonconsequentialist approach to ethics is involved with deciding whether an action is good independent of the outcome. This approach is based in the work of the German philosopher Kant. In addressing the question, "What makes an act a good act?", Kant suggested that the answer involves a three-step progression. Firstly, an act must be motivated by a sense of duty rather than from personal inclination, thus distancing the decision from subjectivism. The next progression is based on the question: "What is my duty?". Duty is derived from some externally framed "law" which may, but not necessarily, be interpreted as civil law. The external law may also be framed in terms of a religious belief, or a set of regulations or guidelines, which may be written or unwritten. It is the third progression which characterises Kant's approach. This is the categorical imperative. Scruton (1995) summarises this process:

> Find your reasons for acting only after all 'empirical conditions' have been discounted. If you obey this imperative you will be doing what reason requires: your action will be referred to reason alone not to your individual passions and interests. (pp. 284–285)

Therefore nonconsequentialists recognise an act as a good one only if they would wish it to be universally applied. That is, they would wish everyone confronted with the same set of circumstances to make the same decision. If a decision is based on consequences or could not be universally applied, it should not respected as a reasoned or good one. In a situation such as occurred at Lyme Bay in 1993, with tragic loss of life, the decision to canoe at sea rather than on a stretch of inland water failed to satisfy the categorical imperative. Few instructors would wish such a group to paddle in the conditions prevailing at that time.

Now that the philosophical groundwork has been established we can look at specific ethical issues in outdoor education.

The risk-benefit equation in Outdoor Education

This section is concerned with the ethical basis of decisions about whether it is acceptable to expose people to activities which could kill or injure them in order to achieve educational benefits.

Lee (1987: p. 22) has defined risk as:

> ...the likelihood that an accident (an unintended event with an adverse outcome) will occur during a given period of exposure, compounded by the scale of the consequences if it should occur.

Risk is often framed in terms of a statistical probability, although this can be misleading because of the relatively few people who participate in sports which have been classified as high risk. The intervening variable between the risk situation and the unpredictable outcome is the judgment of the practitioner. Hunt (1990) believes that judgment should be removed from the risk-benefit equation. To Hunt, risk means the aspects of the situation which are beyond the instructor's knowledge or control. I believe this view justifies too much. It encourages the view that some things are completely unpredictable. The effects of increased temperature on a snow slope are unknowable but with training and experience they may become more predictable.

The educational benefits of Outdoor Education have been the subject of much debate. Westbury (1992) identified three main areas of learning commonly found in the outdoor adventure experiences. These are:

1. *Cognitive Skill Learning* — the acquisition of procedural and declarative knowledge of skills and skills and techniques in the range of activities offered.
2. *Social Skill Learning* — the recognition and development of social skills such as leadership skills.
3. *Self-Management Skills* — outdoor adventure experiences requiring students to show determination and persistence, confront and deal with their fears. These have been shown to help students deal with situations that occur in their 'normal' everyday lives

The ethical balance that the practitioner needs to maintain involves the assessment of the risks, the probability of negative outcomes against the educational benefits, the probability that learning has occurred. Clearly the situation would be simplified if we could, in some way, quantify the risks inherent in a situation, alongside the educational benefits accruing from that situation. The balance would be easily established. Tables might be drawn-up and thresholds established to clearly identify where activities become unacceptable. Ideally, the aim is a situation where the maximal educational benefits are gained with the minimal risk. Realistically, can this be achieved? Mortlock (1987) provides a model which helps to clarify the nature of this balance between risk and benefit. He discusses risk in terms of objective risk, where a situation is uncertain and the outcomes are really unpredictable, and subjective risk, where the situation seems uncertain and unpredictable but in reality safe and the outcomes predictable (see **Figure 1**).

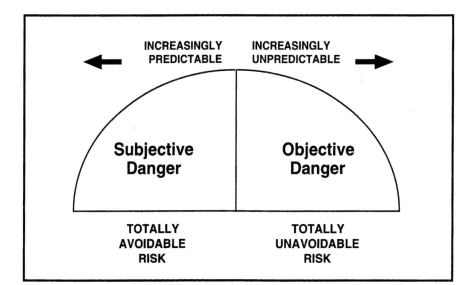

Figure 1   The Subjective-Objective Nature of Risk (From Mortlock, 1987)

Rock Climbing, (using top-rope belay systems) and abseiling (using safety ropes and fixed anchor points) are examples of situations where the novice experiences a high level of subjective risk, but in reality they are objectively very safe since the rope systems are operating under a minimum of mechanical stress. Hunt (1990) argues that if the educational goals can be accomplished by using high levels of subjective risk (and therefore low levels of objective risk), that is the ethically preferable route. The practitioner who chooses a more objective risk situation to achieve the same educational outcomes faces the difficult question: "Why did you place your students at a greater risk than necessary?".

Returning to the language of the ethicist, the nonconsequentialist may argue that the greater good is safety. Any action which may compromise safety is intrinsically bad and therefore unjustified. On the other hand the consequentialist may adopt the position that the greater good is the possible educational benefit to be gained, any act compromising this end is bad. This argument has been used to justify some of the practises used in military training. The conflict exists. The nonconsequentialist position, with its emphasis on the categorical imperative, may justify too little. The consequentialist view, with a utilitarian emphasis, may justify too much.

Informed consent

Informed consent refers to the consent a participant gives having been given a full and accurate account of the risks involved in the activities and the possible benefits which may be gained. The ethical issues begin to become apparent when we explore the extent of consent necessary. Informed consent is premised on participants being given as much information as possible about every activity which they will be required to undertake. From a practical perspective this can be very difficult. A great deal of technical and practical information may be given but in order to interpret it and give consent which is fully informed, the participants must already possess a high level of knowledge and skill, and this is rarely the case. This argument can be further obscured by the fact that the environment in which the activity takes place is ever-changing. It is impossible to give information that is 100% accurate. Adding the participant's lack of expert understanding to the changing environment, it may be argued that consent to participate does not need to be informed. The ethical debate then becomes centred on whether the 'informed state' is better than the 'uninformed state'. It is common practice to keep students uninformed as to the precise nature of what they will be doing in order to maximise the opportunity for the students to learn about adaptability in decision-making and problem solving. In a consequentialist analysis this is a risk which can be balanced against the educational benefits. On the other hand it is necessary to examine the nonconsequentialist perspective. By surprising students with situations to which they have not consented, the practitioner is removing the sense of choice, ownership and self-determination from the student. When the argument extends into the realms of personal autonomy, we need to proceed with care. When does the uninformed state begin to infringe on a person's liberty and free will — for example, in a specific case of paternalism where a practitioner takes an action on behalf of students without their consent and feels justified by the argument that the action best serves the students' needs or welfare. The consequentialist is faced with the dilemma of establishing where the greater good lies. Is it with the denial of information on the grounds that the educational benefits will be greater or with the establishment of rules which in the longer term will benefit more people? The nonconsequentialist might argue that the issue of free-will and choice of action is such a significant one that the categorical imperative should operate; thus the informed state is ethically preferable, despite the education benefit which might be gained.

The arguments regarding informed consent and paternalism are highly pertinent to the everyday practice of those working in outdoor adventure education. An example from my own experience is drawn from my Mountain Leadership training. As an exercise, we were to act as 'typical' group members. This involved all the trainees leaving all their personal equipment in the centre and using boots, rucksacks, tents and other items of equipment from the store. All the group members have personal kit that over years of use they have become familiar with and trust. There were several items I felt completely lost without — especially, my sleeping bag. I knew a store sleeping bag would be comparatively cold and uncomfortable. I was very upset that I had not been informed that this type of exercise would be undertaken. I certainly learned a lot about the confidence, or lack of it, many centre clients have about kit. But should they routinely be told that their equipment is functional rather than comfortable?

Often the tension necessarily set up between risk and benefit governs the type and amount of information that participants are given. Practitioners should try to put themselves in the boots of their group members. Prior to undertaking a task for the first time how much and what sort of information would they like to be given? This is a difficult question as the information will be more meaningful to the expert than the novice.

Secrecy and deception

Recently, while teaching undergraduate students who had selected an Outdoor Leadership module, I deceived them. To promote their sense of ownership, I had set them to devise their own night navigation exercise which they would undertake later in the course. They had returned, having satisfied the criteria, with a course covering less than a mile on easy terrain and including three 90 degree turns and ending at a local hostelry. On the day of the exercise, they loaded into the minibus and gleefully set out. I dropped them off at a point about three miles from their planned route. None of them questioned this, so I left them and parked a further half mile up the road and returned to covertly shadow the group and watch the chaos unfold.

Most practitioners have done something like this. In consequentialist terms, I believe my actions were justified by the educational benefits which the students gained. Initially, they believed they were where they thought they were and could not understand why their navigation was letting them down. They returned to their starting point and realised they were not where they thought they were; after some deliberation they located themselves and successfully navigated to their intended destination. I believed that the act of deception generated a positive end. The nonconsequentialist would argue that the categorical imperative should operate. Would I want my decision to become a universal law that everyone must adhere to? If I do not, then the act is a bad act and I should not have deceived them.

Once again, the wider perspective must be examined. This group was later to undertake a longer expedition which involved crossing Striding Edge, a tricky and exposed ridge walk, in potentially very hazardous winter conditions. Although the group was working independently, I would have ultimately decided whether a planned route, or a safer low-level alternative, was to be followed. Having deceived them once, how confident could the students be in my subsequent decisions? How confident could they be that I would not simply press on in difficult conditions because of the 'educational benefits' which might accrue, but prejudice their safety? It can be argued that any deception necessarily undermines the teacher-student relationship. From the examples given, it is clear that the use of deception as a strategy in teaching is highly problematic and controversial.

Secrecy and deception are related but different constructs. Deception involves actively encouraging people to believe a fact when it is not really true. Secrecy on the other hand is the passive withholding of information. Secrecy is sometimes used in outdoor education, for example when encouraging groups to plan expedition routes. The practitioner may be asked to approve a route, knowing that it will involve a great deal of ascending and descending, whilst a high level route although appearing to be longer would be much quicker. Is the secrecy justified when learning at relatively low risk can occur?

Secrecy may also become apparent in dealing with issues of confidentiality. Examples of this can be drawn from many sources. The rapport that skilled outdoor educators are able to develop with students can encourage self-disclosure of a very personal nature, for example, of abuse within the home, of bullying at school or the breaking of rules within the residential centre. The ethical conflict lies in balancing the public good with the personal secret. In the consequentialist analysis, it is for the practitioner to establish the greater good. For the nonconsequentialist, it is not ethically correct to make a promise that you are not willing or able to keep.

Environmental issues

As users of the outdoors we advocate a lowest possible impact approach, in which we "take only photographs, leave only footprints." However, the reality of extended living in the outdoors often makes demands which makes this rule difficult to adhere to. The building of fires, using natural water sources for washing and the disposal of human waste all present problems of ecological ethics. To the nonconsequentialist the categorical imperative operates. All negative impact on the environment represents an ethically unacceptable decision and must be avoided. However, consider a situation which commonly occurs. A group has walked all day in cold and miserable weather, spirits are low and clothes are wet through. The group members ask if they can build a fire, to dry their clothes and raise their morale. The leader knows the fire will have a positive effect on the group but will have negative consequences on the environment. The nonconsequentialist approach has already been presented. For the consequentialist, the decision that needs to be made is where does the greater good lie in raising the spirits of the group or in avoiding the negative impact on the area? This dilemma has been discussed by Hunt (1990) as a 'conflict of values'. The outdoor educationalist does not need to be convinced of the value of protecting the environment. The difficulties become apparent when the protection of the environment becomes compromised by the needs of human beings. There are no simple answers when considering issues of environmental ethics. Some radical environmentalists suggest that our aim of zero environmental impact is impossible to attain without completely banning access to the outdoors. The compromise position is one of minimal impact, balanced against the human needs of the group. In Hunt's analysis the balance between impact and benefits can be approached in similar terms to the risk-benefit argument already discussed. More benefit may justify more impact. This view is controversial, placing personal or educational benefits to humans higher in the hierarchy of good than maintaining the environment.

Conclusion

This paper set out to present an overview of ethical theory in the context of outdoor adventure education. There is no doubt that confronting and resolving ethical issues is an everyday concern of the practitioner. The examples in this paper have illustrated that. The differing methods which are available to help us resolve issues have also been highlighted. However, the key conclusion I would like to draw is that awareness of ethical issues should be an integral element of practice. Good, safe practice in outdoor adventure education should also be ethically sound. This means that teachers and instructors have to be very clear in their thinking about issues such as risk taking, secrecy and deception, and about their relationship with group members and the environment in which they work. Some of these issues have been raised in recent legal cases involving practitioners. This focuses the mind further. Practitioners are very aware of the fine line they walk between challenge and safety, between play and adventure. They are also aware of the increasing demand for thrills and the 20-second fair ground adrenalin 'fix'. The outdoor environment offers many opportunities for personal development, but will not be able to deliver if challenges are legislated against. At the outset I warned that thinking about ethics is hard. I hope it remains so; because all the time it is hard people have to think about how the natural environment can be used creatively for personal development. I believe that the issues that this paper have raised will aid practitioners to appraise their decision-making and consider in hindsight decisions made in the past. Hopefully it will be useful in future risk assessment exercises and help those working in this exciting area of education to make better decisions in the future.

References

Hunt, J. (1990) *Ethical issues in experiential education*. Boulder, Colorado: The Association for Experiential Education.

Kretchmar, R. (1994) *Practical philosophy of sport*. Champaign, Ill.: Human Kinetics Publishers.

Lee, M. (1987) *Colloquium on risk taking in sport, leisure and recreation*. London: Department of Health and Social Security.

McIntosh, P. (1979) *Fair play: Ethics in sport and education*. London: Heinemann Educational Books.

Mortlock, C. (1987) *The adventure alternative*. Milnethorpe, Cumbria: Cicerone Press.

Peters, R. (1966) *Ethics and education*. London: George Allen and Unwin.

Scruton, R. (1995) *Modern philosophy, An introduction and survey*. London: Sinclair-Stevenson.

Singer, P. (1991) *A companion to ethics*. London: Blackwell.

Westbury, A. (1992) *Curriculum development — An assessment driven summer fieldwork programme for the B.A. Sports Studies Degree*. Unpublished PGCED Project. University of Northumbria.

Wood, R. and Barrow, R. (1977) *An introduction to philosophy of education*. London: Methuen.

II:

ETHICAL ISSUES IN
RESEARCH IN SPORTS SCIENCE

THE PHYSIOLOGICAL ASSESSMENT OF ATHLETES

J. Doust
University of Brighton

Introduction

Physiological assessment, commonly termed exercise testing, provides the sports scientist with a most challenging task that has implications beyond the purely technical. Consider the assessment of maximal oxygen uptake in a professional basketball player. The purpose of testing may be stated simplistically as "Is the player fit enough?". Such a question assumes that a standard can be placed on the level of aerobic power needed for basketball. It assumes that the player is in a healthy condition to undertake a test and that the testing environment allows the player to perform fully. It assumes that there is no risk of a strenuous test causing the player's injury or even death. It assumes that the player is willing to participate and does not feel obliged by pressure from the coach or threat of financial penalty. It assumes that the sports scientist is capable of making accurate measurements with precision equipment. It assumes that the sports scientist is able to interpret the resultant data. It assumes that the sports scientist and the coach will know how to change training as a result of the test and that the player will actually change his or her training behaviour. And what if the player has a high adiposity and needs dietary as well as fitness advice? Is such advice available directly, or should the player be referred to an expert? Will any suggestion that the player is overweight be handled with sensitivity or might the entire process nudge the player towards an eating disorder?

These issues are of topical relevance since the use of exercise testing has become widespread. The British Olympic Medical Centre, the National Sports Medicine Institute, numerous higher education institutions, and commercial organisations offer physiological assessment as part of support services to Olympic competitors and athletes in National or representative teams in perhaps as many as 40 sports. For athletes at a less elite level of performance and for the individual involved in sport and exercise as a means of recreation and health enhancement, physiological assessment is widespread in health clubs and centres.

A number of organisations provide guidance on the ethics and code of practice for investigators using human participants (American Physiological Society, 1993; American College of Sports Medicine, 1991, 1993; The Australian Sports Commission see Minikin, 1991 and Gore, 1993; The British Association of Sports Sciences, 1988 and 1993; British Psychological Society, 1991). The code of the Physiology section of the British Association of Sports Sciences (now the British Association of Sports and Exercise Sciences [BASES]) is attached as an appendix. All of these codes of practice suggest the need for investigators to act with integrity, and with respect for the athlete. General principles of professional behaviour should always apply. Central to the codes are: the need for investigator competence; the obtaining of informed consent; and the need for confidentiality. The purpose of this paper is to elaborate upon these broad principles in the special circumstances of laboratory and field based physiological assessment of sportsmen and sportswomen.

1.   The purpose of physiological assessment

Physiological assessment can serve many purposes. For the individual athlete[1] the primary purpose is ultimately to improve performance. But there are other subsumptive purposes. Physiological assessment provides baseline data (on the athlete's physical strengths and weaknesses) to allow training prescription; it provides monitoring to evaluate the effectiveness of a particular regime of training; and it serves an educational purpose in allowing the athlete to understand more fully the physical demands and requirements of his or her sport. Information may also be obtained about the health status of the athlete. From a wider perspective, physiological assessment provides the general sporting community with greater knowledge of the physiological bases of sports performance and thus helps generically in the development of effective training and performance strategies.

What testing cannot do is act as a magical intervention to suddenly improve performance, and the current state of knowledge concerning the growth and development of athletes places severe limitations on testing as a means of identifying talent. Moreover, since performance in sport is a complex blend of physiological, psychological, biomechanical, and social factors, it is naive to suggest that testing alone will predict performance or should act as a single criterion for selection purposes.

A primary question then must be why is an athlete being tested? For the athlete's needs? For the coach? For the selector? For general advancement of knowledge in the sport?

2.   Proficiency of investigators

Proficiency encompasses competence in the appropriate and safe use of techniques and equipment, and expertise in the interpretation of the gathered data.

Some guidance is given by law where regulations such as those established by the Committee on Substances Hazardous to Health (COSHH) govern the general aspects of laboratory practice and safety. Methods of monitoring quality control are well established in the scientific community. External bodies such as BASES provide a scheme for accrediting competence in physiological assessment, and this type of approach is mirrored elsewhere (Minikin, 1991). These schemes set standards for personnel, equipment and methodology to ensure that assessment is carried out with appropriate scientific rigour. Currently in Britain, however, this type of approach has not been extended to health clubs where proficiency is monitored locally, if at all.

The precision of measurement will be high in a carefully run laboratory utilising sophisticated equipment. The variability of derived data will be low, ranging up to perhaps 5% for maximal oxygen uptake. However, this type of laboratory testing is time-consuming and expensive. Moreover, laboratory testing may rightly be criticised for low external validity. Thus field testing at the athlete's training venue has become extremely popular. In most cases investigators will use less sophisticated equipment and prediction procedures based on measurement of the external work performed rather than direct measurement of the physiological response. In such circumstances, not only are the precision of measurement and the physiological validity reduced, but also attainment of maximal performance is critically dependent on the athlete's effort, which cannot be judged by objective physiological criteria. MacFarlane (1991), in a provocatively entitled paper *Who do exercise physiologists test best — the athlete or themselves?* , suggests that these issues undermine the very basis of quantitative fitness testing in the field. Applying MacFarlane's reasoning to the use of the extremely popular 20m shuttle test of maximal aerobic capacity (Leger *et al.,* 1988) with a test variability of ±10%, the following data might apply (Table 1).

Table 1

	Sample athlete before training	Sample athlete after training
Field test VO$_2$max (ml. kg^{-1}. min^{-1})	54 — 66	62 — 76
'True' VO$_2$max (ml. kg^{-1}. min^{-1})	60	69

With a true change of +15%, the assessment procedure could show the change to be anything between -6% and +41%! A clear dilemma is apparent; pictured by Figure 1 below. Never can all three apexes be attained simultaneously. In the field, precision must be compromised for cheapness and convenience. The laboratory cannot exactly replicate the sporting environment. The more a test directly mimics a sports situation, the more it becomes contaminated by skill and the less will it reflect only a single physiological capability.

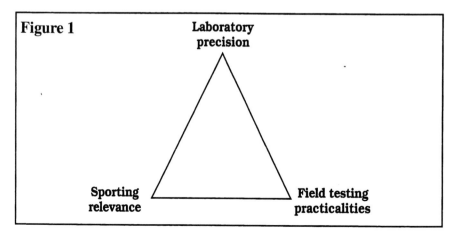

Figure 1

Extensive efforts are being made by sports scientists to resolve this dilemma through the development of valid field tests which precisely estimate physiological function in a sports-specific manner. But this approach is inherently limited since physiological function itself is not being measured. Part of the resolution of the dilemma must remain with the scientist, athlete and coach appreciating that, although compromise is inevitable, through discussion the nature of the compromise can be agreed and the resulting data interpreted accordingly. Testing should be thought of less in terms of seeking a definitive assessment of current physiological status, and rather more in terms of the other purposes of assessment described in section 1.

In the course of assessment it is common for the athlete or coach to seek advice about allied matters such as medical conditions and nutritional advice. Moreover, during a physiological assessment the initial screening questionnaire (see section 5) and observation of, say, the electrocardiogram, might evidence a condition of possible medical concern previously unrecognised by the athlete. To what extent should advice be offered and of what nature? To what extent has the sports scientist a duty to raise with the athlete any suspicions of a possible medical condition when the sports scientist has not been trained in diagnosis (yet may well be more knowledgeable about the electrocardiogram during exercise than the average General Practitioner). When injured, all too often the athlete is faced with medical advice "to rest". Yet for the athlete this is anathema, so the sports scientist's advice is sought on how to achieve an early return to training. Is the sports scientist in a sufficiently knowledgeable position to give such advice? Similarly, body weight and composition are commonly determined during fitness testing as part of the profile of assessments and discussion of percentage body fat requires sensitive handling. Eating disorders are now recognised to be of significant importance and sources such as the IAAF (1989) and Brownell *et al.* (1992) discuss this topic in detail.

Sports scientists need to be aware of the boundaries of their own competence and "should only employ equipment and techniques which they are qualified to use" (BASS, 1993). Advice should be given with care, and caution exercised as the boundaries of competence are reached. Thereafter, it would seem unacceptable simply to refuse to assist further and leave the athlete stranded. Rather, a network of contacts should be established so that appropriate referral may be made to a suitably qualified expert such as a physician, physiotherapist, or nutritionist.

3.   Informed consent

Since physiological assessment procedures necessitate some invasion of an athlete's physical and psychological independence, the athlete must grant consent to this invasion if his/her freedom is to be recognised. This is usually achieved by an athlete reading and signing an informed consent form[2]. In the simpler conditions of a field assessment this is usually attained verbally. Informed consent means that the athlete willingly agrees to the procedures and recognises the purpose of them. But the consent must be both *true* and *informed*.

By true consent is meant consent freely given with proper understanding of the nature and consequences of what is proposed. Assumed consent or consent obtained with undue influence is valueless, and, in this latter respect, particular care is necessary when the (athlete) stands in special relationship to the investigator (Medical Research Council, 1964).

For the athlete the purpose of testing is critical if true consent is to be obtained. The purpose must be clear and the involvement of the coach established. Testing should not be considered judgemental and should not be used solely for selection purposes. This is a particular risk since the apparently 'objective' results of a 'fitness test' can provide a ready opportunity for coach and selector to rationalise away extremely complex and difficult decisions when choosing teams.

Informed consent can act as an important means by which investigators can help ensure the ethical soundness of their work. Although investigators can attempt to consider in advance the ethical issues involved in their work with athletes, the wide variety of sporting subcultures and the multi-cultural nature of society may mean that investigators simply will not have a full understanding of the implications of their actions. The best judges may well be the athletes themselves, and this is the judgement that is gained from consent.

4.   Confidentiality

Legislation such as the Data Protection Act makes certain requirements of confidentiality. Scientific journals require that if work is to be published then individuals should not be identifiable, unless this is critical to the work and has been agreed in advance with the individual concerned. In physiological assessment the greater issue concerns to whom the data are confidential. Normally, the athlete will, as a matter of course, have a right to a copy of his or her results. But what about access by others such as the coach or doctor? Do *they* have a right to the results? Clearly there could be serious discontent if an athlete learns that the coach has been informed without that athlete's knowledge or permission. If drug use becomes apparent serious consideration needs to be given to the nature of confidentiality between the athlete, coach, and sports scientist. Unethical practices by physicians and Sports Scientists have been seen recently in the Ben Johnson affair, and are strongly suggested in national drives to athletic excellence by some of the former Eastern Bloc countries. What is the right action? Singer (1993:100) questions for whom is the Sports Scientist is working — the athlete? The coach? The sports administration? Understanding about what is to be communicated, and to whom, should be determined before any services are rendered.

And what about observation by team mates and others *during* the test? This is often encouraged for motivational reasons. During field testing whole teams may be tested simultaneously with consequent pressure on an individual not to be the first to drop out. Feedback of results will often incorporate norm scores to allow cross-sectional comparisons. Although the very nature of competitive sport involves open competition with others, the self-esteem of the athlete may be extremely vulnerable in, what seems to them, the unusual and threatening circumstances of physical testing. This effect may be exacerbated by the presence of the coach, and possibly the selectors. For professional athletes, the source of their salary complicates matters further. In such circumstances, what is the true worth of the BASS (1993) ethical guideline that: "the athlete is free to withdraw at any point without prejudice..."?

Total confidentiality and freedom of choice for the individual athlete appear to be unattainable and unrealistic goals. Perhaps the only solution is pragmatic. The sports scientist must consider the issues involved and pre-negotiate the delimitations of the assessment procedures with the athlete, coach and others.

5. Risk

Activities of daily life constantly involve risk of accident or death but these risks are usually within an individual's control and individuals continually make decisions according to their perception of the risk. As soon as an individual commences an exercise test this control is, at least partially, removed. It is incumbent on the investigator to assess the risks involved in physiological assessment procedures. It is naive to suggest that physiological assessment involves no risks. The important principle is to consider whether procedures increase the probability of athletes coming to harm. This assessment requires two considerations: first, the inherent risk of physical exertion; second, the steps that can be taken to identify an individual who is at greater risk.

Strenuous exercise involves a risk of death or injury that is very small indeed though, acutely, this risk is greater than that experienced by the individual that is not exercising. On the basis of many studies (e.g. Vuori *et al.*, 1978; Kaltenbach *et al.*, 1982) it may be estimated that the acute risk of death or of a serious medical event during exercise is about twice as high as for the non-exerciser (see Table 2). However, the medical benefits of exercise have been well established (Fentem, 1992) and thus, while not exercising, the risk to the athlete is lower. On balance, epidemiological evidence confirms that the overall risk ratio is in clear favour of those who exercise regularly. Moreover, since individuals undergoing physiological assessment are usually involved in strenuous exertion on a daily basis as part of their involvement in sport and exercise, it is reasonable to conclude that the risk of the assessment procedures is similar to those encountered in *their* daily life.

Table 2   The risk of strenuous exercise: results of typical studies of various groups of individuals

Author	Sample; Risk of death	Deaths: exercise bout
Vuori *et al.* (1978)	1,030,000 performances during ski-hikes in the general population	1:128,750 ·
Kaltenbach *et al.* (1982)	353,638 healthy young athletes during exercise testing	No deaths recorded
Epstein and Maron (1986)	Asymptomatic young athletes	1:200,000
Foster (1988)	Exercise tests in individuals with known or suspected cardio-vascular disease	1:10,000

Nevertheless, there will be some individuals for whom strenuous exercise does involve risk. Kenny and Shapiro (1992) discuss sudden cardiac death in athletes. In the young (less than 35 years), congenital cardiovascular abnormalities such as hypertrophic cardiomyopathy and congenital coronary abnormalities are the most common cause. Coronary atherosclerosis is the major cause in older, and occasionally in younger, athletes. This increases the risk of exercise and the mortality ratios are considerably greater (see Table 2).

To these cardiac risks must be added the risks associated with acute viral or bacterial infection, asthma, and diabetes. The issue for the investigator is whether these risks are identifiable. Pre-test screening is the absolutely essential step in identification (BASS, 1988), followed by appropriate investigation of symptomatic individuals by a medical practitioner. For the asymptomatic individual the paradox of sudden death in an apparently fit and healthy athlete appears unavoidable since "screening of young athletes would not appear to be useful or cost effective due to the low incidence of sudden death in this population and the relative insensitivity of screening techniques" (Kenny and Shapiro, 1992).

This discussion is of special importance when physiological assessment is used as a screening procedure for older individuals or individuals with known coronary risk, prior to participation in a programme of exercise. This type of assessment has increased in popularity with the growing promotion of exercise as a therapy. Here, since the risk is *known* to be greater than in younger and healthier populations, greater responsibility lies with the investigator to ensure that procedures minimise the risk of an event. The American College of Sports Medicine offers extensive guidelines (ACSM, 1991) and these guidelines have been confirmed empirically by Kohl *et al.* (1990).

6. Legal matters

What is the position of the sports scientist should an athlete die or become injured during an exercise test? In the clinical arena medical intervention and clinical trials are well covered by law, professional practice and insurance. No case is known in Britain of a sports scientist being taken to court following an incident in a sports science laboratory and until such a case arises it is impossible to be definitive. *Duty of care* requires that facilities should be 'reasonably' safe for the purposes for which they are used. *COSHH regulations* and the *Health and Safety at Work* Act provide more specific requirements for laboratory environments. The defence of *volenti* to a claim of negligence has been used in the sporting context where athletes implicitly 'volunteer' to participate in sport and thus accept the inherent risks involved (Collins, 1984). *Vicarious liability* also places some liability on the employer where an employee is negligent. Clearly the sports scientist has a duty to fulfil the specific demands of the law, and has a professional responsibility to act with integrity and in a manner which places as paramount the safety and welfare of the athlete. Competence (section 2), an understanding of the risks (section 5), and the use of true informed consent (section 3) are obligatory.

7.   A note on children

Several factors make matters more complex with children than with adults. The gaining of informed consent must involve the parent or guardian. Most testing of children, particularly in schools, uses field tests. Not only will the data therefore be inherently variable but also this variability will be increased in children due to poorer motor control and differing perceptions of maximal effort compared to adults. In comparison to what is known about adults, knowledge of children's responses to exercise is comparatively poor and this makes interpretation of data and assessment of risk more difficult. This problem is exacerbated by the need to know both chronological age and developmental age since a large proportion of cross-sectional differences and longitudinal changes in physiological status will relate to growth and must be appropriately scaled to partition out size (Jakeman *et al.*, 1993). Developmental age is most easily assessed by visual examination of the chest and genitalia for development of the secondary sex characteristics. The consequent need for consent, care and sensitivity is patently obvious. Other techniques are available such as wrist x-ray, peak height velocity, and level of salivary testosterone — but each has its own problems. The difficulties associated with assessing developmental age have lead many investigators to avoid the issue altogether and rely solely on chronological age. However, it could then be reasoned that this approach advantages the early developer over the late developer and leads, in turn, to ethical dilemmas of a different nature. For example, Brewer *et al.* (1992) demonstrated a significantly skewed distribution in the birth month of young boys selected for the Swedish U17 national soccer squad. They attributed this skew to the selection being made at a single, fixed point in the year which consequently favoured those boys born in the early months of the selection year. Burwitz *et al.* (1993) provide further thoughts on talent identification and selection. They conclude with support for the development of player profile schemes aimed at longitudinal development — "all who have the capacity and desire to improve their performance levels deserve appropriate support rather than simply those who may be identified as "talented"' (p. 29).

For these types of reasons, the Physical Education Association (1988) has argued that the use of fitness testing in schools is only appropriate within the wider objectives of education. It should be used not as a means of assessment, but as a means to encourage positive attitudes towards health-related fitness and to promote a lifetime commitment to a healthy lifestyle. As discussed earlier in this paper — the *why?* of testing again becomes a critical consideration.

Conclusions

The growing provision of physiological assessment services by sports scientists requires a parallel growth in consideration of the ethical issues involved. The practice of science cannot be removed from the social context in which it is performed, and this is particularly true when working with humans in sport and exercise where there is a complex interaction between the individuals involved and sporting and societal structures. The athlete may be strongly focused on a uni-dimensional outcome — improved performance — but the scientist must be aware of the underlying multi-dimensional fabric. Difficulties and dilemmas will arise and these will need resolving. Legal requirements and codes of practice provide a certain amount of guidance but the sports scientist must go further and consider fully other dimensions of his or her work if a professional service of high ethical standard is to be provided.

Notes

[1] The term "athlete" is used generically to indicate a performer of any type of sport or exercise.

[2] The nature of the information that should be detailed in an informed consent form is well described in the documents referred to in the introduction.

References

American College of Sports Medicine [ACSM] (1991) *Guidelines for exercise testing and prescription.* 4th ed. Philadelphia: Lea and Febiger.

———(1993) 'Policy statement regarding the use of human subjects and informed consent', *Medicine and Science in Sport and Exercise* 25: p. vi.

American Physiological Society (1993) 'Guiding principles for research involving animals and human beings', *Journal of Applied Physiology,* 73: appendix.

Brewer, J., Balsom, P. D., Davis, J. A. and Ekblom, B. (1992) 'The influence of birth date and physical development on the selection of a male junior international soccer squad', *Journal of Sports Sciences* 10: pp. 561–562.

British Association of Sports Sciences [BASS] (1988) *Position statement on the physiological assessment of the elite competitor.* Leeds: BASS.

——— (1993) *Sports physiology ethics and code of conduct.* Leeds: BASS.

British Psychological Society (1991) *Code of conduct and ethical principles and guidelines.* Leicester: The British Psychological Society.

Brownell, K., Rodin, J. and Wilmore, J. (1992) *Eating, body weight and performance in athletes: disorders of modern society.* Philadelphia: Lea and Febiger.

Burwitz, L., Moore, P. M. and Wilkinson, D. M. (1993) *Future directions for performance related research in the sports sciences: an interdisciplinary approach.* London: Sports Council.

Collins, V. (1994) *Recreation and the law.* 2nd Edition. London: E & F. N. Spon.

Epstein, S. and Maron, B. (1986) 'Sudden death and the competitive athlete: perspectives on preparticipation screening studies', *Journal of the American College of Cardiology* 7: pp. 220–230.

Fentem, P. (1992) 'Exercise in the prevention of disease', *British Medical Bulletin* 48: pp. 630–650.

Foster, C. (1988) 'Sudden death and the graded exercise test', in Hall, L. K. and Meyer, G. C. (eds) *La Crosse exercise and health series: Cardiac rehabilitation: exercise testing and prescription,* Vol. II. Champaign, Ill: Life Enhancement.

Gore, C. (1993) *Proficiency requirements for exercise physiology laboratories: draft position paper of the Laboratory Standards Assistance Scheme.* Belconnen, Australia: Australian Sports Commission.

International Amateur Athletics Federation [IAAF] (1989) *Too thin to win: an information booklet on eating disorders.* Monaco: IAAF.

Jakeman, P. M., Winter, E. M. and Doust, J. (1993) *Future directions for performance related research in sports physiology.* London: Sports Council.

Kaltenbach, M., Schrere, D. and Dowinsky, S. (1982) 'Complications of exercise testing: a survey of three German speaking countries', *European Heart Journal* 3: pp. 199–202.

Kenny, A. and Shapiro, L. M. (1992) 'Sudden cardiac death in athletes', *British Medical Bulletin* 48: pp. 534–545.

Kohl, H. W., Gibbons, L. W., Gordon, N. F. and Blair, S. N. (1990) 'An empirical evaluation of the ACSM guidelines for exercise testing', *Medicine and Science in Sports and Exercise* 22: pp. 533–539.

Leger, L. A., Mercier, D., Gadoury, C. and Lambert, J. (1988) 'The multistage 20m shuttle test for aerobic fitness', *Journal of Sports Sciences* 6: pp. 93–101.

MacFarlane, D. (1991) 'Who do exercise physiologists test best — athletes or themselves?', *New Zealand Journal of Sports Medicine* 19: pp. 13–15.

Medical Research Council (1964) 'Responsibility in investigations on human subjects', *British Medical Journal* 2: pp. 178–180.

Minikin, B. (1991) *Laboratory standards assistance scheme: requirements and recommended practices for laboratories conducting physiological and sports performance testing.* Belconnen, Australia: Australian Sports Commission.

Physical Education Association (1988) 'A position statement on health-related fitness testing and monitoring in schools', *British Journal of Physical Education* 19: pp. 194–195.

Singer, R. (1993) 'Ethical issues in clinical services', *Quest* 45: pp. 88–105.

Vuori, I., Makarainen, M. and Jaaselainen, A. (1978) 'Sudden death and physical activity', *Cardiology* 63: pp. 287–293.

Appendix:

BRITISH ASSOCIATION OF SPORTS SCIENCES SPORTS PHYSIOLOGY SECTION CODE OF CONDUCT

1 Introduction

This document sets out the broad principles of conduct and ethics which should guide working practices in sports physiology. All members of the British Association of Sports Sciences (BASS) Sport Physiology Section, by being accepted as members of BASS, automatically consent to abide by this code of conduct. This code of conduct should be read in conjunction with the guidelines on physiological assessment of the athlete which provide elaboration on experimental techniques and protocols, and give examples of informed consent and medico-legal clearance procedures.

The sports physiologist must balance three considerations.

i   Sports physiologists work with human subjects who have the right to expect the highest standards of professionalism, consideration and respect.

ii The pursuit of scientific knowledge requires that research is carried out with integrity.

iii The law requires working practices to be safe and the welfare of the athlete to be paramount.

2 The Competence of the Sports Physiologist

i   Sports physiologists will only employ equipment and techniques which they are qualified to use; and they will meticulously restrict interpretations of results, offered in their professional capacity, to those which they are qualified as physiologists to give. In particular, any problem whose essence appears to lie within another specialist field such as biomechanics, physiotherapy, medicine, or psychology, must be referred to an appropriate professional.

ii The accreditation process is a key means by which sports physiologists may demonstrate that they have achieved professional competence, and members of the physiology section should seek to achieve accredited status.

3   Professional Relationships

Sports physiologists will be sensitive to the needs and concerns of subjects and colleagues. Particular attention must be paid to the potential conflict between the need of the physiologist to gather data and the need of the subject to exercise, train or compete. The latter must be considered paramount at all times.

4   General and Specific Ethical Clearance

Ethical clearance must be obtained for all work. The division between general and specific clearance will be determined in relation to the policies of the local Ethical Committee. General clearance should be sought for all routine procedures. Specific clearance must always be obtained before the imposition of any unusually severe physical demand or psychological stress, the administration of any ergogenic aid to be taken internally, work with subjects having disabilities, or the employment of biopsy or venipuncture. Specific clearance is also often required in many areas for work with children, and in some areas for the sampling of capillary blood.

5   Informed Consent

All subjects must give informed consent prior to participating in a project. Informed consent is the knowing consent of a subject (or legally authorised representative in the case of children) so situated as to exercise free power of choice without undue inducement or any element of force, fraud, deceit, or coercion.

In most cases informed consent would be obtained by having the subject read and sign a document presenting all the information pertinent to the investigation. This would normally include a description of the investigation and its objectives; the procedures to be followed; the risks and benefits; an offer to answer any queries; an instruction that the subject is free to withdraw at any point without prejudice; and an explanation concerning confidentiality.

In the case of simple field tests such informed consent may be obtained verbally.

6   Confidentiality

Confidentiality will be observed with appropriate measures taken to ensure that, unless necessary for the project and clearly so stated on the informed consent form, all materials will be securely and safely held. All subjects will have a right to a copy of their results; as the norm, subjects should be given such a copy on a routine basis after each test session. The question of access by other persons, such as coaches and doctors, should wherever possible be agreed with the subject in advance. It is normal practice, and to be encouraged, that the coach is involved in full. Nevertheless, on no account may such access be granted at any time against the subject's wishes.

7   Data Protection & Publication

Storage and use of individually-identifiable data must follow the Data Protection Act. Within this constraint, however, investigators in sports physiology should seek always to maximise the accessibility of research findings, and whenever appropriate to publish them, in the interests of both science and sport. Contracts of secrecy should be entered upon only where the investigator is satisfied that desirable scientific guidance cannot otherwise be made available to the subject(s) concerned.

8   COSHH Regulations/Guidelines

These must be followed in all respects.

INFORMED CONSENT? A CASE STUDY FROM ENVIRONMENTAL PHYSIOLOGY

Graham Mcfee and Paul Mcnaught-Davis
University of Brighton

The question of how scientists proceed *ethically* is both a vexed one and one of considerable importance. In environmental physiology — where the risks to subjects are considerable — this question is posed especially sharply. For the study of human functioning in cold or hot climates, or under increased or decreased pressures or humidities, may well involve approaching the limits of what is *safe* as well as what is comfortable: SCUBA and saturation diving research, for example, might involve the risk of decompression sickness (the bends) or of hypothermia. How should any researcher *constrain* the research practice in order to proceed ethically?

Further, the relative importance of the topic of research may play a part here. Perhaps extreme procedures are warranted in cases where the outcome of the research may be of universal benefit to mankind: but for *sports science* one *might* argue that a further constraint was imposed by the (comparative) triviality of the topic.

Nevertheless, sports science researchers must proceed ethically, and therefore a discussion of the ethics of such research is warranted. In this paper, we approach that question obliquely, by discussing the practices and problems of a group of researchers as described in the BBC *Horizon* programme, "Bitter Cold" (BBC, 1986)[1]. By exploring the notion of *informed consent* as it might be thought to apply (or not apply) in cases derived from the television report of this research, we pose questions — and consider answers — as to how ethical research in environmental physiology might be conducted. We begin by presenting a general framework often employed in such research.

111

1.   The issue[2]

The whole question of the ethics of human research might be posed in terms of a tension between, on the one hand, the rights of subjects and, on the other, the principle of academic/intellectual freedom and the public right to know. And this issue is both a practical one — what to do in one's own research — and a theoretical one about the research process. Suppose that a group of researchers insist on performing a particular experiment (say, as a result of the demands of academic freedom): has due weight been given to the rights of the subjects to be used in this experiment? Similarly, if a topic represents a legitimate interest of the public (as, for example, in some sociological research) it does not follow that the topic *must* be researched: the rights of subjects might again be invoked. (Think here of, say, discussion of 'invasion of privacy' by tabloid journalists and the like.)

To clarify the issue, we will need to address the standard mechanism by which — in line with many professional codes[3] — ethical research is 'ensured': namely, *informed consent*. Before that, however, it is worth saying *something* about the idea of a *right* as it appears in this context. Of course, this discussion could be protracted, so we will simply offer a *strong*[4] account of rights: if I have a right to X (for instance, a right to work) then you must give me X, or let me do X, even if my having X or doing X is against the general or public good. If this is what it means to have a *right*, then there will indeed be rights of subjects: we might wonder whether there can be a *public* "right to know", since its satisfaction could not so easily be contrasted with the *public good*. However that is resolved, we should recognise the centrality of the rights of subjects: and this is just what the principle of *informed consent* invites us to do.

2.   Informed consent

The idea of informed consent is succinctly stated in the Nuremburg Code:

> The voluntary consent of the human subject is absolutely essential. This means that the person involved should have legal capacity to give consent, should be so situated as to be able to exercise free power of choice, without the intervention of any element of force, fraud, deceit, duress, over-reaching or any other ulterior form of constraint or coercion; and should have sufficient knowledge and comprehension of the

elements of the subject matter involved as to enable him to make an understanding and enlightened decision. (quoted Homan, 1991: p. 69)

In one form or another, this idea is enshrined in most of the codes of research practice.

What this implies is fairly clear, at least superficially (for further discussion, see Homan, 1991: p. 71): (a) the subjects must give *consent*: therefore, they must be the kind of people who *can* consent — not children, and not coerced, for instance; and this condition implies that their consent can be withheld. In this way, it puts the researchers in the hands of the subjects; and (b) the consent must be *informed*: that is, the subjects must understand what is going on.

But both these requirements are hard to be precise about, and not easy to implement. To clarify this point, it is useful to see the requirement that the consent be *informed* as including at least the following four conditions:

- *First*, that one should announce one's role as researcher. This will standardly be straightforward in the case of research in environmental physiology — one's appearance in the lab, perhaps in a lab coat, carrying records, thermometers, electrodes and the like may make one's role obvious. But this represents one set of considerations which, in other kinds of investigation, might be circumvented, and covert methods come into play.

- *Second*, that one should announce one's research topic. This may be rather more problematic — can one's subjects fully understand the *technical* presentation in one's experimental protocols? Is an *informal* presentation really getting one's topic across to them? Is verbal on-the-spot agreement really *informed* consent? Again, this is a procedure which covert methods might not follow: so that subjects knew that one was a researcher but not (precisely) what one was researching — for example, if their knowing would itself contaminate the data. Equally, it is worth here reflecting on a common procedure of, say, interview schedules: the placing of sensitive questions at the end. By that time, subjects have invested sufficient time answering the 'safe' questions that they answer the sensitive ones. In this way, nothing is hidden *exactly*, but neither is the full extent of the questionnaire made explicit when the subject's consent is sought.

- *Third*, that one make plain the *future* of the research, whether it will be published or disseminated in whatever form to what groups or bodies .

- *Finally*, that one announce any implications the research might have: in particular, any hazards there might be. This is the area most usually considered in the context of the *informing* for informed consent. But, again, it is not easy to implement. As we will see, what one researcher might consider a hazard (and therefore inform subjects concerning it) another researcher might not (and hence not inform subjects).

It is worth noting in passing that the principle of informed consent may in practice be by-passed in research by the use of gate-keepers (Homan, 1991: pp. 84–87) who give a 'second-party' consent. This may apply directly, for example if teachers' consent were sought to use pupils as subjects, or indirectly, as when registering for a particular option-course in higher education commits students to participation as experimental subjects. So that, again, the *apparent* force of the moral stricture of informed consent is in practice less constraining (and hence less of a guarantee of the rights of subjects) than is sometimes supposed[5].

3.   The case: "Bitter Cold"

The *Horizon* television programme from which we have extracted our case-study concerned the 1980 International Biomedical Expedition to the Antarctic[6]. This Expedition involved a phase where the whole research team lived in tents in the extreme cold of the high ground of the interior of Antarctica. Further, each researcher contributed an experiment (or group of experiments) for which he was responsible, but each also acted as a research subject in his colleagues' experiments.

Do the experimenters, as described, have informed consent for their researches? One would think that this is perhaps the ideal research community, so that the answer must be a resounding "yes". The consent is clearly given in the willingness to participate in the experiments. The subjects are informed, one can imagine, in all of the ways listed above. So that they know (first condition above) that the others are experimenters; and they know (second condition above) what is to be done — they have had a chance to study the protocols of the various experiments in which they will be involved, and are sufficiently expert to understand them in technical language. Moreover, they know what will be done with the results of the research — they know its publication destination and (likely) audience (in line with the third condition). Finally (fourth condition), they are aware of any hazards: after all, they are fellow scientists who understand such hazards and risks and have access to details of the experiments.

Certainly, too, the "guinea pigs" were compliant to some degree: they should be taken to have understood:

- the importance of the research topics;

- the centrality, for good research on that topic, of suitable equipment (as one researcher said: "we're all perfectly aware of the importance of rectal temperature");

- the inevitability of some discomfort — as for example when one researcher records another saying "I am comfortable" when he was obviously not: "here was this guy totally strung out but totally co-operating".

Surely, one might think, this represents to the highest degree the research-use of *informed consent.*

Into this rosy picture of the informed consent of the experiments, the film quickly introduces a certain amount of despondency: one particular experiment (the noradrenalin experiment) rapidly produces complaints — the subjective experience is deeply unpleasant for at least some subjects. As one reported it:

On the first run of noradrenalin, I got this very strong reaction that ... my chest started to get tight. I then felt like I was going to vomit. My head was really hot — I could feel the pressure on my head like there was a great balloon inside pushing it open.

Some refuse to continue with this experiment, despite its acknowledged "technical merits", because of "a very strong emotional reaction". However, the fundamental idea here — as a debate later in the film made plain — was of respect for the rights of subjects in ways fully consistent with *informed consent*:

The general ethics of human experimentation must apply to this group. And this is terribly important. And the general ethics of human experimentation is that the final arbiter of stopping an experiment is the subject. If the subject says 'no' at any time ... the experimenter is *bound* to stop the experiment.

And, of course, this means that the experimenter is "honour bound" to stop rather than that it will automatically happen! Still, that commitment impinged on practice in a number of different ways. First, were subjects allowed the opportunity to refuse? One might think so: yet the film includes cases which run in the opposite direction. In one such, a subject on a cycle ergometer is vigorously encouraged to continue:

> ... keep going, you're doing well! Now push, push, push ...! Keep it going! Ten seconds more!

Of course, there is nothing automatically reprehensible here: the subject may need to be encouraged. Yet is this subject *really* being allowed to withdraw his consent at any time? One might feel not. And that danger is explicitly recognised when the research team is described as, "a group of very highly motivated people, ... not likely to say 'no' because of loss of face and all sorts of these things". The impression that subjects might feel under an obligation to continue is reinforced by two further claims:

- "Personally, myself, I wouldn't have bailed out": one of the researchers gives the impression that the technician who did withdraw from the experiment was in some senses a quitter.

- The motivation for staying was "to succeed and push this thing through" since "lots of trust, lots of investment, lots of work and background" had been put into it.

But meeting one's obligations in this way is, one might well think, not straightforwardly consistent with being able to withdraw one's consent at any time. Finally, the fact of the research base being many miles from home committed them to at least some level of discomfort even if they had decided to withdraw from the experiments as such.

Consider, then, the issue of subjects being (suitably) *informed.* A key factor here, and one supporting the claim of the research team to have been behaving ethically, is that some subjects did withdraw from the noradrenalin experiment. And an illuminating side-effect was that some of the researchers began to review their own past practice. In a revealing story, one researcher asked his colleagues to consider the way that the medical profession regularly subjects hospital patients to unexplained, or not adequately explained, tests:

> Imagine a patient, who knows nothing about this, going into a hospital. And he is in fact assaulted like this from the very moment he comes in. ... Just imagine the stress this causes him ....

But even withdrawal from the noradrenalin experiment was not regarded universally as wholly justified:

> People can get themselves into great states of apprehension about their fears, real or imagined. Fears do not kill you. The dangerous things in experimentation, objective ones like excessive rises or falls in body temperature, excessive rises or falls in blood pressure, ... are the things which ethical investigators have to make it their business to monitor extremely carefully.

The idea here is that the dangers or hazards one should be alerted to, and hence which play a part in one's being informed, are those the researcher *sees as dangerous*[7]. Thus, the researcher may well feel that monitoring heart rate and core body temperature guarantees one's well-being; whereas, as a subject, one might place much greater weight on the subjective experience of that research — on the discomforts and fears one feels.

Further complications become apparent in the programme itself. First, in addition to the specific discomforts of that one experiment, the researchers registered a more general dissatisfaction associated with a failure to *know* (or perhaps to recognise) the precise conditions under which experiments were to take place: for instance, the placing of tape (to secure instrumentation) on the "short and curlies", as one subject put it; or the intrusion of privacy implicit in the male scientist being filmed (by female photographers) inserting a rectal thermometer. So there were not just the specific hazards at issue, but also the conditions under which the research was to be conducted. Had the subjects given informed consent here too? Clearly some felt they had not. Again, a central factor emerged: the importance of the *trust* the research subject places in the researcher. One subject in particular recognised "how vulnerable I was", and for him "the question of trust is now one that is raised". For he felt misled — that he had not been informed of *all* that he might be experiencing (again it was the noradrenalin experiment). Here too the implication is far wider: for, as the case (mentioned before) of patients entering hospitals suggests, a trust in those who are research-ing can only provide a limited guarantee of the ethical nature of their procedures — they may not recognise *as disturbing* factors that *do* disturb the subjects.

It is not essential to further discuss this whole case, for it shows clearly the slipperiness of the idea of informed consent: that one might seem to have it, believe (with some justice) that one had it, and yet still end up infringing the rights of subjects in ways the principle of informed consent was designed to prevent.

One could conclude, of course, that *genuine* informed consent was not obtained in the "Bitter Cold" cases. But, if one thought that, surely it would follow that genuine informed consent was *never* obtained (for these are nearly ideal conditions for both informing and consenting). Better, instead, to conclude that informed consent merely provides a *framework* which may permit one to give due regard to the rights of subjects, and hence to conduct one's research ethically.

4.   Ethical practices

In the light of this review it becomes clear why *informed consent* does not represent a cure-all. At best, it can offer us issues to be addressed. Notice, though, that restricting our investigation to research methods which are *necessarily* overt — as in much environmental physiology — automatically avoided some of the pitfalls associated with informed consent. We could be sure that our role as researchers was clear, and that the outlet of research, if not explicit, was at least not hidden. Further, our research was into *individual subjects*: hence we could realistically ground our appeal to informed consent in the rights of such subjects. (As Homan [1991: p. 72] notes, the possibility of legitimate research into groups or societies means that not all accounts of informed consent can take this form.)

Nevertheless, the cases from "Bitter Cold" pose clearly a number of the remaining problems to be faced by the researcher wishing to be an ethical investigator into environmental physiology. In particular, it has highlighted some of the limitations implicit in a reliance on the notion of informed consent. For we have seen how easily the *spirit* of informed consent is (1) abandoned by subjects, either so that they are not thought 'quitters' or when they give way to (implicit or explicit) pressure from investigators to continue with the experiment, or (2) infringed by investigators — either through a failure to grasp what subjects need to be appraised of (for instance, feelings of discomfort) or through a conception of the dangers to subjects that differs from the subjects' own. And we have recognised how this latter infringement, even when unintentional, nevertheless represents a genuine danger to subjects. For what the experimenter deems to be crucial — say, changes in heart-rate or blood pressure — might differ quite radically from the concerns of the subject. And only from the most positivistic of positions on the nature of science could one guarantee that the psychological reactions of subjects were *never* of relevance in experiments with human subjects, even those in environmental physiology. In fact, as the "Bitter Cold" cases illustrate, a major danger here derives from the ways in which *subjects* might be less attentive to their own rights than the *idea* of informed consent requires.

Within institutions of higher education, research on environmental physiology will regularly use students as subjects. Such students, having studied physiology, will typically be better informed than the general public about both dangers and discomforts. But that is not always a safeguard. Imagine a case in which a student, having graduated with a sports science degree and having taken environmental physiology courses as part of that degree, acts as a subject in an environmental physiology experiment involving exposure to cold. One might suppose that such a subject would be well-placed to assess the risks of the experiment and hence to withhold consent to any procedures that seemed dangerous. But it is easy for such a subject to assume that, because one understands the risks, one is somehow immune to them. In such a case, asked for permission to conduct the experiment without the monitoring of deep-body temperature (via a rectal thermometer), the subject might be foolhardy enough to agree — and, as a result, permit a dangerous procedure. In this case, not only should the experimenters know better (they have had the dangers clearly explained to them) but the subject should also know better. Yet this does not preclude such cases arising.

Notice that, in the case as presented, the subject was aware of the dangers, and that compliance went beyond what was taken to be safe. Notice too that here there may well be a time-lag between the procedure and its effects: by the time the dangers were recognised, the physiological processes involved may be well advanced. Thus, even though the subject might be well-aware of the 'time-lag' phenomenon, confidence in the ability to recognise when all is not well has the potential to lead to foolhardiness. So the 'familiarity' which results from understanding represents a danger in itself.

This hypothetical case, then, highlights both the way in which an assumption of informed-ness might be misplaced (seen too in the "Bitter Cold" cases) and that these are problems in the laboratory as well as the field setting. Indeed, one might even think that there was an increased importance for explicit informed consent in the lab: in going to the Antarctic, the field researchers might be thought to have considered the situation fairly fully. It also re-emphasises that the responsibility here remains with researchers, however knowledgeable the subjects.

Here, therefore, it is worth extending the discussion by raising three further — related — issues[8]. The first concerns the use of informed consent in double-blind experimentation, where neither subject nor experimenter knows whether a particular subject is in the experimental group or the control group. Of course, such an experimental design may be difficult to manage for environmental physiology, where simply entering, say, the environmental chamber may place one in one group rather than the other. Still, if we can formulate such a design, it is important to notice that the same considerations (concerning informed consent) continue to apply: now, though, the responsibility for ensuring both that there is consent from subjects, and that it is based on appropriate information, rests with someone in the research team *other than* the researcher. That I have not personally seen the consent form signed is not relevant, as long as I can be sure that it has been signed: indeed I could even oversee the signing of these forms, as long as I do not know which subjects will be in which group. (And there might be a good reason, brought out by the "Bitter Cold" discussions, for my doing so — that it improved the likelihood of trust on the part of subjects.)

Second, it is worth saying something about the use of placebos (for example, 'harmless' tablets which look similar to those under trial) since it is clear that here too consent must imply willingness both to be or to not be a member of the experimental group. This point is most sharply made by a piece of *covert* research at a family planning clinic in North America (described by Homan, 1991: p. 97), where many of the women receiving the placebo had the 'unfortunate' side-effect of becoming pregnant: clearly, this was precisely what they would not have consented to! And while experiments in environmental physiology will typically not be covert (as noted above) it is important to recognise that consent — as we saw earlier — must invoke all consequences, not only those the researcher deems potentially harmful.

The final major issue turns on the cumulative effects of being an experimental subject — that here again one must pursue an enlightened informed consent. For example, we now know that repeated involvement in saturation deep diving research experiments (as undertaken in naval establishments) may have a cumulative effect: that repeated exposure to situations, each of which produces only a minimal risk of bone necrosis, can produce in a particular (unfortunate) subject extensive bone necrosis — to the point where bones can shatter if subjected to such minor stresses as getting out of bed. In such a situation the ethical investigator will require that any genuinely informed consent accommodate these considerations by enquiring into the subject's previous involvement in similar experiments. Note, though, that an element of the responsibility here must lie with the prospective subject, for he/she must recognise the danger. This in turn means that relevant factors must be part of any information provided by the researcher (they must constitute part of the 'informing').

Additionally, we should be aware of a further aspect of informed consent: the degree to which it can be seen as guarding ourselves — that is, the researchers. For, while the primary concern in respect of informed consent is the rights of subjects (as noted earlier), it also serves to indemnify the researcher; whatever befalls is then — to some degree at least — the subject's own responsibility. And this point has a wider application. For instance, as *The Observer Magazine* March 28, 1993 reports, when discussing the first human recipient of an artificial heart (in 1982), the surgeon:

...was looking for someone who was sufficiently ill to take a chance on the largely unproven device but sufficiently well to give it a fighting chance of success. He wanted someone with the intelligence to give informed consent and the pioneering spirit to inspire future patients whatever the outcome of his own operation. (p. 49)

Assuming the accuracy of this report, we see both the requirement of informed consent and the ways in which the giving of consent might involve more than just a willingness to participate in the experiment. Indeed, a parent signing a form allowing the child to do some activity (for example, for a school ski trip) could be seen as consent: therefore some of the problems that confront the use of informed consent as a safeguard for research might occur in this context too — has the parent sufficient knowledge of the detail of the activity, the conditions of supervision, and the like, to understand what is being consented to?[9]

5. Some brief remarks on covert investigation

The borderline between overt and covert research is typically not as sharp as is sometimes supposed. Indeed, we believe that much ostensibly overt research will not satisfy all the conditions for informed consent listed earlier: in particular, that subjects are often not told the precise research topic. (Equally, a researcher might not mention that the research was funded, and that the company was the final arbiter of the destination of the research.) In environmental physiology, it may be that the subject typically could be fully informed — that the research protocol would not thereby be undermined. Our point is that the subjects are, as a matter of fact, often not so informed.

Therefore, it may be useful to say something about covert investigations; and for two reasons. First, they provide the backdrop to much that is said here. Second, it is a thesis of Roger Homan (whose ideas have provided much stimulation for this essay) that covert methods have a lot of morality in them, (even) when contrasted with overt methods, since (a) covert methods have moral strictures, and (b) overt methods have less strictures than is sometimes supposed — in support of this second contention Homan would cite difficulties for the thesis of informed consent of kinds we have identified here.

At the heart of the discussion are two ideas, familiar from our discussion thus far. The first concerns doing justice to subjects' rights, which may typically include (a) the avoidance of physical harm, (b) a clarification of the situation after the fact [for example, by debriefing] where this is possible, and (c) preserving anonymity, as far as possible. The second involves doing no harm to their more general rights; to their rights as people or as citizens — for example, by not invading (justified) privacy. (For cases where such injunctions are not well obeyed, see Homan, 199: pp. 96-104.) But it is to precisely these notions that we have been appealing throughout: for informed consent is designed both to empower the subjects in terms of possible consequences (by informing them) and to avoid infringing their general rights (by obtaining subjects' consent).

Conclusion

This paper should be seen as part of a debate around the nature and research-role of informed consent: as offering neither simple prescriptions nor proscriptions. However, it may be helpful to draw together some of its major thrusts:

- Our approach has built on a case study from the "Bitter Cold" programme. The issues and questions thrown up by this programme apply to some degree to much scientific research with human subjects. Further, it vividly illustrates the eminent and experienced falling into the 'traps' inherent in the need to research ethically.

- We have urged that the idea of *informed consent* is both complex and difficult to guarantee, even in apparently 'ideal' situations (such as that the programme presented). We have recognised how easy it is to pay lip-service to the idea of informed consent. In this light, ethics committees would do well to investigate thoroughly any claims to have achieved genuine informed consent. Simple formulaic presentations of consent may well be inadequate, even when provided by, for example, some well-intentioned governing body of sport. As we have seen, it is all to easy to oversimplify both the issues of informed consent and its achievement.

- The constraints on research suggested by the notion of informed consent, and especially its implicit respect for the rights of subjects, are worth thinking deeply about — even when we agree that full informed consent is not achieved/achievable. Indeed, its (justified) emphasis on the rights of subjects suggests to us — topically — a *subjects' charter*! Understanding the ethical basis for decisions concerning the rights of research subjects is, we are sure, one of the major virtues of having thought-through the idea of informed consent.

- The assumption that scientific research — in particular, research in environmental physiology — was necessarily completely overt was challenged by our enquiries, although that idea was not fully explored here. Still, it should give one pause when thinking about the adequacy of informed consent as a guarantee of ethical research.

Overall, then, we have seen consideration of informed consent as a way of sharpening one's awareness of the ethical underpinnings of research. This paper lays out some key themes for such underpinning.[10]

Notes

1 All unattributed quotation in this paper is to this programme.

2 Throughout this paper we recognise a debt to Roger Homan. (See Homan, 1991).

3 See, for example, British Sociological Association [BSA] (1992). The discussion of informed consent is on pp. 704-5.

4 See Dworkin, 1978, esp. p. 224. For a fuller treatment, see Dworkin, 1977, esp. p.92.

5   Informed consent may also be circumvented by, for example, the signing of
    the Official Secrets Act: researchers on deep diving in naval institutions
    would not typically be approached for further consent.

6   We recognise that the *Horizon* programme inevitably represents a selection
    from the original footage, with the associated implications of the pr-
    ogramme makers' agenda.

7   It might be thought that these were all that *were really* dangerous; but that
    assumes that the researchers know for sure all the relevant cause-and-effect
    relations (scarcely the usual situation). Indeed, one might introduce a
    distinction between, say, *danger* and *distress* — as though it were clear that
    mere distress was not really injury/life-threatening. This is scientism of the
    kind we are opposing here.

8   There is a fourth issue, concerning the place of financial or other incentives
    for subjects. The use of students and prisoners as research subjects exploits
    a principle well captured in the film *The Dirty Dozen* in which prisoners,
    with the inducement of a pardon and therefore freedom, are pitched into an
    impossible war mission: prisoners are literally a 'captive audience' while
    students typically find financial inducements impossible to refuse. But such
    abuses of research ethics are not our main concern here.

9   In this context, it would be interesting to follow-up the impact of the *On The
    Line* television programme, "Jobs for the Boys" (BBC, 1993), which
    investigated how easy it was to gain employment as an instructor on sports
    activity holidays: in spite of public concern over the deaths of four children
    in an accident at Lyme Bay on the Dorset Coast in April 1993, few checks
    were made on the reporter who posed as a candidate for positions looking
    after children on sports activity holidays.

10 We would like to thank all those who commented on earlier drafts of this
    material, thereby saving us from numerous mistakes; especially Roger
    Homan. Also, thanks to the generations of students whose response to this
    material convinced us of its continuing usefulness.

References

British Broadcasting Corporation [BBC] (1986) 'Bitter cold', *Horizon*, BBC 2,
    Monday 13th January; producer — David Parer for the Australian Broadcasting
    Corporation [*Horizon* editor: Robin Brightwell].

British Broadcasting Corporation [BBC] (1993) 'Jobs for the boys', *On the line,* BBC 2, Wednesday 14th July; producer — Jonathan Jones.

British Sociological Association [BSA] (1992) 'Guidelines for good professional conduct' and their 'Statement of ethical practice', *Sociology* Vol. 26, No. 4 (November): pp. 699-707.

Dworkin, R. (1978) 'Philosophy and politics' in Bryan Magee (ed) *Men of ideas.* Oxford: Oxford University Press, pp. 210-228.

Dworkin, R. (1977) *Taking rights seriously.* Cambridge, Mass.: Harvard University Press.

Homan, R. (1991) *The ethics of social research.* London: Longman.

PROBLEMS OF REFERRAL AND TIME IN APPLIED SPORT PSYCHOLOGY CONSULTANCY

Stephen J. Bull
University of Brighton

Introduction

Applied sport psychology has developed significantly in recent years. Many sports teams and individual athletes now seek advice from practising sport psychologists and the Sports Council's Sports Science Support Programme has facilitated the implementation of an educationally-based sport psychology service to a wide range of National Governing Bodies. These programmes usually involve the teaching of various psychological skills associated with the optimisation of athletic performance such as goal setting, imagery, attentional control, confidence enhancement and anxiety management (Miller, 1991). The dramatic increase in the provision of applied sport psychology services over the past decade has been accompanied by the emergence of certain ethical and professional issues (Biddle, Bull and Seheult, 1992). The purpose of this chapter is to consider two ethical problems of current concern. First, the problem of crisis intervention and making referrals. This becomes a problem when athletes appear to require the services of a professional with either different, or more, expertise than the primary sport psychology consultant. Second, the problem of dividing consultant time between athletes in a squad when different sorts of intervention are needed and when available time is severely limited.

Crisis intervention and referral

Nideffer (1981) explained that a crisis intervention in sport psychology involves a situation when an athlete requires some type of outside intervention in order to regain control over feelings and the ability to perform. Anshel (1992) suggested that the sport psychology profession should create formal guidelines with regard to an organisational policy for referral. The purpose of these guidelines would be to facilitate the referral process by assisting individuals in judging their own professional limitations — an issue which LeUnes and Nation (1989) claimed has been a problem in sport psychology for many years.

Codes of conduct associated with professional psychology bodies are intended to guide the practice of individual members. The British Association of Sport and Exercise Science's Code of Conduct for psychology states that accredited sport psychologists "... must recognise their limitations in qualifications, competence, experience, and expertise and should operate within these limits" (Biddle, Bull and Seheult, 1992: p. 75). This recommendation clearly suggests the need for referral when a situation presents itself which is deemed to be outside the competence boundaries of the individual in question. However, further guidance on how to recognise personal professional limitations is not provided. This is perhaps not surprising given the subjective nature of the problem, although some guidelines have been offered by the Association for the Advancement of Applied Sport Psychology ("AAASP Passes", 1990). Nevertheless, these guidelines still contain ambiguities as they merely list activities which are deemed to be outside the scope of a certified sport psychology consultant without clinical training. The list includes coaching, diagnosis and treatment of psychopathology, treatment of substance abuse disorders, marital and family therapy and the use of restricted psychological tests.

Much of the problem in this area is linked with the use of counselling psychology techniques in sport psychology consultancy. Sport psychology consultants typically serve a counselling, rather than a clinical, role because they are dealing with mentally healthy people (Morgan, 1988). Nevertheless, drawing the line between a problem requiring a medically-based clinical approach as opposed to an educationally-based counselling approach, can be extremely difficult. Parry (1975), in his book *A Guide to Counselling and Basic Psychotherapy*, begins each chapter with a cardinal principle. These vary from "There is nothing so obvious that it can be accepted without question" to "There is no Santa Claus". Parry begins a chapter focusing on problems for the therapist (one of which is identified as "second opinions") with the cardinal principle of "For some situations there are no cardinal principles". The implication here is that there are certain situations which may arise in counselling for which it is very difficult to stipulate rules and restrictive recommendations. Earlier in the book, Parry explained how Michael Balint claimed that psychotherapy is about personal skill rather than theoretical knowledge and Anshel (1992) suggested that many sport psychology specialists who are extremely effective in counselling athletes, coaches and parents have little academic training. In his rather provocative article, Anshel (1992) makes a case against the certification of sport psychologists by claiming (amongst many other things) that certification does not guarantee expertise and that sport psychology is not an exact science. This is an extremely contentious issue and is outside the scope of this chapter although interested readers are advised to read Anshel's (1992) article as well as a rebuttal paper which presents the contrary view (Zaichowsky and Perna, 1992).

The issue of concern in this chapter is how we can assist practising sport psychologists in their ability to make informed decisions about their own expertise and boundaries of competence. The commonly stated recommendation that, if in doubt referral *should* take place, is a sensible starting point although it does not go far enough. There are often occasions when an athlete has built up a trusting relationship with a consultant, feeling totally at ease and willing to discuss very personal problems. When a referral is then suggested, the athlete rejects the idea of beginning the process of building a relationship with another individual and refuses to be referred. The consultant is then left with the problem of persuading the athlete to see another individual. This can be either a very long-term, or sometimes an impossible, task. A complicating factor is the grey area between when a problem can be dealt with by an educationally-based counselling approach and when a clinical intervention is necessary. As pointed out by Biddle, Bull and Seheult (1992), when does a mild eating disorder become a serious eating disorder? When does persistent post-performance disappointment become clinical depression? Inexperienced consultants may make one of two mistakes. They may wish to refer an athlete in order to err on the side of safety, when they do actually possess the counselling skills required to help the athlete. Alternatively, they may overestimate their counselling abilities and continue working with an athlete when a referral to a clinician is the correct course of action.

An additional problem may relate to the counselling style adopted by the two consultants. It is conceivable that the referral consultant may assume a more or less directive approach than the primary consultant. The athlete, therefore, having complied with the bold step of being referred, may find the contrasting style uncomfortable and be reluctant to continue the counselling process with the new consultant. Conversely, of course, the new approach may be exactly what is needed and the athlete may make rapid progress towards resolving the issue. However, this scenario is perhaps less likely given the athlete's satisfaction with, and dedication to, the primary consultant.

The issue of counselling style is an important one for consideration by applied sport psychologists and will be examined again later in the chapter.

Nowell-Smith (1954) explained that students of ethics are often disappointed to find that although the subject has been studied for over two thousand years, it has not produced established truths which are comparable to those in mathematics and the natural sciences. He goes on to explain how Aristotle believed that one could not make people good by lecturing on ethics or writing a handbook. In response to someone asking Aristotle for a moral code by which to live, he would have replied by advising the individual to go and watch other people who are deemed to be good and wise, and then copy their behaviour. This principle can be applied in sport psychology. Rather than attempting to create a handbook which explains how to operate ethically as a consultant, inexperienced sport psychologists could work closely with established consultants and observe how they operate. In effect, this is the model which the British Association of Sport and Exercise Sciences has adopted. In addition to meeting the conventional requirements necessary to be granted accredited status as a sport psychologist (such as an appropriate higher degree and experience in sport) applicants must now serve a supervised experience period of three years. During this time they must work with an experienced individual who acts on a mentor-type basis. During this period, the applicant is deemed to be working as a trainee sport psychologist. For further details on this accreditation scheme, the reader is advised to contact the British Association of Sport and Exercise Sciences at the address given at the end of this chapter.

Dividing time

Most sport psychologists work with National Governing Bodies on a part-time basis. When working under the auspices of the Sports Science Support Programme, consultants are allocated a number of days per year for which they are paid to work with athletes who are usually members of the national squad. Due to obvious and unavoidable financial restrictions, the number of days is often comparatively small in relation to the number of athletes on the squad. A dilemma immediately emerges. How does the consultant divide the allocated time? Several philosophies towards this dilemma exist:

1. The winning philosophy

Spend the majority of time with those athletes who are most likely to achieve medals and international recognition.

Advantage: This will enhance the profile of the sport which will benefit all participants in the long run. The success of athletes who use a sport psychologist is also a quick way of eliciting interest in the provision of sport psychology services and encouraging developing athletes to be open-minded about the use of mental training techniques.

Disadvantage: It is an elitist policy, denying many athletes access to what can be a highly useful form of training. There are also occasions when members of the support team, such as coaches and managers, may require psychological support. Denying these individuals access to the sport psychologist may lead to resentments and conflict, resulting in disruptions to team cohesion.

2. The egalitarian philosophy

Spread the time equally between all those athletes and support staff who wish to opt into the training programme.

Advantage: Psychologists should have the welfare of all athletes and support staff as a priority and therefore if an individual wishes to receive help, then it should be given. The psychologist will thus be seen to be helping everyone and resentments are unlikely.

Disadvantage: Spreading limited time thinly may lead to minimal effects and consequently psychological support is not seen to be useful.

3. The "means test" philosophy

Spend the majority of time with those athletes who seem to need psychological training the most.

Advantage: These athletes are probably going to demonstrate the largest performance increases and therefore the time is being spent very productively.

Disadvantage: Will this approach win medals? The argument may be made that an athlete requiring a great deal of assistance from the psychologist does not possess sufficient amounts of mental toughness required to perform at the highest levels. This is clearly a debatable point but not an insignificant one. From a perceptual standpoint, recent research has demonstrated that derogation of athletes who use a sport psychologist still exists and a negative halo effect is often evident (Linder *et al.* 1991; Linder *et al.* 1989; Van Raalte *et al.* 1990). The sport psychology profession, therefore, still has some way to go in eliminating negative perceptual biases among some coaches, athletes and administrators. Assuming the "means test" philosophy would not, presumably, combat this problem in the way the "winning" philosophy might.

4. The investment philosophy

Spend the majority of time with the youngest and most promising athletes. **Advantage:** These are the athletes of the future and therefore must be viewed as an investment. They are perhaps also less likely to harbour sceptical and suspicious attitudes regarding mental skills training as compared with older, more experienced, performers.

Disadvantage: The observable rewards and recognition are long-term and therefore delayed. This is a problem in an area which is still establishing credibility in the athletic world and may suffer from the same disadvantage just described in relation to the "means test" philosophy.

A survey of practising sport psychologists would probably demonstrate a range of views relating to these philosophies and indeed probably yield a further list of alternative philosophies regarding mode of delivery. To date, detailed discussion on this issue has not taken place amongst experienced professionals in the field. Many individuals would view the issue as an ethical one and therefore rigorous debates designed to inform thinking would be extremely useful.

A further point of interest regarding limited time and delivery of sport psychology services relates to counselling style. A sport psychologist may be faced with a crisis situation, particularly during a major championship, when a pragmatic and rather directive approach seems to be the best option due to very obvious time constraints. If this individual is accustomed to a more relaxed, non-directive, approach in non-crisis situations, a problem may arise. He/she may not feel comfortable, or indeed particularly competent, with the directive approach and consequently may wish to suggest a referral. At a major championship, this may be highly undesirable and perhaps logistically impossible. The importance of ensuring that sport psychologists are able to adopt a flexible style is therefore apparent. This would seem to be particularly relevant for individuals acting as on-site consultants during competitions. It is during these occasions when a host of different crisis scenarios can arise and a reactive style is essential. The methods of gaining the necessary experience to assume the on-site role effectively present another professional issue with ethical implications. This is once again where the British Association of Sport and Exercise Sciences supervised experience scheme is so important. It is interesting to note also, that the British Olympic Association has implemented a separate register of accredited individuals. The criteria for membership of this register are more stringent than the BASES requirements, due to the perceived additional demands of working within the Olympic framework.

In conclusion, it was not the purpose of this chapter, and indeed it would not have been possible, to provide answers to the ethical problems which have been considered. But these problems do exist, and the recommended course for future action is that the problems continue to be considered, reviewed and discussed by those accredited professionals who have a wealth of relevant experience and expertise to offer any debate. In 1990, the British Association of Sports Sciences (now British Association of Sport and Exercise Sciences) staged an "Ethical Considerations in Sport Psychology" workshop. Subsequent workshops have been held to consider specific aspects of accreditation and supervised experience. These workshops must continue as a forum for debate if important issues such as quality control and philosophy of service delivery and, in particular, problems of referral and time, are to be allocated the attention which they definitely deserve.

References

AAASP passes certification criteria. (1990, Winter) *AAASP Newsletter*, pp. 3, 8.

Anshel, M. H. (1992) 'The case against the certification of sport psychologists: In search of the phantom expert', *The Sport Psychologist*, 6: pp. 265–286.

Biddle, S. J. H., Bull, S. J. and Seheult, C. L. (1992) 'Ethical and professional issues in contemporary British sport psychology', *The Sport Psychologist*, 6: pp. 66–76.

LeUnes, A. D. and Nation, J. R. (1989) *Sport psychology: An introduction.* Chicago: Nelson-Hall.

Linder, D. E., Brewer, B. W., Van Raalte, J. L. and De Lange, N. (1991) 'A negative halo for athletes who consult sport psychologists: Replication and extension', *Journal of Sport and Exercise Psychology*, 13: pp. 133–148.

Linder, D. E., Pillow, D. R. and Reno, R. R. (1989) 'Shrinking jocks: Derogation of athletes who consult sport psychologists', *Journal of Sport and Exercise Psychology*, 11: pp. 270–280.

Miller, B. (1991) 'Mental preparation for competition', in S. J. Bull (ed) *Sport psychology: A self-help guide.* Ramsbury: The Crowood Press, pp. 84–102.

Morgan, W. P. (1988) 'Sport psychology in its own context: A recommendation for the future', in J. S. Skinner, C. B. Corbin, D. M. Landers, P. E. Martin and C. L. Wells (eds) *Future directions in exercise and sport science.* Champaign, IL: Human Kinetics, pp. 97–110.

Nideffer, R. M. (1981) *The ethics and practice of applied sport psychology.* Ithaca, NY: Mouvement.

Nowell-Smith, P. H. (1954) *Ethics.* Harmondsworth: Penguin Books.

Parry, R. (1975) *A guide to counselling and basic psychotherapy.* Edinburgh: Churchill Livingstone.

Van Raalte, J. L., Brewer, B. W., Brewer, D. D. and Linder, D. E. (1990) 'Perceptions of sport-oriented professionals: A multidimensional scaling analysis', *The Sport Psychologist*, 4: pp. 228–234.

Zaichkowsky, L. D. and Perna, F. M. (1992) 'Certification of consultants in sport psychology: A rebuttal to Anshel', *The Sport Psychologist*, 6: pp. 287–296.

Address for information regarding sport psychology accreditation:
British Association of Sport and Exercise Sciences
c/o Sports Science Education Programme
114 Cardigan Road Headingley, LEEDS, LS6 3BJ (UK)
Tel: 0113 230 7558   Fax:0113 275 5019

III:

ETHICAL ISSUES IN RESEARCH
IN THE SOCIOLOGY OF
SPORT AND LEISURE

QUALITATIVE RESEARCH INTO YOUNG PEOPLE, SPORT AND SCHOOLING: THE ETHICS OF ROLE-CONFLICT

Scott Fleming
Cardiff Institute of Higher Education

In this paper[1] I consider some of the ethical issues and dilemmas that were encountered during an ethnographic research project[2] that was based at an inner-city secondary school in North London, and was concerned with South Asian male youth and sport (Fleming, 1992). The issues raised are not, however, unique either to this specific study, or to investigations of South Asian males. On the contrary, the central theme of 'role conflict' is much more pervasive than this, and undoubtedly affects many researchers engaged in qualitative work.

A background to the research

The significance of sport in some cultural groups is not fully understood — and in some cases remains unexplored. Among the factors and influences that impact upon young people in particular, the importance of school-based activities should not be under-estimated. It is through frequent exposure to formalised physical education (PE) lessons, organised extra-curricular clubs and teams, and informal 'play', that many young people have the opportunity to formulate their own realities of sport (Fleming, 1991).

The absence of research on South Asian youth and sport meant that the study was of an 'exploratory' kind (Phillips and Pugh, 1987), but it was intended to have practical applications by informing policy-making decisions. An ethnographic approach had been used to good effect in the study of the lifestyles of young people in schools to produce valid and high-quality data (e.g. Willis, 1977; Corrigan, 1979; Mac an Ghaill, 1991). Thus, for a number of reasons — some theoretical (the well-established case-study paradigm in sociological research), some strategic (a multi-cultural pupil profile and well resourced local sports facilities), and some pragmatic (proximity to an underground station) — Parkview School[3] in North London was chosen as a research base for the fieldwork in 1988 and 1989.

Choosing the role(s)

When studying young people, the adult researcher is faced with a problem of gaining access. Participant observation may be one of the most effective research methods for gathering data of this kind, but there are many difficulties associated with it. Mandell (1991: p. 39) concludes that: "The central methodological problem facing an adult participant observer of children concerns the membership role adopted by the researcher". Even if it were desirable (and ethically justifiable), it is doubtful whether even a physically small adult could convincingly masquerade as a much younger person (Mandell, 1991).

Access to young people can be gained through the established institutions where both young people and adults are present; in this case Parkview School. The role I adopted was that of a member of the PE department in the school, but this created two unavoidable sets of problematic social relations. First, the host-guest relation that the researcher has with the institution and its gate-keepers. Second, the implicit teacher-pupil relation that the researcher has with the subjects of the research. These complex interactions create real ethical dilemmas and predicaments, which in turn influence the behaviour of the researcher, and so therefore the shape and direction of the reseach itself.

The host-guest relation

An entrée to Parkview School was negotiated through two important gate-keepers (a contact at the Sports Council and the Local Education Authority PE Adviser). From the earliest contact the tone of the dialogue was that of a mutually beneficial relation, in which the school would receive an unpaid but qualified support/supply teacher in return for providing me with an opportunity to research some groups of young South Asians. This inevitably created the sort of real researcher-teacher role-conflict that others have identified (Peeke, 1984; Mac an Ghaill, 1991). The discussion returns to this later.

There were also some of the understandable concerns that guests have about upsetting or offending their hosts, and making themselves unpopular. The arrangement from the start was that the research would take as long as it needed; but towards the end of each term there was a point at which continued presence in the school was re-confirmed for the following term. It became incumbent on me, therefore, not to 'blot my copybook' and so jeopardise the research. Moreover, as time passed this dilemma became more acute: on the one hand, I was establishing a good research rapport with a number of young people, and would have welcomed the opportunity to distance myself from the authority and officialdom of the school further; and on the other, when an increasing amount of time had been invested, there was so much more to lose had the necessary permission been withheld, and the necessary access been discontinued.

During the time I spent at the school I was also aware that (at least) some of the teachers were affected by my presence. There were those, for example, who modified their own behaviour (and the behaviour of others) in my company; and treated me with the caution accorded to a 'vigilante racist-language spotter'.

Mr. Jenkins: "I've got a good joke. It's a bit racist, but it's a good one".
Ms. Taylor engaged me in eye-contact, and looked embarrassed.
Ms. Taylor: "No, we've probably heard it. And I bet it wasn't funny in the first place".   I think she was very conscious of my presence — partly because it might have provided me with some data that I could use; and partly because I think she sensed my uneasiness. (Field-notes, 12/7/ 1988)

Fortunately Ms. Taylor's action spared me the dilemma of having to choose between challenging one of my hosts — and so cause offence; or ignoring (and therefore tacitly condoning) something that offended me. In such circumstances there is a personal ethical dilemma to be confronted. Failure to act is an abdication of principles in order not to offend, and so allow the research to proceed smoothly. It is an illustration of the 'means and ends' argument in which the justification of such inactivity would presumably be that it would eventually lead to a greater good. That is, the ends justifying the means. But are strongly held principles so easily circumvented? Are individual consciences so readily appeased?

The other concern that I had as I wrote those notes was that my presence caused this person to feel uncomfortable. How many others were experiencing the same feelings?

The teacher-pupil relation

The role of the teacher is an easy one for a credible (and qualified) adult to fill, and provides a point of contact to a 'captive audience'. It is clear though, that real access goes beyond mere physical proximity (Hammersley and Atkinson, 1983), and necessarily requires trust and cooperation (Fine and Sandstrom, 1988; Shaffir and Stebbins, 1991). Developing this trust and cooperation can pose significant problems to the teacher-researcher, especially when the subject matter of the research is of a sensitive kind. As Paul Corrigan (1979) explained in his rejection of the 'teacher' role:

> The gap between teacher and taught would preclude me from obtaining some of the more sensitive information about the boys which I felt was essential. (Corrigan, 1979: p. 12)

Amongst the young people at Parkview School I was identified as a member of the PE department, but my precise role was unclear. There was evidently a good deal of confusion and misinformation about my presence at Parkview. A colleague in the PE department once remarked to me that he had overheard one of the young people who attended the school refer to me as: "the tall geezer that's here to make sure we react proper". For some time I actually traded on the ambiguity of my role, and would frequently respond to the question "are you a PE teacher?", with a rather unsatisfactory and unconvincing "sort of". My purpose was not to deceive curious enquirers, but rather to offer a factually accurate and brief response[4].

As far as the subjects of the research were concerned, therefore, I was a 'sort-of PE teacher'. But the authority structure in schools, and the power position of the teacher vis-à-vis the pupil, meant that even this ambiguous and vague role was not entirely satisfactory. I was concerned with sporting involvement, attitudes and perceptions; yet I was also concerned with other facets of the leisure lifestyles of young South Asian males, and these caused other ethical predica-ments. Some concerning 'guilty knowledge' (Fetterman, 1989) were relatively minor, and are addressed in the section that follows. What I would have done had I been given confidential hearsay evidence of serious criminal activity, for example, remains an unanswered hypothetical question. But importantly for this discussion, the factors that would have influenced the decision-making process would probably have been governed by the need for researchers to "protect ourselves and our informants from possible criminal actions and ethical disquietude" (Cromwell *et al.*, 1992: p. 104) — not, perhaps, the best motives upon which to make ethical judgements.

As a 'sort-of PE teacher' my main strategy was to attempt to reduce social distance with my informants. In an attempt to negate the power position that adults occupy in the school, and thereby gain the real access that I sought, I adapted the 'least-adult' role proposed by Mandell (1991), into a 'least authoritative' role. This did not pose great problems. Personal appearance can, as Hammersley and Atkinson (1983) observe, present a problem for the ethnographic researcher that can jeopardise the whole project if mis-managed. Fortunately my role in the PE department necessarily required that I adopt the appropriate clothing — a tracksuit and training shoes; and this was the garb worn by many of the young people at Parkview School. I also found myself slipping easily into conversations about football and television. Conversations gave way to good-natured banter when they discovered that I came from the Midlands (which they immediately labelled the 'North'), and that I was a fan of Brian Clough and the Nottingham Forest football team, The basis for very informal dialogue therefore existed, and comments about the *EastEnders* and *Grange Hill* television programmes were traded for remarks about flat-caps and whippet-racing. This process was not consciously planned, but had it been part of a coordinated scheme to develop rapport, it could hardly have been more effective.

The real ethical issues associated with the development of rapport, however, are the ways in which subjects are duped into revealing more of themselves than they otherwise would, as a direct result of the tactical decisions made by the researcher in order to break down 'barriers'. This whole area of the researcher behaving in such a way as to facilitate informants 'opening up' is a well established research technique, but it is difficult to resist Homan's (1991: p. 58) conclusion that "it is unethical to probe around issues that respondents are reluctant to talk about". He adds, somewhat provocatively, that techniques which attempt to put respondents in a more cooperative mood are "an abuse of professional conduct" (Homan, 1991: p. 125).

Role conflict and the dereliction of the teacher's 'professional' duty

The teacher's professionalism[5] is a concept that is constantly reinforced to student teachers throughout initial teacher training. But whatever the acceptable 'professional' standards of behaviour are, Mac an Ghaill (1991) is quite clear that in doing his own school-based research into the perceptions of young people, he was faced with researcher-teacher role conflict. This was my experience too.

At the outset, in order to gain acceptance in the PE department, it was incumbent on me to demonstrate some sort of professional competence as a teacher, and this necessarily included the adoption of the departmental standards. Initially I enforced the departmental regulations (for example, with regard to PE kit and showering), and employed the appropriate sanctions when these were not observed. But it soon became apparent that my behaviour was gaining the trust of the people who were, at most, only peripheral to the main focus of the study. Here then, was an ethical and professional dilemma. For though I was establishing my professional credentials with departmental colleagues, I was also distancing myself from the young people on whom the research was focused.

My response, which was more pre-meditated than the "self-presentation" (Shaffir, 1991: p. 77) described earlier, was to divest myself of authority status, and adopt the persona of an interested and approachable anti-authority figure. I began to judiciously select opportunities to disregard departmental protocol. I discovered too, that in the privacy of the interview situation, the most effective mechanisms for reducing social distance were the unprofessional behaviours of swearing (when it was deemed that the informant would not be offended), and joking about members of staff (with comments about personal appearance being especially valuable). The effect was that I, as the interviewer, was able to take the informant into my confidence, demonstrate my trust in him by sharing a non-deferential climate of scepticism towards authority, and break down barriers by sharing a common language as a means of communication.

Whether this is seen as effective fieldwork strategy, or unethical manipulation and exploitation of informants, depends on the ethical standpoint adopted. The point here, though, is not an ethical or professional evaluation of researcher conduct; but rather to draw attention to some of the practical dilemmas that resulted. Most of these were based on my responses to particular situations, but the decision-making process was seldom straightforward.

First, I was prepared to tolerate nick-names (some unflattering) and jokes at my expense. I was, for example, likened to 'Johnny Metgod' — the follicularly challenged footballer[6]; and occasionally greeted with "beam me up Scottie" — a reference to a character in the popular science-fiction television programme *Star Trek*. Not in themselves cause for a great deal of concern. But, as I wrote in field-notes at the time, I would not have allowed them had I been concerned about my 'professionalism' as a teacher. More significantly, when these instances occurred in front of PE department colleagues — as they sometimes did — my conduct was the subject of both professional and informant scrutiny. There was an apparent dilemma: was I to jeopardise the rapport that I was developing with the subjects of my research in order to maintain the professional standards of key gate-keepers? Or was I to break the professional trust of colleagues in order to sustain the personal relations developed with key informants? In the end I did neither, and compromised; but in doing so ran some risk of damaging my credibility in the eyes of both parties.

Second, there were the issues of professionalism in enforcing departmental policy:

4A collectively are causing problems for themselves by not bringing the correct kit — including a towel. Ms. Webster read them the 'riot act' this morning. It was thought to have been more effective before a football lesson since "that's the only one they care about". Anyone without full kit had to write 'lines' instead. Mahmood did not have a towel, but had told Ms. Webster that he did; she asked to see it, so he went to the changing rooms to get it. He did not have one, and immediately came into the office asking me to lend him one. At that moment Mr. Dennison arrived, and because there were other kids around too, I didn't risk undermining Ms. Webster's authority too flagrantly. I found myself in an awkward situation, and only resolved it by challenging Mahmood's problem-solving ability. If Ms. Webster wanted to see a towel, then I wasn't bothered where he got it from, but he wouldn't get it from me. This was the best compromise that I could come up with, but I sensed that Mahmood lost some of the confidence that he had in me, and probably felt betrayed as we'd been getting on so well. (Field-notes, 25/1/1989)

I was in no doubt that had we been alone, I would have given Mahmood the towel, and probably even encouraged him in the deception. Mahmood did not appreciate the subtle delicacy of the complex social relations in which I was engaged. What then, was he to make of this behaviour, which was apparently at odds with some of our previous interactions?

As time passed, the public face of the teacher, and the more private face of the researcher became increasingly difficult to sustain simultaneously. As Peeke (1984: p. 24) remarks: "to be a successful researcher can demand a lessening commitment to the task of teacher". I would go further, and endorse Burgess' (1985) view that there is a continuum on which the roles of the teacher and the researcher are located at either end. My persona moved along that continuum from an initial point where my affiliation was slightly with the teacher role, to the point where I identified almost exclusively with the role of researcher. An important consideration is to query the extent to which this chameleon–like transition affected the subjects of the research. As a researcher I was preoccupied with the research, but did I exploit these young people as informants to such an extent that they suffered as a result[7]? Had I, for example, through my ambiguous persona, undermined the status of the teachers so much that they were no longer seen as credible? Had I caused doubts to be raised about the trust-worthiness of the teachers?

'Guilty knowledge', researcher intervention and role conflict

The notion of 'guilty knowledge' — "confidential knowledge of illegal or illicit activities" (Fetterman, 1989: p. 130) — is particularly relevant to researchers concerned with criminal or deviant groups (Cromwell *et al.,* 1992; Shaffir and Stebbins, 1991; Punch, 1993). And in the rule-governed institution of the school, various regulations were also frequently being broken. Again I was faced with a dilemma of the 'sort of teacher'-researcher role, and risked accusations of unprofessionalism if my failure to intervene was ever discovered by members of the teaching staff. In one such instance some of my informants were smoking behind some school buildings. I was now being torn in (at least) three directions: to maintain the rapport and trust that had been developed with them; to be seen to enforce school rules; and to express my disapproval of an activity that I believed to be harmful to them. As ever, I compromised. I merely expressed my view about their health by commenting semi-seriously that: "It stunts your growth, you know", and added: "don't let anyone else catch you!" The ethical issue remains: the role of researcher was of greatest importance to me, but at what long-term risk to those being researched?

There is a general principle for researchers engaged in qualitative work that: "Noninvasive ethnography is not only good ethics, it is also good science" (Fetterman, 1989: p. 120). This may be a useful starting point, but it does not go far enough. It is clearly preferable for the researcher not to affect the research setting; the reality is, however, that this is rarely possible. Even when researchers are able to immerse themselves in the field, it is naive to believe that the field is unaffected by their presence (cf. Moore, 1980; Pryce, 1986).

Fetterman (1989: p. 120) provides further guidance: "[The] code [of ethics] specifies first and foremost that the ethnographer do no harm to people or the community under study". It is perhaps a useful supplementary clause to add that 'the ethnographer might *also* act so as to prevent such harm', as failure to do so might be seen as unethical. For example, if a researcher finds out — albeit in confidence — that someone is suffering serious physical or psychological harm, then there is a moral obligation to act.

The difficulty for the researcher lies firstly, in deciding on the seriousness of the harm being suffered; and secondly, in the sort of action to take. Patently there are issues that require little (if any) moral debate — for example physical and sexual abuse. But others are less clear. Whilst at Parkview School, I was aware that some informants were 'bunking off' occasionally. It was my judgement that this was not serious enough to require my intervention, and I did nothing about it (though I did discuss it with them). I chose to turn a 'blind-eye' to this, and other examples of what I considered to be relatively minor breaches of the school rules. I did not suffer any pangs of guilt, but there are questions that need to be addressed, not least the very pertinent: what frequency of truanting *would* cause harm?

There was one final concern that I had about the study of a relatively small sample of the entire school's population: the effects of my attention to these people on the rest. In particular there was one group of Bangladeshis who were victimised in different ways by their peers. I did not want to put them at further risk because of my interest in them. My interactions with them might easily have been misconstrued as favouritism, and I was anxious not exacerbate the situation. This was perhaps the only instance when the interests of the researcher were compromised, for it was important that I was seen to be acting in an even-handed way. It would have been easy to court favour with these particular informants, but at what cost to them?

Conclusion

The roles of the researcher doing fieldwork are complex. The exemplars that have been used in this discussion are from the school situation, and here the potential for role-conflict is especially acute. Other role–conflicts in school-based research do exist (Burgess, 1985; Stanley and Sieber, 1992), but these have not been addressed here — partly because I did not experience them myself, and partly because the purpose has been to consider the *sorts* of role-conflicts that exist. But whatever the research setting the sorts of predicaments and dilemmas outlined here are, at the very least, possible.

It is evident that the research strategies adopted were designed to achieve particular outcomes, for whilst my persona and conduct at the school were intended to minimise social distance, they were also techniques to minimise potential conflicts in the attempt to sustain the dual roles of 'sort-of teacher' and researcher. It is easy to be critical and point to behaviour that could be described as unethical. As a fellow contributor to this volume remarked to me, "I didn't realise how unethical I'd been until I wrote about it!" The ethical considerations and concerns of sport-related social research are not merely confined to the specific contexts of sport and leisure, they apply much more generally to wider research communities. Guidelines for good practice in qualitative research settings can seldom go beyond generalities (e.g. Kemmis and McTaggart, 1981); but different forms of human interaction and the complexity of social relations mean that it is impossible to be prescriptive. In attempting to reach solutions, common-sense and honesty are valuable commodities (Cromwell *et al.,* 1992).

With the benefit of hindsight, the research that I conducted in and around Parkview School involved some instances of ethically questionable behaviour. Perhaps some of the ethical concerns that I experienced at the time were suppressed by the desire to gather data at almost any cost; and had I been challenged about this I would doubtless have argued most indignantly about the 'greater good' being served by my contribution to the body of knowledge in this area of study. Specifically with regard to the role of the researcher and role-conflict, however, I would reject accusations that I behaved unethically. In many of the issues outlined above, there are no 'rights' and 'wrongs', just realistic and pragmatic solutions. Importantly too, many of them were undertaken without the sort of moralising and philosophising that this paper permits. I can say, though, that I am not aware of any harm that came to any of the subjects or indeed the wider community as a consequence of the research (though it is also true to say that I never explicitly sought information of this kind from them). When tensions arose, as they did in the PE department, my belief is that they would have occurred sooner or later, regardless of my presence. I am less convinced, though, that other researchers could exactly replicate the study in the same setting. In the research of 'sensitive' and/or 'controversial' issues, it may be that the researchers almost necessarily 'muddy the waters' for anyone wishing to follow them.

My own feeling is that I was rather lucky in the way that my research progressed, and in the way that real confrontations were avoided. Had I been less fortunate, it might have gone horribly wrong. To use the sporting cliché, it may be that 'you make your own luck', and that is part of the skill of the researcher.

Notes

1 I am grateful to Alan Tomlinson and to Lesley Lawrence for their constructive comments on an earlier draft. The final product is, of course, entirely my own responsibility.

2 This project was undertaken in collaboration with the Greater London and South East Regional Sports Council.

3 Pseudonyms have been used throughout.

4 There were other times during the research when I flagrantly deceived people about my true role. Indeed in some of the local sports clubs at which other parts of the work were also conducted I traded variously on being a teacher or not being a teacher as I perceived the situation to demand. This caused me some real soul-searching at the time, firstly about the ethics of the deception, and secondly — and perhaps more importantly — about the danger of being 'caught out'.

5 The concept of 'professionalism' is one that I grappled with as a student, as a researcher, and as a lecturer in higher education. Rather like the common-sense approach to ethics, I have my own set of standards, and I have to live with my conscience if I flout them. Yet to decide whether an action is professional (or ethical) is, for me at least, problematic. It is much easier to conclude that actions are **un**professional (or **un**ethical). These are those

actions that violate my code of acceptable behaviour. Like Homan (1980), I reject a simplistic ethical-unethical dichotomy, for I am not yet convinced that everything 'not unethical' is ethical, and that everything 'not unprofessional' is professional; there are theoretical and practical grey areas.

6   Like Johnny Metgod, a Dutch footballer with Tottenham Hotspur Football Club at the time, I am, as *The Official Politically Correct Dictionary and Handbook* puts it, "hair disadvantaged"!

7   In affiliating strongly with the role of researcher I did not abdicate my teacher responsibilities. Rather they were undertaken in an almost mechanistic way, exercising the 'duty of care'. But the role of researcher was always at the forefront of my consciousness.

References

Burgess, R. G. (1985) 'The whole truth? Some ethical problems of research in a comprehensive school', in R. G. Burgess (ed) *Field methods in the study of education*. Lewes: Falmer Press, pp. 139–162.

Corrigan, P. (1979) *Schooling the Smash Street kids*. London: Macmillan Educational.

Cromwell, P. F., Olson, J. N., and Avary, D'A. W. (1992) *Breaking and entering*. London: Sage.

Fetterman, D. M. (1989) *Ethnography step by step*. London: Sage.

Fine, G. A. and Sandstrom, K. L. (1988) *Knowing children*. London: Sage.

Fleming, S. (1991) 'Sport, schooling and Asian male youth culture', in G. Jarvie (ed) *Sport, racism and ethnicity*. London: Falmer Press, pp. 30–57.

Fleming, S. (1992) *Sport and South Asian male youth*. Unpublished Ph. D. Thesis, Brighton Polytechnic, CNAA.

Hammersley, M. and Atkinson, P. (1983) *Ethnography: principles in practice*. London: Tavistock.

Homan, R. (1980) 'The ethics of covert research — Homan defends his methods'. *Network*. January, 4.

Homan, R. (1991) *The ethics of social research*. London: Longman.

Kemmis, S. and McTaggart, R. (1981) *The action research planner*. Victoria, Australia: Deakin University Press.

Mac an Ghaill, M. (1991) 'Young, gifted and black: methodological reflections of a teacher/researcher', in G. Walford (ed) *Doing educational research*, London: Routledge, pp. 101–120.

Mandell, N. (1991) 'The least–adult role in studying children', in N. C. Waksler (ed) *Studying the social worlds of children*. London: Falmer Press, pp. 38–59.

Moore, R. (1980) 'Becoming a sociologist in Sparkbrook', in C. Bell and H. Newby (eds) *Doing sociological research*. London: George Allen and Unwin, pp. 87–107.

Peeke, G. (1984) 'Teacher as researcher', *Educational Research* 26, pp. 24–26.

Phillips, E. M., and Pugh, D. S. (1987) *How to get a PhD*. Milton Keynes: Open University Press.

Pryce, K. (1986) *Endless pressure*. 2nd edition. Bristol: Bristol Classical Press.

Punch, M. (1993) 'Observation and the police: the research experience', in M. Hammersley (ed) *Social research*. London: Sage, pp. 181–199.

Shaffir, W. B. (1991) 'Managing a convincing self-presentation: some personal reflections on entering the field', in W. B. Shaffir and R. A. Stebbins (eds) *Experiencing fieldwork*. London: Sage, pp. 72–82.

Shaffir, W. B. and Stebbins, R. A. (1991) (eds) *Experiencing fieldwork*. London: Sage.

Stanley, B. and Sieber, J. E. (1992) (eds) *Social research on children and adolescents*. London: Sage.

Willis, P. (1977) *Learning to labour — how working-class kids get working-class jobs*. Aldershot, Hants.: Gower.

RESEARCHING SPORT AND SEXUAL HARASSMENT: THE ETHICS OF COVERT PARTICIPANT OBSERVATION AND OPEN METHODS

Ilkay Yorganci
University of Brighton / Roehampton Institute of Higher Education

This chapter is based on my doctoral research into gender, sport and sexual harassment (Yorganci, 1994). Doing research on a sensitive issue such as sexual harassment has not been an easy task. It was not just hard to get people to "open up" to a total stranger, to me, about personal and in some cases very painful experiences, but it was also difficult since no substantial research has been done in this area before. Since there were no precedents for me to follow, my first task, I felt, had to be exploratory empirical work in the area. In order to achieve this, I felt that participant observation, in the context of an ethnographic phase of my study, was the most appropriate method to use.

I felt that participant observation would not only provide me with a better understanding of the phenomenon, but would also yield some additional information that other research methods might not provide to the same extent. For example, participant observation is the only method which provides the opportunity to observe the harasser and the harassed at the same time. Participant observation also provides opportunities to examine the environment which women are part of, and, therefore, does not look at women's experiences in isolation.

Having decided to use participant observation, I chose to adopt a covert role (that is, to gather data without the knowledge of those being observed). There are, of course, some very central ethical concerns involved with the use of covert methods and it is opposed strongly by sociologists like Dingwall (1980). Researchers are known to go to great lengths to gather information, and some, in the process of doing so, were involved in great deceptions and role adaptations. Bulmer (1982) and Homan (1980) cite celebrated examples of this. Caudill posed as a mental patient; Lofland's graduate students posed as alcoholics; Festinger and his colleagues joined a gathering of mystics by professing religious beliefs they did not hold; and Humphreys adopted the role of lookout-voyeur to observe homosexual encounters in men's toilets, taking the registration numbers of his subjects' cars in order to trace and interview them under the pretext of a social health survey. Some researchers hid under students' beds to listen to conversations and some went as far as having operations to alter their appearances.

Such dramatic role adaptations were not necessary for me since I was already using the same facilities as the groups I chose to observe. In fact I did not adopt any new role. I continued to be what I was, namely an athlete among other athletes. I was simply an athlete who was interested in my environment, or had an additional role as a researcher.

The British Sociological Association (BSA) guidelines state:

> Participant or non participant observation in non-public spaces ...of research participants without their knowledge should be resorted to only where it is impossible to use other methods to obtain essential data. (BSA, 1992: note 2)

My research adhered to these guidelines, as the participant observation was carried out in a public space (an athletics track).

Adopting a covert role eliminates the possibility of any alterations in behaviour patterns of those observed — the classic "Hawthorne effect" that haunts many social researchers. The BSA is conscious of such problems and allows covert methods to be used where:

> for instance, difficulties arise when research participants change their behaviour because they know they are being studied. (1992: note 2)

I believe that if the group knew that I was looking at sexual harassment the harassers would have altered their behaviours. It was very likely that they would have stopped harassing. This may especially occur when the nature of the harassment is easily identifiable or when the person being harassed is under age, since this might lead to fear of complications with the law. Therefore, it can be taken for granted that, if the members are unaware of the researcher's purpose or existence, their behaviours are unlikely to be affected. Thus, it may be possible to record the "authentic/typical" behaviours of the group. Therefore, covert observation could provide me the opportunity to observe normal behaviour. The extent to which the known presence of the observer alters the research situation is a serious consideration.

Another reason for the use of covert methods was the belief that this might be the only way that the researcher can acquire a record of the actual re-actions of the girls/women (rather than how they claim that they re-act) to the actions/words in question. Although this is an inherent problem with any questionnaires and interviews gathering reported or retrospective data, it becomes even more of a problem when researching sexual harassment. This is because girls/women may be reluctant to explicitly accuse and, ergo, alienate, male peers in, or, the coach of, the group. Alternatively, the girls/women may be reluctant to acknowledge that they are being harassed, because of the fear of being held to be culpable (as is often the case with women who have been raped and who have, in turn, been accused of "asking for it").

Finally, sexual harassment is often considered as part of everyday activity since such behaviours occur in schools, at home, on the street, at the work place, and in all other spheres of our life. The result is that although some women do not like it, for a number of reasons they do not challenge it. Therefore, to uncover the extent of behaviour which may be construed as sexual harassment in sports settings requires direct observation of the people in that environment. Where such behaviour is observed it may then be possible to conduct interviews with or distribute questionnaires to the females involved to establish whether or not these women felt that they were being harassed.

I also claim that by doing covert research in such a public environment I was not invading the "privacy" of those being studied. I was not trespassing on my subjects' environment. I was not only part of that environment but it was also a public place where anyone could go and join in. As Homan said, "the community which declares 'All are welcome' thereby forgoes its privacy" (1980: p. 57). Furthermore, if there was anyone who was overstepping the privacy of others, it was the harassers. Towards harassers I felt no moral obligations.

When examining ethical issues, McCall and Simmons (1969: p. 58) wrote:

> If a social group under observation has a newcomer's role which permits the practice of participant observation, and if the long-run functioning of the group is not disrupted by the unsuspected observation made by the

investigator and his subsequent departure from the group, then there would appear no violation of prevailing ethical norms. This statement assumes of course, that the investigator's report does not "damage" any respondent or subject, nor does it make it impossible for another investigator to enter this group as a participant observer at a later date. If all these conditions hold, standards of both the local group and the larger society would appear to be met.

The BSA guidelines state that the "physical, social and psychological well being of research participants "should not be" adversely affected by research " (1992: note 1a).

The above criterion is very useful when gathering data on "unproblematic" areas, in circumstances when the safety of the subjects is not under threat. However, where research is being conducted on sexual harassment and women in an athletics club and it is concluded that some women and girls are sexually harassed by their coaches, then it may be in the interests of those suffering from harassment that "the long-run functioning of the group" is disrupted and "the investigator's report" can be used to expose the damage being done to the victims of harassment. In short, I am morally forced to reject the view of McCall and Simmons that the investigator's report ought not to "damage" any subject if that subject is, in turn, damaging someone else. I believe that it is appropriate to publish a report which contributes to the exposure of and potential decrease in or cessation of sexual harassment in sporting environments, so that women have a safer environment in which to train. This is more important than to act in terms of some pseudo-neutral ethical code. This also raises an ideological question. Dingwall argued:

> In theory, the researcher is neither a journalist nor a crusader with a mandate to titillate or moralise. His main thrust is to report the "good reasons" which subjects adduce to account for their actions and, thereby, to furnish the context within which their conduct, however objectionable, becomes rational. (1980: p. 881)

I disagree with Dingwall's assumptions about research aims (and with any, however unintended, implication that the researcher is exclusively male!). I do not accept that my aims in doing research are only to "report the 'good reasons' which subjects adduce to account for their actions and, thereby, to furnish the context within which their conduct, however objectionable, becomes rational". It is also my aim to establish whether the actions of the harassers have an inimical effect on the objects of their actions, and if these actions do, to propose ways of stopping these actions perpetrated by the harassers. Consequently, whilst it is important to know why men sexually harass women, the aim of finding out these reasons is not just to report them, but also to formulate ways of eliminating or reducing such harassment. As Marx, in *Theses on Feuerbach*, said:

The philosophers have only interpreted the world, in various ways; the point is to change it. (McLellan, 1987: p. 158)

I also disagree with Dingwall's assertion that the researcher should not "moralise", if by this it is meant that the researcher should not conclude that a group of people is subject to actions which have deleterious effects on them. In particular, if the researcher discovers that sexual harassment occurs in sport and that it hinders the attempts of women to achieve athletic excellence or that it affects the number of women participating in sports by driving some out and keeping others away, then there is little point in the researcher gathering such information without also endeavouring to establish the causes of and potential remedies for the harmful behaviours recorded.

It should be made clear, however, that the objectivity of the researcher who advocates remedies to the problems revealed by her/his research cannot be questioned because of this advocacy. It is a *non sequitur* to conclude that the suggesting of ways of removing or reducing problems experienced by female athletes invalidates the findings of the research which established the existence and context of such problems.

Another objection to the use of covert methods is the notion of deception. Bulmer (1980) implies that the use of covert methods amounts to deception in research which, in turn, constitutes a betrayal of trust. He states:

If the personal relationships are based upon falsehood, this may harm the subjects of the research. (1980: p. 60)

In addition, the BSA guidelines state that:

research relationships should be characterised, wherever possible, by trust. (1992: note 1a).

Bulmer's assertion that covert methods involve deception is not one with which I want to quarrel; however to say that such methods involve a betrayal of trust which may be harmful to the subjects is probably going too far. For example, if one joins a group of athletes without revealing that the reason for so doing is to conduct research, then that is deception. But, using information gathered in this manner is no more a betrayal of trust than another member of the same group revealing the same information (in the form of gossip) to other non-group members, as is usually the case with groups of people.

In the case of my research, I was not a formal member of a group; I simply trained at the location frequented by various groups of athletes which I observed. Further, any information provided to me in the course of conversations with members of these groups was not given in confidence. Indeed, I was only one of several people to whom this information was imparted. Deception is inherent in the covert observer's role. But that does not automatically imply a betrayal of trust, for to use or talk about the data of everyday interactions is part and parcel of normal everyday life.

The second research method I employed was the use of questionnaires. As Homan (1992) claims it is not only the covert methods of research which can be unethical; there are unethical aspects to open methods too.

Homan (1992) questions the practice of "personal" questions being left at the end of the questionnaire. He calls it a "dubious practice" and suggests that in some ways the privacy of the respondent is invaded. I disagree with Homan entirely. My argument is that at any stage in the process of completing the questionnaire, the respondent can decide not to answer any questions that she/ he does not want to answer. This point has been emphasized by the number of people who chose not to answer certain parts of my questionnaire.

The BSA guidelines state:

> As far as possible sociological research should be based on the freely given informed consent of those studied. This implies a responsibility on the sociologist to explain as fully as possible, and in terms meaningful to participants, what the research is about, who is undertaking and financing it, why it is being undertaken and how it is to be promoted. (1992: note 1b).

I agree with the contents of the above guidelines and adhered to them when distributing my questionnaires. In particular, attached to the front of each questionnaire was a note explaining the aims of the research and providing a reference to my identity. Further, when the questionnaires were handed to the potential respondents, I explained the source of any sponsorship of which I was a recipient. These questionnaires were administered by me, but were designed for self-completion. This is less intrusive than probing for personal data in a face-to-face interview, for the respondent can browse, reflect and make unpressured decisions as to how to respond. But 'personal' questions need not be an invasion of privacy — even in face-to-face interviews — if anonymity can be guaranteed.

The BSA guidelines also state, "Research participants should understand how far they will be afforded anonymity and confidentiality..." (1992: note 1(b)). I accept the contents of these guidelines, and they were particularly germane in the case of my research since some of the questions in my questionnaire were of a sensitive nature, and potential respondents were more likely to answer these questions if they were assured of anonymity and confidentiality. Throughout my research, I followed the practice of informing potential respondents that they would remain anonymous. I have kept this promise.

The ethical and moral problems I faced during interviews were of a different nature.

Homan claims that it is unethical to break down the resistance of the interviewee by the "purposeful sequencing of questions, the development of rapport and trust between investigator and respondent and the presentation of the researcher as credible" (1992: p. 320). Unlike Homan I do not believe that it is unethical to develop rapport and trust with my respondents; or to choose the order of my questions. Instead I argue that they are necessary strategies for successful data gathering. Unless the interviewee trusts the investigator, the interviewee will not provide the information needed. However, what is unethical is the betrayal of that trust, for example, by revealing a subject's identity having promised not to do so.

Homan also seems to believe that there is something wrong in using a "degree of charm, empathy or friendliness" while conducting an interview (1992: p. 327). What is the alternative, not to be friendly?

However, I do agree with Homan's assertion that it is unethical to "probe around issues that respondents were reluctant to talk about" (1991: p. 58). As Lynda Measor wrote,

> If respondents have decided they do not want to tell you why they never
> married, failed to get promotion, or left their boyfriend last week, they

have a right to privacy. It is unethical to poke around the issue, trying to pressure them for the data you want. (1985: p. 72)

Although I respected the interviewees' right to privacy and refrained from pressuring them for data they did not want to give, I have, on occasion, rephrased questions. This was a necessary part of the interviewing process since, for example, some women were reluctant to use the phrase "sexual harassment", yet they were willing to refer to such experiences as "unwanted", "offensive", or "horrible". Indeed, if such a strategy was not used, the analysis would have been simplistic and meaningless to the point of futility.

Homan (1992) criticises Finch for invading the privacy of her subjects because her subjects were willing to talk to her since she was a woman like them and therefore they could identify with her. For Homan, this questions the ethics of doing feminist research. I disagree with Homan that this is unethical in any way. There is nothing unethical about women being more willing to talk to a female researcher because she feels more relaxed in female company or identifies more with a woman. Women are not forced to give out information and they are free to withhold any information they do not want to pass on.

Finch (1993), herself, felt some moral dilemmas in using the data obtained during her interviews with other women, since these interviews were made easy because of her identity as a woman. She felt that she "traded on that identity" (1993: p. 173). She also felt that, "there is therefore a real exploitative potential in the easily established trust between women, which makes women especially vulnerable as subjects of research" (p. 174). Finch believes that these techniques can be used to great effect to solicit a range of information (some of it very private), which is capable of being used ultimately against the interests of those women who gave it so freely to another woman with whom they found it easy to talk. This information can be used against women either by unethical researchers or once the information is published by people other than the researcher in ways the researcher does not approve of. She argues that for a feminist doing research on women, it is not merely individual interest which is at stake since this could be relatively easily secured with guarantees of confidentiality, but it is far more difficult to devise ways of ensuring that information given so readily in interviews will not be used ultimately against the collective interests of women. Finch argued:

The dilemmas which I have encountered therefore raise the possibility of betrayal of the trust which women have placed in me when I interviewed them. I do not really mean "betrayal" in the individual sense, such as selling the story of someone else's life to a Sunday newspaper. I mean, rather, "betrayal" in an indirect and collective sense, that is, undermining the interests of women in general by my use of the material given to me by my interviewees. It is betrayal none the less, because the basis upon which the information has been given is the trust placed in one woman by another. (1993: p. 177)

I do not accept that there is anything undesirable about the possibility that female researchers are more likely to succeed in getting female interviewees to provide information than are male researchers. This is only one of the ineluctable variations resulting from the fact the researchers vary not only by gender, but inter alia, by personality and thoroughness.

As far as Finch's point that the information provided to her by her female interviewees may be used against these interviewees is concerned, then it is the researcher's responsibility to ensure that s/he has a theoretical framework in which to place and explain her/his findings. Certainly, the researcher should not suppress her/his research findings because they conflict with her/his beliefs.

As a feminist doing feminist research, Skeggs (1992) also faced some personal dilemmas. She wrote:

When you continually experience dominant ideological views and remain silent you give these views a legitimacy. (1992: p. 17)

She argues that sexism is reproduced and legitimated every day through the process of collusion. Should, she asks, the researcher be part of that process?

It is my view that however much the researcher finds the views of the interviewee to be repugnant, it is not acceptable for the researcher to attempt to persuade the interviewee that her/his views are unacceptable. The researcher has to record the views expressed. However, if the researcher feels strongly, then s/he is at liberty to engage the interviewee in a debate once the interview has been concluded. Alternatively, the researcher may endeavour to explore the source of the repugnant views expressed by the interviewee by challenging such views.

Skeggs (1992) also raises the question of what do you do with sexual harassers. She argues that:

Dealing with either of these issues (i.e. sexism and racism) can easily jeopardise research, but what debts do we owe those who have trusted us with their most intimate problems? (1992: p. 17)

My suggestion for dealing with such a dilemma is that if it is clear that one of my interviewees is being subject to harassment which is causing her great distress, then I should advise her that there are several ways of dealing with such a problem and proffer guidance if she wants it. This would be done in my capacity as a fellow human being and not my capacity as a researcher. The offering of such advice would be made only at the completion of the interview and so would not influence the responses provided by the interviewee. However, if during my research I discover that a number of young people are being sexually harassed, then I would either report it to some form of authority or, if possible, draw it to the attention of the parents.

Conclusion

In conclusion, certain ethical issues arise when using covert methods as part of participant observation and when distributing questionnaires or conducting interviews. Such ethical issues must be recognised and thought through, but do not preclude the use of such methods. Indeed, research in some areas would not be possible without resort to these methods. In the case of my research, I concluded that it was essential to use covert methods in observation of harassers and the harassed, to obviate the possibility of modified behaviour as a result of those being observed knowing that they are being observed.

My second method was questionnaire-based. A well-explained questionnaire, particularly when designed for self-completion, allows the respondent to decide what and how much detail is provided. If the aim of the research is clearly explained, including details of who is undertaking it, financing it, and anonymity is assured, then ethical integrity in the use of the questionnaire is assured.

As far as the use of interviews is concerned, I reject the idea that establishing rapport with the interviewee as a result of sharing the same sex or being friendly is undesirable. These are excellent ways of eliciting information without coercion.

I also maintain that where research reveals that the behaviour of some people has a deleterious effect on other people, then the researcher should be concerned for those being harmed and not for those perpetrating the harm.

Acknowledgement

The doctoral research on which this article is based was conducted at the Chelsea School Research Centre, and supported by the Economic and Social Research Council (Postgraduate Research Studentship No. R00429124306).

References

British Sociological Association (BSA) (1992) 'BSA statement of ethical practice', *Sociology* Vol. 26, No. 4: pp. 703–707.

Bulmer, M. (1980) 'Comment on "the ethics of covert methods"', *British Journal of Sociology* Vol. 31, No. 1: pp. 59–65.

Bulmer, M (ed) (1982) *Social research ethics*. London: Macmillan.

Dingwall, R. (1980) 'Ethics and ethnography', *Sociological Review* Vol. 28, No. 4: pp. 871–91.

Finch, J. (1993) '"It's great to have someone to talk to": Ethics and the politics of interviewing women', in M. Hammersley (ed) *Social research: philosophy, politics and practice*. London: Sage: pp. 166–80.

Homan, R. (1980) 'The ethics of covert methods', *British Journal of Sociology* Vol. 31, No. 1: pp. 46–59.

———(1991) *The ethics of social research*. London: Longman.

———(1992) 'The ethics of open methods', *British Journal of Sociology* Vol. 43, No. 3: pp. 321–32.

McCall, G. J. and Simmons, J. L. (eds) (1969) *Issues in participant observation*. USA: Addison–Wesley.

McLellan, D. (ed.) (1987) *Karl Marx: selected writings*. Oxford: Oxford University Press.

Measor, L. (1985) 'Interviewing: A strategy in qualitative research', in R. Burgess (ed) *Strategies of educational research: qualitative methods*. London: Falmer Press.

Skeggs, B. (1992) 'Confessions of a feminist researcher', *Sociology Review* Vol. 2, No. 1: pp. 14–17.

Yorganci, I. (1994) Gender, Sport and Sexual Harassment, PhD thesis. Chelsea School, University of Brighton.

COVERT ETHNOGRAPHY AND THE ETHICS OF RESEARCH: STUDYING SPORTS SUBCULTURES

Belinda Wheaton
University of Brighton

I have been involved in a research project investigating the changing nature of sport and leisure practices in the 1990s. Ethnographically-rooted field work on leisure lifestyles conducted over a 14 month period focused on windsurfing and surfing sub-cultures. The specific idiosyncrasies of ethnography give ethical issues a "distinctive accent" (Hammersley & Atkinson, 1995a), especially issues surrounding informed consent and intrusion of privacy. These issues will be discussed in the context of this fieldwork, and I will illustrate how I have tried to deal with the ethical and moral dilemmas that have arisen.

Ethical problems are those that emanate during the research process when faced with making a decision "regarding standards of what is morally right or wrong" (Barnes, 1979). Ethical issues are, as Rees (1991) highlights, prevalent in most research, and they exist throughout the research process, from obtaining funding to publishing results. Yet, ethical issues, both predicted and unexpected, are particularly significant in cases involving covert methods or deception, such as in this research project.

The methodology adopted in the first phase of the research involved an extended participation observation period, to be followed by in-depth interviews. Before an ethnographer can enter the field-work site s/he must forge a role in the community to gain access to the group. Although there are several different observational strategies possible[1], as I am an active member of the subculture under study, the favoured approach was adopting a 'complete participant' role (Hammersley & Atkinson, 1995a). This involves 'total immersion' in a native culture; the researcher cannot just pass as a group member, s/he must become one (Hammersley & Atkinson, 1995b). But the researcher's real intentions are concealed from the group, which involves playing a covert role. Other researchers studying sport subcultures have adopted similar strategies, especially if they are a member of the group under study (see Donnelly, 1993).

The main advantages of the 'complete participant' strategy are that the researcher can easily obtain insider knowledge without the obstacles of gate-keepers and gaining access; and that the effect of the researcher on the environment s/he is studying is minimised (Hammersley & Atkinson, 1995b). The practical limitation of covert observation is that the researcher becomes entwined in the group's social practices, so it is harder to control situations and behaviour to aid data collection (Hammersley & Atkinson, 1995b).

Some commentators argue that it is the researchers' ethical obligation to obtain consent from all the subjects to participate in the research (see Warwick, 1982). Homan (1991) has defined 'informed consent' as:

> ... the principle [...] that the human subjects of research should be allowed to agree or refuse to participate in the light of comprehensive information concerning the nature and purpose of the research. (p. 69)

But covert participant observation is a conspicuous departure from the principle of informed consent. Almost all of the group members were unaware that the research was taking place, so it was impossible to get their consent.

But this insistence on informed consent is an extreme view in a debate where commentators differ markedly[2]. Other commentators deny the relevance of ethical considerations, arguing that deceptive methods are necessary to do 'good' research in the unethical social world in which we operate (see Douglas, 1976). Moreover, the whole notion of informed consent is practically problematic in ethnographic field work. For example, frequently researchers can only speculate about the potential hazards or demands on their subjects.

As Rees (1991: p. 146) argues, taken literally 'informed consent' seems an impossibly tough requirement in most social research situations. Thus abdicating the principle seemed justified in this research. Firstly, as discussed it would have been difficult to obtain informed consent without changing the behaviour of the subjects (the placebo effect), and thus adversely affecting the results.

Secondly, the 'complete participant' role was the only possible observation option for gaining full access. As a female researcher studying a very male-dominated subculture, my role as an active and competent windsurfer was vital in gaining access. Status in the windsurfing subculture seems to be related to commitment, proficiency and gender; that is individuals who commit time and effort to the activity, and so are skilled, have status (and tend to be predominantly men). So to get full access to the predominantly male activities, my status in terms of commitment and proficiency was vital: in many ways my subcultural role was as 'one of the lads' (Moore, 1994).

Had I been a female' non-participant observer, it is doubtful that I would have been able to get such useful data. This was borne out by my observation of surfing groups at the same locations, which yielded less rich data. Although I did go out 'surfing', the craft I used was a 'boogie-board' which many surfers consider inferior to the surf board. This, in conjunction with my moderate competence at the sport, denied me the same access I had to the windsurfing subculture.

Thirdly, obtaining informed consent does not necessarily resolve this ethical obligation to inform the subjects. In practice many researchers are satisfied with giving their subjects 'half-truths'- enough information to satisfy moral obligations, but not enough to dissuade the subjects from participating. Moreover, once consent is obtained, researchers can make it hard for the subject to drop out. So several commentators have rightly suggested that the real purpose for the formal consent procedure is to protect the researcher, not the subjects, especially in potentially risky experimental or psychological work. By obtaining a signature, or verbal consent, the researcher feels s/he is relieved of responsibility, as it becomes a disclaimer (Homan, 1991). Moreover, as Roth (1962) argues, all research falls along the continuum between the completely covert and completely open; even within the same project the degree of openness may vary between subjects (Hammersley & Atkinson, 1995a) and in my project, between different phases of the research.

So although my research was mainly covert, and involved some deception (as I was an active member of the group before the research began) my intrusion of privacy was minimal. Moreover, my subjects were not subjected to any risk. As Hammersley & Atkinson (1995a) argue:

> In our view, an element of not telling the whole truth, even of active deception, may be justifiable so long as it is not designed to harm the people researched and so long as there seems little chance that it will. (Hammersley & Atkinson, 1995a: pp. 282–283)

Even had I decided that the covert approach was ethically unacceptable, due to the informal non-regulated environments that I was researching, I did not have sufficient control over the research process, to ensure that all participants were freely consenting and fully informed.

Ethnographic interviews will present similar concerns. Obtaining written consent could spoil the rapport between researcher and subjects, especially in informal focus-groups, and consequently could be detrimental to my response rate. The acceptable ethical minimum seems to be informing my subjects of the broad area of research, explaining my involvement, and what the research is for. However, due to the covert nature of the participant observation phase, and my unease about the intrusion of privacy, I do not intend to reveal that I have been operating as a covert observer.

I will offer to give all my subjects an interview transcript, and ask their consent to use the data in other publications, especially the more prominent members of the windsurfing community. However although all names, places and dates of incidents will be disguised, I cannot guarantee all my subjects' confidentiality. In a relatively small, insular community like that of the wind-surfers, anonymity is nearly impossible, especially when dealing with prominent places and windsurfing/surfing-media celebrities.

Privacy and intrusion

> Even when cover is successfully maintained, though, the researcher engaged in covert research has to live with the moral qualms, anxieties, and practical difficulties to which the use of this strategy may lead. (Hammersley & Atkinson, 1995a: p. 72)

Although all social research has an element of intrusion, in ethnographic research this is heightened as very private events become available for public consump-tion (Hammersley & Atkinson, 1995a), which can cause anxiety and a sense of insecurity for the researcher. However what constitutes 'public' and 'private' space is rarely clear cut (Hammersley & Atkinson, 1995a). In this research context, many interactions were observed at the beach, usually considered to be a 'public' place. Yet some of the subjects I observed were friends, which amplified these concerns. In particular I felt very uneasy reporting events that occurred in my home, which seemed a particular encroachment of privacy and confidentiality, especially when these incidents and conversations involved other people living in the house, and their visitors.

Social practices and expected behaviour

As discussed above, Hammersley & Atkinson (1995b) warn that the complete participant researcher becomes so involved in the groups' social practices, that s/he 'must behave in expected ways', which can be counter productive to data collection. This limitation soon became apparent in my field work in several ways, and prompted unexpected ethical decisions.

Firstly, although my role as a proficient and active windsurfer was vital in gaining access to this male-dominated subculture, it also affected the amount of time I could spend 'hanging out' on the beach for observational purposes. To retain my legitimacy in the subculture as a participant, I had to go out wind-surfing, at least for a short time. The few times I tried to avoid sailing, other members in the subculture made it difficult for me. Comments like "Are you an actor or a windsurfer?", or "Stop being such a girl and get out there" were made. This problem was perpetuated in the Autumn and Winter. It was so cold that 'hanging out' on the beach was out of the question; windsurfers turned up to sail, changed and left. Short of faking a long-term injury (an unethical as well as difficult scenario to depict), it was almost impossible not to windsurf myself.

The second set of social practices that I had to observe were those regarding attitudes and practices of drinking, and using soft drugs, especially marijuana (see Renneker, 1987, regarding the widespread use of illegal drugs in surfing subcultures in California). Within certain sections of both subcultures, marijuana use is quite widespread. Although some other researchers studying surfers seem to have ignored illegal drug use (or perhaps this aspect of the subculture wasn't detected due to the researchers' non-participant roles), as "countercultural" activities (Donnelly, 1993: p. 134), this seemed an important part of the culture, and one that I shouldn't omit. Consequently, at social gatherings I had to decide whether or not I had my 'researcher' hat on. If I did, then I had to try and mask the fact that I was not getting 'involved' in these practices, so that I was still alert enough to observe. Of course this wasn't always a conscious decision. For example, if I was relaxing in the evening with a beer, and unexpected visitors arrived, I had to revert to a mode of observing and recording data.

Journalist and researcher: the implications

My participation in the subculture was complicated by my dual role as a sports journalist and researcher. In the past I have worked as a freelance journalist, which has included regular contributions to a Windsurfing magazine. I decided to continue this involvement during the research as one of my aims was to examine the relationship between the subculture and the media. Working for one of the windsurfing magazines made me privy to invaluable information, albeit under-handedly, especially about how the media operates, and the specific economic and political influences.

My 'journalistic' role also aided data collection on many occasions. For example, at the beach strangers would come up to talk to me on, and chat about windsurfing, often in relation to the windsurfing media. On several occasions I attended windsurfing competitions for observational purposes, but I was also reporting on the event for a magazine. My role as a journalist was a useful alibi here, and gave me a legitimate reason for carrying a dictaphone and note book on the beach, and for the occasional informal 'interview'.

Commentators have suggested that researchers usually investigate those that are less powerful than themselves, thus the relationship between researcher and his/her subjects is hierarchical, even if the researcher has an emotional and intellectual commitment to the group members (Hammersley & Atkinson, 1995a). Similarly, the journalist-interviewee relationship is often one of unequal power, and potentially equally exploitative. However in this context the group that I studied, and others who knew me, seemed to realise that my position as a columnist for the magazine didn't put me in a position of 'power' within the community. The windsurfing magazines are dependent on advertising revenue from within the windsurfing industry; thus the journalists have limited influence over editorial content and direction. Consequently I don't think that I was denied information or access on the basis of being a 'journalist', nor was I able to coerce informants to give information unwillingly. Perhaps if I held a more influential position, like the magazine editor, the situation would have been different.

During the research period the magazine editor approached me, and asked me to edit a new monthly column aimed at giving women who windsurf a 'voice' in the magazine. He felt it would be an inappropriate job for the 'male' editorial team. Although the idea of a 'separatist' women's section was, in my view a non-ideal solution to the problems of women's under-representation in the magazine, it was still a very positive initiative, and one to which I felt an ethical commitment, (and excitement). As Duncan and Hasbrook (1988) argue:

> We as sport and leisure educators have an ethical obligation to try and change the structures of sport-to strongly encourage female participation [...] to petition the media to present sporting women as athletes and not as objects of sexual gratification. (p. 20)

So although I felt uneasy, both about the time commitment, and whether ethically I could combine these two roles, I decided to accept the offer, especially as it would give me access to all the letters, and comments written to the magazine about women windsurfers. As it has turned out, my involvement in the magazine has been very useful in terms of the 'documents' to which I now have access, and readers' reactions to the concept of the column.

My ways of dealing with the ethical dilemmas — both practically and emotionally — are less clear. Firstly, I have discussed my research aims with the magazine editor, who has no objection to me using the documents. Although I would like to contact all the contributors to the magazine to ask for permission to use their letters in my research, not all contributors include their full name or address, so it is not always possible. Some commentators would argue that I am exploiting my subjects, but as Hammersley & Atkinson (1995a) argue, this is always a matter of judgement that is hard to evaluate. Finch (1984) and other feminists argue that feminist researchers, should try to give back something, or empower their (female) subjects through the research process. It could be claimed that there are benefits for my female subjects, and female windsurfers generally. My involvement in this research, and my 'voice' in the magazine's editorial office, have contributed to this initiative to give women windsurfers a voice in a sexist, male- dominated sport-media product.

Hammersley & Atkinson suggest that the ultimate goal of research is the "production of knowledge" (1995a: p. 263), but not at all costs. Although in this, and other reported cases of covert research, the benefits of the research do seem to outweigh ethical considerations, it is a fine line between paternalism and the subjects' 'right to know'. The point is that: "There is a balance here which has to be struck by each researcher as an individual" (Rees, 1991: p. 146). In every situation, the researcher must find a compromise between purist ethics and pragmatic judgement, based on an awareness of how the 'real world' operates.

Hammersley & Atkinson point out that some debates about ethics in social research exaggerate the potential harm to which subjects are exposed, and are premised on an idea that social researchers should have "a heightened ethical sensibility and responsibility" (Hammersley & Atkinson, 1995a: p. 285).

> Underlying the treatment of any procedures as absolute ethical requirements are assumptions about how social settings ought to be that may neglect how they actually are. (Hammersley & Atkinson, 1995a: p. 279)

This is not a carte blanche for researchers to behave like tabloid journalists; but nothing would ever get done if unrealistic ethical standards were adhered to. Perhaps, as Rees (1991) proposes, the acceptable balance is 'half-informed consent'. If researchers ignored every unethical social practice then academics are surely at risk of becoming stuck in their 'Ivory Towers'.

Acknowledgement

The doctoral research on which this article is based was conducted at the Chelsea School Research Centre, and supported by the Economic and Social Research Council (Postgraduate Research Studentship No. R00429334379).

Notes

[1] See Hammersley & Atkinson (1995a: 99-109) for a discussion of the different possible field roles in ethnographic research.

[2] See Homan, (1991: p. 71) for a full discussion of the informed consent principle, although it should be noted that diverse positions exist in this debate, which are reflected in, for instance, the ethical guidelines of professional bodies.

[3] For a discussion of the issues and problems caused by the publication of ethnographic accounts see Homan (1991), and Hammersley & Atkinson, (1995a).

[4] Renneker (1987) notes that in California, deviant behaviour has been blamed for the high drop-out rates from school of obsessive surfers. Although there is no available published study on windsurfers' or surfers' drug use, an informal survey in California suggests that around 90% of surfers "got loaded" on marijuana, alcohol, or other drugs at least once a week" (Renneker, 1987). However there is no formal evidence relating to the British context.

References

Barnes, J. (1979) *'Who should know what?'*, *Social science, privacy and ethics.* Harmondsworth: Penguin, cited in Rees, T. (1991).

Donnelly, P. (1993) 'Subcultures in sport: Resilience and transformation,' in Ingham, A. and Loy, J. (eds) *Sport in social development: Traditions, transitions and transformations.* Champaign, IL.: Human Kinetics Publishers, pp. 119-147.

Douglas, J (1976) *Investigative social research.* California: Sage: cited in Hammersley, M. and Atkinson, P. (1995a).

Duncan, M. C. and Hasbrook, C. (1988) 'Denial of power in televised women's sports', *Sociology of Sport Journal* Vol. 5, No. 1: pp. 1–21.

Finch, J. (1984) '"Its great to have someone to talk to": The ethics and politics of interviewing women,' in Bell, C. and Roberts, H. (eds) *Social research: Policies, problems and practice.* London: Routledge and Kegan Paul Ltd, pp. 70–87.

Hammersley, M. and Atkinson, P. (1995a) 'Ethics', in *Ethnography: Principles in practice*, 2nd ed. London: Routledge, pp. 263–287.

Hammersley, M. and Atkinson, P. (1995b) 'Field relations', in *Ethnography: Principles in practice*, 2nd ed. London: Routledge, pp. 99–123.

Homan, R. (1991) *The ethics of social research.* London: Longman.

Moore, D. (1994) *The lads in action: Social process in an urban youth subculture.* Aldershot: Arena/Ashgate Publishing.

Rees, T. (1991) 'Ethical Issues,' in Allan, G. and Skinner, C. (eds) *Handbook for research students in the social sciences.* London: The Falmer Press, pp. 140–151.

Renneker, M. (1987) 'Surfing: The sport and the lifestyle', *The Physician and Sports Medicine*, Vol.15, No. 10: pp. 156–162.

Roth, J. (1962) 'Comments on "secret observation"', *Social Problems*, Vol. 9, No. 3: pp. 283–284: cited in Hammersley, M. and Atkinson, P. (1995a).

Warwick, D. P. (1982) 'Tearoom trade: Means and ends in social research', in Bulmer, M. (1982) (ed) *Social research ethics.* London: Macmillan.

PRIVATE PARTS: ETHICAL ISSUES
IN THE OBSERVATION OF WRESTLERS

Roger Homan
University of Brighton

For many observers of social behaviour, the occupation of a ringside seat at a 'wrestling spectacular' might be considered to pose greater personal hazards than ethical problems: the prospect of involvement is not welcome to those who are trained to defend themselves in rational argument rather than physical encounter.

The observation of wrestling highlights the sense in which ethical issues are borne in the mind of the field researcher but are not a factor in the social reality constructed by those to whom it belongs. Whereas the notion of privacy is intrinsic to the gynaecological encounters observed by Joan Emerson (1973), the homosexual encounters observed by Laud Humphreys (1975) and the students whose bedroom conversations were eavesdropped by Henle and Hubble (1938), wrestlers and their spectators do not bring with them sensitivities about being seen.

Scruples of an ethical kind intruded in the observations reported in this paper largely as a consequence of a sociological definition of the situation and of its classification within a frame or typology imported from other fields. One weeknight evening in the summer of 1991 I attended in the conscious role of sociological observer a prayer meeting of the Gospel Standard Strict and Particular Baptists in a seaside town in the south of England. This was held in a Victorian chapel built for a rather larger congregation than now occupied it. In the late twentieth century, the solemnity of Calvinists at prayer tends not to compete well with other leisure attractions. The following evening, however, I went to the town hall to watch the wrestling, more out of nostalgia for an interest which compelled me in my youth than with a view to collecting more field notes. I discovered a crowd fewer in number than the congregation at the previous night's prayer meeting. The hall was larger but the crowd was missing; a faithful remnant hung on against the trend. The parallels were so striking that my intentions as a spectator were immediately surpassed by sociological purpose. Performers, fellow spectators and organisers became subjects. I resolved to revisit and interpret.

In the 1960s wrestling claimed the heart of Saturday afternoon on the commercial television channel: special events such as tag-matches or celebrated anti-heroes such as Jackie Pallo and Mick McManus were billed immediately before the Cup Final to attract viewers from BBC. But in the 1990s wrestling does not attract the quantity or quality of viewer advertisers want to interrupt. Old fashioned wrestling has been displaced by the glamour of the American style and the mystique of Sumo.

The withdrawal of television has left the sport stranded and ageing. Newcomers to the ring cannot count upon a television début: they must cultivate their reputations in one place at a time. The phenomenon of the 'big name' which can pull a crowd has diminished. And in small provincial halls organisers cannot effect the hype that is observable in major television sports events such as boxing and American football. The atmosphere is not the same when wrestlers play to an empty house and a flagrant breach of the rules fails to elicit murmurs of disapproval.

So it is in history that the organisers of professional wrestling find their inspiration. The home-grown media are like old boys' newsletters. They feature obituaries and report retirement parties. The theme of much reporting is 'Where are they now?'. Pat Roach has played the part of Bomber in 'Auf Wiedersehen Pet', Danny Lynch filmed in 'Robin Hood' and Tony Rudge appeared in an episode of 'Boon'. And:

> "Talking of one-time greats of wrestling, 'Dazzler' Joe Cornelius is now mine host at the Turners Arms in London's West End".

In conversations with fans I found that some wrestlers were distinguished as a superior class because they 'used to be on the television'.

The issue of privacy

The expectation of a public and professional event is not realised. It is the aspiration of the faithful but not the reality. Wrestling today is provincial and relatively private. Its publicity is by correspondence, posters and telephone. The various tasks of master of ceremonies, ticket sales, amplification of sound and so on are conducted by a small group known by their first names to the regulars. If the music does not sound to herald the entry of a wrestler, there are calls from the audience of 'Come on Dave, have you lost the tape?'. At the first event I attended there was a raffle in which the main prize was a basket of fruit. Before the interval, the MC announced from the ring:

"Numbers are a little down tonight so you might stand a better chance of winning something in the raffle. You can get your tickets from [Dorothy]."

On another occasion,

"I should say before we draw the raffle that the lovely cake has been donated by our dear friend Mrs [Hawkins]. Shall we give her a round of applause?"

Familiarity is also evident in greetings exchanged at the door between the promoters and regular spectators. These at times come close to the warm and solicitous welcome offered to those arriving at a mission hall:

"Haven't seen you for a long time. Have you been keeping all right?"

There is a corresponding loss of confidence and authority. On one occasion a fight appeared to be ended but the MC in his bow tie was not available to give the announcement. The word came that he was in the toilet. The wrestlers were asked to continue for another round after which the timekeeper made the announcement. On another, the announcement of a knock out was disapproved by the crowd. There was a consultation between the organisers who evidently wanted the crowd to be happy, small though it was: in response to public opinion the decision was reversed. Wrestling promoters formerly angered the crowd but today they have lost their nerve.

The structures and appearances have not changed in thirty years. The poster outside the town hall looks just the same. The rules and parameters within which the sport is conducted are constant. The language is persistently that of the mainstream sports: there are championships, timekeepers and heavyweights and those who appear in provincial community centres are British and European title holders. But wrestling has devolved from a national phenomenon to a family business. Deprofessionalised wrestling poses a series of ethical issues for the sociological spectator. There are moments when the amateurism and domesticity of the situation are so conspicuous to the observer that he is mindful of having intruded. This feeling, however, is achieved only by virtue of the definition of the situation as in some sense private. That definition is resisted by its providers who aspire to be public and even publicised. It may look like a family holiday to the sociologist but it is not defended as such by those who arrange it.

The sense of decline and loss is comforted by an historic mythology and sustained by a hopeful vision. These are both principles of the motivation of religious communities. But the prophets of the wrestling community have no systematic ideology within which to locate a hopeful message, no millennial insight, no sense of a divine plan, no notion of human error or failure, no concept of a Devil save those who play such a part in the ring. Where these explanatory factors are available, one can as a researcher broach with subjects the problem of falling congregations, for example. Where they are not, it takes the nerve of a trained counsellor to pick at scars and open wounds. If the nostalgia and contemporary myth of wrestling sustain its faithful, we do not have to probe about lost glory and the relative success of its modern rivals.

In any case, comparisons with professional sports past and present are not pertinent to the question of the legitimacy of old-fashioned wrestling in modern times. It has changed its clientele and transformed its purpose. It neither asks for a public spotlight nor deserves the critical attention that would follow it.

My own sense of invasion was aggravated by another factor. I am registered blind and use a small telescope in public places like the theatre. The spectacle of a man sitting in the front row watching a pair of female wrestlers through a telescope was for some fans more interesting than the action in the ring: I became aware of nudges among those sitting near me and their amusement was on occasion audible. So I desisted and relied upon hearing. Although a half guilty self-consciousness is in some measure endemic to all forms of covert observation, the identity of voyeur was only effectively conveyed to me through the responses of fellow spectators to my own behaviour — which I believed to be misinterpreted by them. I am reminded of research students who gained admission to mental institutions and who were suspected of being sane not by the doctors but by fellow patients.

The issue of belief

The ambiguity of wrestling is a moot point. For the faithful, it is a sport: knocks are for real, characters are authentic, it is a dangerous business. For sceptics, it is a form of drama, with scripts agreed beforehand and kicks and punches not making contact. I remarked to another spectator that a particular wrestler was not restrained by the referee for a habit recognized by the crowd to be illegal; there was a prompt insistence that the wrestler knew how to operate on the blind side of the referee. Loyal followers of the sport would report from previous experience 'he is dirty' rather than 'he always plays a dirty part'. There would be calls for the disqualification of wrestlers even though those who broke the rules provided the best entertainment. The wrestling audience, like the pantomime audience, enjoyed the participation of warning the innocent to look out behind them and the ritual verbal abuse of anti-heroes. They came not to cheer but to boo. This being the understanding, it falls to some wrestlers such as the Warlords — billed as 'the notorious rule benders' — to give them the pretext.

Demythology, however, was not the purpose of the research. What is more, consensual belief on the matter was not negotiable and I found no evidence that the entertainment could be enjoyed if the illusion was not shared. I never heard in wrestling, as one does elsewhere, 'it's just a bit of fun' or 'at least it's a good night out'. Indeed, so much is belief the condition of entertainment that it is assumed in all who attend. There is no mechanism for testing the beliefs of newcomers or inducting them in appropriate attitudes.

Those who doubt that wrestling is for real are sometimes invited to enter the ring to find out. It was not for fear of this invitation that I concealed my unbelief, even to the point of affecting the normal reactions of believers. In the post-television era the reality of wrestling has transformed. It is now viewed without a commentator so that the modern audience is less educated in the sport than that of the 1960s: they may not know what a 'Boston crab' is and so are restricted to non-technical cheers of the 'come on, Danny' and 'chuck him out ref' calibre. Further, live sport is (much more than televised sport) self-selective of those who are convinced by it. Modern audiences for wrestling are predominantly working-class, hardly sophisticated and often include numbers of young children. The official programme also advertises speedway and stock car and banger racing. In some places there are large numbers of disabled persons in the audience. Spectators, including children, rise to their feet to protest at the habits of such as Cyanide Sid Cooper of Soho and their participation and influence affords the sense of empowerment. It is arguable that wrestling is not only an entertainment but a social service and a therapy. It is only effective in these functions if it is also honoured as a sport. I therefore saw no purpose in distancing myself from the prevailing belief that it was so.

Discussion

The case is therefore being made for a *situational* research ethic. The principle of the situational ethic is that the relativism and therefore validity of values is recognized in a context in which other values may be in conflict. A classic example is that if one visits one's grandmother for tea and she has taken care to prepare what proves to be an inedible cake, one lightens the truth and even pretends to have enjoyed it while declining a second piece and concealing the first in one's pocket. There are, in this situation, more important things than candour. To simulate beliefs and feelings may be deceptive but it is sometimes more sensitive than to come clean. So it was in the outward subscription to a system of beliefs about truth and appearance that constitute the essential myth of wrestling.

The professional codes, it may be noted, are not so much situational but in many instances based around moral absolutes. They identify values such as truth and openness and they operationalise these in terms of standard procedures. Their purpose is in part to foster a professional reputation that will engender trust and respect by those who use social research. The codes do not trust the researcher to judge what is right, sensitive or appropriate in a given situation. On these grounds my posture in the field might have been a violation of the letter of the 'law':

> [An anthropologist] shall undertake no secret research or any research whose results cannot be freely derived and publicly reported.
> (American Anthropological Association)

> Participants in a research study have the right to be informed about the aims, purposes and likely publication of findings involved in the research…   (British Educational Research Association)

I have argued elsewhere that ethics represent a narrow formulation of the kinds of value that should be respected in social research; what is necessary is the cultivation of a research *morality* in which the values are made explicit and the means of achieving them left to the researcher (Homan, 1991). This is more achievable by means of an educative code than through the implementation of regulatory codes (Homan, 1990).

What is being argued here is consistent with those previous attempts to soften the rules of professional engagement. In particular, I was mindful that subjects were exposing private needs, motives and relationships within a public space and I was sensitive of the vulnerability of the beliefs on which their entertainment depended. These inclined me to invoke an ethic of protection of subjects which has since Nuremberg and the case of Stanley Milgram been more developed in codes for psychologists than in those governing social research. Accordingly the concern of sociological codes for revelation took a lesser priority. There was no sitting on the fence of whether this was sport or illusion. To vacillate would have been to signify a negative disposition and I did not relish the probable style of the ensuing discussion.

Marginal groups such as pool-room hustlers (Polsky, 1969) and the criminal community observed by Hobbs (1988), religious and political organizations and individuals in positions of power (Mullan, 1980) are mindful of the crises of their own legitimacy, of the boundaries of their own space and of the possible consequences of adverse reporting. The ethical principles which a researcher may take to those fields connect with dimensions of self-interest already made explicit within them.

The wrestling community, however, is not so aware. One first has to establish the sense in which transactions within it are private before negotiating the conditions of invasion.

The raising of the level of consciousness to the point of informing consent involves an educational process which is not in keeping with the rationale of the group. The ethics of openness and informed consent are as disturbing of one's leisure as having to fill in an evaluation questionnaire when one only went into a pub for a drink. The option of invoking the ethic of protection has the merit of nonreactivity: subjects do not have to be involved in decisions about observation, nor is the researcher indemnified against the hazards and consequences of research. Where the subject group is relatively unreflective about the condition and context of its place in contemporary culture, it may not be sufficiently informed to make decisions.

Note

[1]   Here and following, text surrounded by double quote-marks ("...") denotes passages quoted by the author from fieldnotes.

References

American Anthropological Association (1971) *Principles of professional responsibility.*

British Educational Research Association (1992) *Ethical guidelines for educational research.*

Emerson, J. (1973) 'Behaviour in private places: sustaining definitions of reality in gynaecological examinations', in G. Salaman and K. Thompson (eds) People and Organizations. London: Longman, pp. 358-371.

Henle, M. and Hubble, M. B. (1938) 'Egocentricity in adult conversation', *Journal of Social Psychology,* pp. 227-234.

Hobbs, D. (1988) *Doing the Business: Entrepreneurship, the Working Class and Detectives in the East End of London.* Oxford: Clarendon.

Homan, R. (1990) 'Institutional controls and educational research' *British Educational Research Journal* 16, 3: 237-248.

———— (1991) *The Ethics of Social Research.* London: Longman.

Humphreys, L. (1975) *Tearoom Trade: Interpersonal Sex in Public Places.* Chicago: Aldine.

Milgram, S. (1974) *Obedience to Authority.* London: Tavistock.

Mullan, B. (1980) *Stevenage Ltd: Aspects of the Planning and Planners of Stevenage New Town 1945-78.* London: Routledge.

Polsky, N. (1969) *Hustlers, Beats and Others.* Harmondsworth: Penguin.

INSIDER DEALING: RESEARCHING YOUR OWN PRIVATE WORLD

Ben Pink Dandelion

University of Brighton

Amidst the theoretical debates of the nature and validity of insider, as opposed to outsider research, there are particular closed or semi-closed settings which only allow insider research. The following article by Pink Dandelion draws on his experience as a Quaker undertaking some four years of research into his own religious group. Whilst he refers specifically to a semi-closed religious setting, there are obvious parallels in the points he makes to other 'private worlds', such as those in sport and leisure where only insiders have access to respondents.

Insider research

The term 'insider research' is widely used to refer to research undertaken on a group or constituency by a member of that constituency (for example Becker, 1963; Polsky, 1967; Ianni and Reus-Ianni, 1972; Krieger, 1985). It does not refer to non-members who disguise themselves as members, with the knowledge of the group (Wolf, 1991), or without it (Ditton, 1977; Pryce, 1979; Fielding, 1981; Van Zandt, 1985).

There are four types of insider research: overt research by an 'insider to the group', or an 'insider to the context', and the covert equivalents. The terms 'overt' and 'covert' are not always distinct, but they serve to delineate research which is sanctioned by the group, and that about which the group knows nothing.

The distinction between the researcher being an 'insider to the group' and an 'insider to the context' can be noted by comparing Shaffir's study of Chassidim

(1974), and Heilman's survey into synagogue life (1980). Shaffir, who had to change his dress-sense and negotiate his way into the group (1974: pp. 29–40) writes:

> Although I was a practising Jew, my personal background in Judaism was remote from the chassidic way of life (1974: p. 29).

Shaffir was an insider to the context. Heilman researched life in his own synagogue (1976), and is best described as an insider to the group.

Hobbs's work on the entrepreneurial nature of the East End of London was based on his own knowledge of the area and its personalities. He did not personally know the whole of his constituency, nor was he familiar with the practices and rituals of the group he studied until he began his research (1989). Hobbs's research is best described as an example of 'covert insider (to the context) research'. Holdaway began his research on the police after nine years in the Force. He was an insider to the group in the sense that he knew the rituals and practices, as a member of the group, before he began to explore them from a sociological perspective (1982).

Figure 1 illustrates the typology of insider research, and lists an example of each kind.

COVERT INSIDER TO THE CONTEXT (Hobbs, 1989)	OVERT INSIDER TO THE CONTEXT (Shaffir, 1974)
COVERT INSIDER TO THE GROUP (Holdaway, 1982)	OVERT INSIDER TO THE GROUP (Heilman, 1976)

Figure 1:   A Typology of Insider Research

I was an insider to the group (and the term 'insider' is used in this sense hereafter), having attended a Quaker school and regularly attended Quaker Meetings for five years prior to carrying out this research. I was formally a Member, and during the period of this research, held, amongst others, the following posts: Preparative Meeting Assistant Clerk; General Meeting Assistant Clerk; Co-Clerk to Young Friends Central Committee; Elder. I was employed part-time, and later full-time, on separate national Quaker projects.

Hayano, in his work on auto-ethnography, describes varying levels of outsidership (1979: p. 100). This analysis is useful in understanding how an insider can be more of an insider in one setting than in another. For example, I was more of an insider in those Meetings I was well acquainted with, than in settings I visited for the first time as part of this research.

As the 'weight' of the roles given to me by the group increased, so my profile changed. Levels of outsidership, within any setting, decreased. Figure 2 describes a 'shorthand' version of the stages of insider identity. The term 'national' is used to refer to the whole of Britain Yearly Meeting.

Year 1	Local / national involvement	Unemployed / active committee member
Year 2/3	National / local involvement	Part-time Quaker employee
Year 4	National involvement	Full-time Quaker employee

Figure 2:   Stages of Insider Identity During this Research Process

Degrees of insidership vary between different sorts of insiders, between settings, and between different stages of the research process. The more involved an insider becomes in her/his group, the greater the consequent advantages, disadvantages, and ethical complications of insider research become. These three components of insidership are discussed in turn.

Advantages of insider research

a) Access

The basic advantage of formal Membership was the access this offered. Only Members have an automatic right to attend Quaker business meetings, and Members are more likely to be involved in the committee work of the group (Meeting for Sufferings Minute 8, April 1992).

Quaker Faith and Practice describes the criteria for the attendance of non-Members at Yearly Meeting:

> Permission for the attendance of non-members at one or more sessions may be given at the discretion of the clerk, if he [sic] is satisfied that their presence is likely to be of service to the Yearly Meeting. Such permission should be sought well in advance of Yearly Meeting and should be supported by one or more elders to whom the applicant is well-known. Last minute requests should not be made. (1995: 6:12)

One respondent offered the following information on applications to attend Yearly Meeting by those involved in academic research:

> In reality, the Recording Clerk refers letters to the Clerk of the Yearly Meeting, when the applicant is doing academic research. Permission has always been refused if the non-member is doing research and not otherwise committed to the ways of Meeting for Worship. (Personal Correspondence)

A researcher was refused the right to attend in 1992 (Personal Correspondence). The non-Member researcher has four choices: i) to attend Yearly Meeting under the pretence of being a Friend; ii) to operate covertly at a local level and secure the support of local Elders in the application to attend Yearly Meeting; iii) to assimilate with sincerity; iv) to be overt about the research motive and risk the denial of access to certain Meetings.

As a Member, I had no problems of access to research settings. Indeed I had almost unrivalled access. For example, because I was appointed as one of two Young Friends representative on Meeting for Sufferings, the small executive body of the group in Britain, I was one of only two Quakers eligible to be a part of both groups.

b) Familiarity

Insider status obviates routine fears over entry into the group (Sanders 1980: p. 158), and the possibility of brainwashing, or conversion (Robbins et al. 1973: p. 265, Van Zandt 1985: p. 71).

Technical problems of understanding the context are diminished. Poll attended a Chassidic rabbinical school before observing Chassidim in Brooklyn and claimed that this helped him 'in comprehending the group norms and the significance of various Hassidic activities' (1962: p. 267).

Flanagan comments on how a religious context provides particular problems for the sociologist:

> Because the actor can pretend to be what he is not, and could conceal what he ought to be, in a ritual performance that deals with the intangible, deciphering the truth or falsity of his act can pose acute sociological problems of interpretation. (1991: p. 15)

Snow felt this all the more acutely in an environment he did not feel a part of:

> I felt as though I constantly had to have my eyes open and my ears finely tuned, that if I was not constantly monitoring what was going on about me, then perhaps I might miss something. (1980: p. 108)

Heilman offers a useful summary of the advantages of insider-status which, in part, counters the problem identified by Flanagan, and the paranoia experienced by Snow:

> ... as an insider, I could supply, both through introspection and a sense of the relevant questions to ask, information about dimensions of inner life not readily available to pure researchers. (1976: p. xi)

Superior knowledge is, thus, not confined to the acknowledgement of events and actions. As well as knowing what to ask, the insider knows who to ask. The idea that only insiders have access to knowledge (as described by Merton, 1972: p. 11), or the idea of privileged access (Agassi. 1969), are unconvincing. Rather, insider familiarity helps achieve knowledge of a situation, which might take an outsider longer to gain. This is particularly true of research into religious groups, where structure, activity, and language are not necessarily coherent (Godlove 1989: p. 2); and is certainly true of specialist subcultures and committed cultural groups.

I was able to watch central figures at critical moments in Yearly Meeting discussions. A knowledge of intra-group politics allowed data collection to be focused. As Burgess states, an insider may be her/his own 'key informant' in the early stages of a research programme (1982: p. 77).

Where the researcher is known to the group in the way in which the group is known to the insider, the knowledge of familiarity is mutual. Interview respondents, and those filling in the open-ended sections of the questionnaire were able to talk in 'Quaker-speak' without the need to translate. 'In-jokes' helped 'break the ice' at interviews.

c) Trust of motives

There are two kinds of access. First, there is physical access to the research setting, described above. Second, there is the data access offered the researcher by respondents. Whilst I had the automatic right of attendance, the right to research had to be negotiated with the group. At this level, the trust of the researcher (and the motives of the researcher) are crucial to the degree of access given. Oakley writes:

> ... personal involvement is more than dangerous bias — it is the condition under which people come to know each other and to admit others into their lives. (1982: p. 58)

Insiders are at an advantage where personal involvement and mutual familiarity help build an attitude of trust towards a researcher.

> Having originally joined the congregation with no ulterior motives of research, I had established a degree of intimacy with the insiders which is rare even among the most dedicated of participant observers. (Heilman, 1976: p. xi)

There was no need for me to be covert, and the mistrust of research, experienced by those in other religious settings (Wallis, 1976; Homan, 1978; Greeley, 1989), was not a feature of my research, until some of the findings were shared with the group.

I experienced life as an outsider in my requests to survey non-Quaker groups, and the purpose of this research, and the destination of the research findings, was a common source of concern. The reputation of the insider can ease anxieties in a way which is not open to the outsider. When one Quaker Meeting had concerns over my motives and character, it was able to contact another Meeting who knew me better, for more information.

Constraints of insider research

a) Knowing too much

Smircich has described the challenge of field-work in terms of the problem of remaining a learner (1983: p. 167). This challenge is amplified in a situation where an insider researcher is initially required to learn how to become a learner. Heilman described the problem of the insider as an 'epistemological liability of taking too much for granted' (1976: p. xi). The science-fiction novel, *Pennterra*, includes the following quotation which illustrates the problem:

> Having lived in an isolated community of Friends for so long, it wasn't obvious ... what an outsider would find strange. (Moffett 1987: p. 91)

Insider or outsider, it is debatable how far any researcher can achieve the necessary analytical distance. Krieger comments:

> We bring biases and more than biases. We bring idiosyncratic patterns of recognition. We are not, in fact, ever capable of achieving the analytic 'distance' we have long been schooled to seek. (1985: p. 309)

Similarly, Stanley and Wise note that "no researcher can separate herself from personhood and thus from deriving second order constructs from experience" (1979: p. 361). Everyone is an insider to the context of human existence.

As such, it is unclear how far a lack of distinction between researcher and sample undermines the validity of the research findings. Frank and Hackman have demonstrated that there is no generality in the proposition that similarity between interviewers and interviewees leads to biased interview judgements (1975).

I asked other trained sociologists to accompany me on field work visits on two separate occasions to act as 'shadow ethnographers'. The exchange of field notes following the participant observation opportunities was reassuring, confirming that my analysis was sociological rather than Quaker, and that my insider knowledge allowed a more accurate reading of research settings. For example, one shadow ethnographer described the vocal ministry as lacking in a Christian message. I, with a greater comparative knowledge of the Quaker setting, 'read' the ministry as particularly Christian (relative to other fieldwork data).

b) Saying too much

One problem rarely discussed in the insider literature is the one of affecting the sample under research. This is a problem for all participant-observers, and is described by Schwartz and Schwartz as 'affective participation' (1955: p. 350).

The problem, for the insider, is not one of assimilation (see Griffin 1977 as an extreme case of attempted outsider assimilation), but of presence.

Where the researcher is in a key position of influence, active participation, or a sudden lack of it, has the potential to alter the situation under research. In my own research, I found myself noting down decisions of the group which I had initially suggested.

Where the research is overt, the group may wish to be updated. An insider may feel more compelled to assent to such requests. In these cases, a discussion of the findings of the research with the group might change the direction of the group's activity. This phenomenon was illustrated when planning for a weekend on 'life-after-death' started after I had described belief in reincarnation as 'one of the great conspiracies of silence' (Field Notes). In this instance, the sharing of results began a chain reaction which contradicted the original finding. Participant observation became action research.

It is ironical that a greater distance from the group under study, within the framework of insider-research, can foster a greater risk of affective participation. Margaret Fraser, on a visit to an American Yearly Meeting of a different tradition, expected to be able to observe the proceedings from the discretion of a seat at the back. She was concerned that she should not induce a halo effect on the behaviour of the group, as an insider from outside. In this instance, her presence as an 'insider-outsider' from overseas led to an invitation to address the Meeting (Fraser 1993). In this way, insiders can generate their own data.

I attempted to take a marginal role (see Freilich 1970) in discussions under observation. Total silence was not possible. First, it may have alerted the sample to my new role, and caused a reactive effect. Second, I was often called upon to offer my viewpoint.

c) Premature saturation

Bryman notes 'the growing difficulties researchers experience of finding the space in their home and work lives for prolonged immersion' (1991: p. 209). The problem can be the opposite for the insider.

Parry (1990) discusses the problems of participant observation in a 'greedy institution' (after Coser 1974). There is also the problem of the greedy researcher. Wax describes 'an almost irresistible urge to gather more data' (1971: p. 45). Living in the field increases the chances of subject-saturation and premature withdrawal.

When I began full-time work for the group, my research life, work life, and worship life were all oriented around the Quaker group. Fortunately, the partial demands of each within the daily routine, and the distinct tasks they involved, prevented a loss of motivation. The problems associated with this pattern of work were connected more with the problem of role identity.

d) Observer and participant

One of the problems faced by the insider is role-identity. The lack of explicit tension between the subject of the research and the life of the researcher can mask a confusion over the nature of participation in the group. Cassell's claim that there is no form of differentiation between insider-observer and observed (1977: p. 413) is, on the basis of my own fieldwork, naive.

In the Quaker setting, the concept of researching during worship was replaced by the reality of research replacing worship. The need of the sociologist to observe (passive activity) undermined the requirements of worship (active passivity) and I found it impossible to combine the two.

The presentation of a paper to a group of academics and Quakers highlighted the lack of a single role. I turned down a private request for silence from one of the audience before the event on grounds of inappropriateness. At the end of the seminar, however, in the absence of the Chair, one of the Elders present used the end of the time for questions to ask for silence. The group, including the non-Quakers, fell quiet until I ended the silence with the usual words 'Thank you, Friends'. My role had been transformed from one of academic to one of Quaker Elder.

Sociologists are called to doubt informants and to investigate the reality behind the mythologised view. Heilman notes a dilemma of loyalties:

There was ... the question of whom I owed the greater allegiance, the academic or religious community. (1980: p. 105)

More significantly, beliefs and customs which were part of my religious life were, themselves, called into question through the analysis from within my research life. Heilman reported feeling insecure and ambivalent towards his community (1980: p. 106). I felt a sense of isolation from the religious meaning of worship, and developed a sense of internal conflict.

My research programme on Quaker culture involved long periods away from my 'home-Meeting', and the cultivation of a research/worship relationship with other Meetings. Towards the end of the field work, I transferred my Membership from one Meeting to another. This was, perhaps, symptomatic of the degree of distance created between me and the group under research, and of my inability to continue a worship-relationship with a group I had sociologically dissected and demythologised. Peter Collins resigned the wardenship of the Meeting he was studying for similar reasons (Personal Correspondence). For me to re-subscribe to the myths which defined participation in the worship event, I had to find a new setting. The legacy of perceiving the group as a sociologist was maintained but a new setting offered a greater chance of rehabilitation.

e) Negotiation of the results with the group

i) Expectations

The overt nature of this research, and the circulation of a questionnaire in particular, drew considerable interest in the outcome of the research, and a regular flow of requests for the results. I was invited to give lectures on the findings. Interest and expectations were supportive but also maintained a pressure. This pressure was increased by the knowledge that the end of this research would mark the start of re-engagement instead of disengagement.

ii) The prevention of negative reception

One influential Friend was particularly critical of the need for this research. I realised that if her support were not given, the group might oppose the project, or marginalise its findings. Heilman was criticised for not being a 'proper Jew' when his research was published (1980: p. 105). It is a danger an insider faces, especially when the group under investigation is small, and when it has a large investment in a particular perception of itself. Hobbs (1989), and Holdaway (1982), both moved to new jobs away from the location of their fieldwork after publication. In order to establish an equivalent distance, I would need to change religion.

The conflict with the respected Friend was resolved by asking her for advice. This strategy, of co-opting dissent, is noted by Wilkof in her study of consensus-generation within organisations (1989). Coincidentally, a favourable book review which I wrote of a work written by the Friend was published in the early stages of correspondence, and further tempered the potential for opposition.

The overt nature of this research, and the lack of disengagement from it, both allowed, and encouraged, the signalling of results. Some researchers have claimed that all the data collected is the property of the respondents and that none of it can be published without it first being checked for accuracy by them (Simons 1984: p. 91). Curry and Kazi have described this as the 'participatory model' (1987: p. 81), Bryman as 'respondent validation' (1988: p. 78). This level of democracy was not adopted. The data are not privately owned by anyone but are public property (subject to contracts of confidentiality). The sociologist is merely an interpreter of a particular type. Sociologists should not imagine that they necessarily describe social relations as they are perceived by the actors involved in those relations. A check for accuracy on the grounds that the respondents own the data would, in certain circumstances, simply offer respondents the right to restate a mythologised view.

The research findings were signalled to the group through a series of talks and a couple of lightweight articles (Dandelion 1991, 1992). I hoped that this opportunity for the group to be reflexive around the research findings would ease the re-engagement process.

iii) Creating uncomfortable reality

The process of negotiation back into the worshipping group was complicated by the mixed reception given to the research findings. The presentation of the idea of a post-Christian Society, in which theological belief is marginal (Dandelion 1993), both pleased, and displeased, members of the group.

The division of attitude to the findings is usefully characterised by the following extracts from two letters to The Friend, the weekly Quaker periodical. The first supports the idea of a pluralist Society:

> I do not ask traditional Christian Quakers to endorse ... humanist reworkings of unfathomably rich religious language. But, as Ralph Hetherington writes...'Without diversity there would be no development,

no adjustment to changing cultural circumstances and spiritual needs and, above all, to new insights. There would then be no life'. [letter to *The Friend* 150 (1992): p. 471]

The second defends a more traditional perception of Quakerism:

The very idea of re-conceptualising God and diminishing the centrality of Christ in the Society, would, I know, be deeply disturbing and offensive to many Quakers — many Quakers whom I love, respect and would grieve to see torn by such a major challenge to their religious orientation. [letter to *The Friend* 148 (1990): p. 1416]

Frequently, I was blamed for the consequences of presenting my findings, and was held responsible for the creation of the conflict, or its cause. My role, motives, and methods were questioned. Such challenges militated against a straightforward re-engagement with the group. They underline the dual nature of sociological and group perspectives which can be problematic for the insider.

The ethics of insider research

So far I have considered the advantages and constraints of insider research. An ethical dimension cuts across these positive and negative aspects. This is explored below, in terms of a) the manipulation of the group, and b) the covert nature of overt methods, as practised by an insider.

a) The manipulation of the group

As far as possible sociological research should be based on the freely given informed consent of those studied. This implies a responsibility on the sociologist to explain as fully as possible, and in terms meaningful to participants, what the research is about, who is undertaking and financing it, why it is being undertaken, and how it is to be disseminated. (Statement on Ethical Practice. British Sociological Association, 1992: §1b)

Any researcher seeking consent will seek to present as positive a picture of her/ his proposal as possible to those considering the request. How overt researchers are in their attempts to secure informed consent is rarely mentioned by those who call for the use of overt methods on ethical grounds. Homan notes that consent can only ever be given on the basis of a partial interpretation of what the research programme will consist of (1992: p. 324).

The potential manipulation of the group, in these terms, is even greater for an insider. The same knowledge of language and of personalities which is an aid to the research process can be used to manage the opposition to requests for consent. Two Meetings had refused permission to tape-record Meeting for Worship. A third Meeting was approached. The request was passed from Preparative Meeting (PM) to two Elders of differing opinions who met with me. A favourable report was made by the Elders to the following PM but the Meeting failed to reach unity, and I was asked to attend Meeting and be available for questions. The matter was then put on the agenda of a third PM.

As Homan states, 'Investigators develop a sense of what details allay fears and what prompt suspicions' (1992: p. 324). It was clear, by the time of my second visit, that consent would not be granted. One Friend in particular was adamantly opposed. It was also clear that those in favour of tape-recording were beginning to withdraw their support because of the amount of time the matter was taking up at business meetings. At this point, I wrote to the Clerk and withdrew the request on the grounds of not wishing to further waste the Meeting's time.

The withdrawal of the request may have been a miscalculation in that the opposed Friend might have withdrawn her opposition, but a third inconclusive business meeting would have alienated the Meeting from the research. The withdrawal of the request was a popular move which guaranteed further co-operation on other aspects of the research process. Familiarity with the group allowed the timing and the wording of the request to be chosen in order to maximise this effect.

> In Quaker decisions, [the] ... moment of withdrawing one's opposition ... so the meeting may proceed is a very important way of preventing polarization and its exercise, therefore, is virtually an art form of graciousness. (Sheeran, 1983: p. 67)

A second manipulation of the group occurred when the focus of the research changed and consent was not re-sought. The ethic of the principle of informed consent is undermined when consent is given for a research project which subsequently changes direction (Homan, 1992: p. 322). At the end of this research programme, some participants in the case-study Meetings were convinced that the research centred on a typology of Quaker theology. They had missed the interim notices that the focus had changed.

b) The covert nature of overt methods

There is a healthy literature on the covert/overt dichotomy (for example Roth, 1962; Barnes, 1963, 1979; Erikson, 1967; Bulmer, 1980a, 1980b, 1982; Homan 1980, 1991, 1992) but few writers have considered the specific ethical problems of insider research. An insider is, to a greater or lesser degree, invisible. S/he can participate fully in an event without anyone realising a researcher is at work.

This phenomenon was apparent in three ways within my research. Firstly, I visited Meetings once, sometimes by chance, where consent had not been sought. I did not lie about my reasons for attending, but was not necessarily asked about this. It was assumed by fellow-insiders that I had come to worship.

In certain other Meetings, permission to research was given by a single gatekeeper. This was the case with Young Friends Central Committee (YFCC), and Meeting for Sufferings. While the Clerk of YFCC and the Recording Clerk (chief executive) knew of the dual purpose of my participation, no one else in the Meeting necessarily did.

In Meetings which had collectively consented to the research, there would still be those who were not party to that decision.

Participants who had been aware of this research were not reminded by me of its fieldwork aspects. Typically, Friends would ask how the research was 'going' without realising that it was under way at that moment. In this sense, I was actually more covert at some Meetings than at the case-study Meetings, where participants, at least initially, equated my attendance with research tasks.

> Once the investigator has briefed participants that research is the purpose, he or she adopts a camouflage that is no more virtuous than a role that was covert from the outset .... (Homan, 1992: p. 326)

It is easier for an insider to adopt a camouflage because it is often given to the researcher by other participants in their ignorance of the research role. This is espe- cially true of friends and others used to falling into conversation with the re- searcher. Heilman notes the dilemma of using friends as informants (1976: p. xi), and Jarvie describes the impossibility of integrity both as a researcher and friend (1982). In this sense, it could be argued that all participant observation is in some way covert, regardless of whether or not informed consent has been gained.

The tension between overt-overt methods and covert-overt methods was exposed when Friends asked about this research in new research settings. Platt describes how informants mention aspects of their interviews outside of the interview situation (1981: p. 78). This phenomenon occurred regularly within this research. The public nature of such references would often embarrass me by alerting those who were not familiar with the work to the fact that a researcher was in their midst.

Homan points out that ethical guidelines about informed consent mask the methodological paradigm of attempting to allow respondents to forget the research-motive and to think of the researcher as a friend to whom they talk openly (1992: p. 324). I attempted to avoid being denoted by participants as an observer, for the reason Homan cites, and to ease the process of re-engagement. If my participation were defined solely in terms of research interests, my involvement in the group in other ways would be marginalised.

Conclusions

While only an insider could have collected the data which featured in my research, insider research entails numerous personal disadvantages, and is not free of ethical complications.

The ethical considerations outlined above have all been around the rights of informants to be informed about the research and to exercise some control over the role of research in their lives. Some Friends would not have been aware of this research whilst it was in progress. Others may have been accidentally misled about the status of conversations. The principle of informed consent remains a standard component of the ethical codes of professional organisations concerned with social research but is ethically problematic.

Ethical systems based on principles are practically inappropriate to human society. The Quaker group face this challenge with their peace testimony and its use in complex scenarios. Homan shows how overt methods are as ethically questionable as covert methods, when a sense of ethic is based on the principle of 'informed consent' (1992). This article has revealed how difficult it is to maintain an ethical stance in all situations without influencing those situations. Whether or not an informant has given their informed consent to the research they are a part of, is less important than the consequences for the informant of having done or not done so.

Professional ethics are, however, not just about the informant's right to consent, but are also concerned with the public right to knowledge. In this sense, there is a complex arrangement of competing rights which codes of practice seek to embody, in principles which claim to offer the most ethical outcome.

Homan (1991) illustrates that the 'public right to know' is a defence invoked against critics of research, initiated to satisfy the motives of the researcher. If the public right to know is a primary consideration, research topics should be selected by the public. Equally, researchers would have an obligation to make their results as accessible as possible.

In this sense, it might be argued that informed consent would follow automatically. The public would select a research topic and then know about the research. This is, of course, a simplistic reading. Concepts of 'the public' and 'informed' are ill-defined concepts rather than specific categories. Who the public are, and what 'to be informed' means, remains unclear. The ethics of the research fall upon the researcher to determine.

> The principle of informed consent from subjects is necessarily vague since it depends for its interpretation on unstated assumptions about the amount of information and the nature of the consent required to constitute acceptable practice. (Social Research Association, Interim Statement on Ethical Issues in Social Research, 1984)

Thus, the ethics of the research situation, whilst guided by principle, are, in fact, pragmatic. I worked within the ethical uncertainties inherent in insider participant observation, and insider research in general, and justified the methods through their appropriateness to the aims of the research, and the perceived consequences of the methods used for those they affected. As the research programme progressed and Quaker interest in the results increased, the 'right to know clause' was invoked as a defence against the ethical uncertainties. My desire to complete a worthwhile piece of original work, and the fear of rebuke from the group, if this was seen to be achieved by unethical means, increased the need for such defence. In other words, the need to balance my continuing involvement in the group with the wish to finish the research led me to rely heavily on the grey areas of research ethics to validate my approach. I could have taken a clearer ethical stance had I not been an insider who wished to remain active within the group. In this sense, the research process carried a high cost in terms of its failure to maintain a clear research ethic and in terms of the confusing mindgames I found myself, the researcher, needing to play with myself, the Quaker.

References

Agassi, J. (1969) 'Privileged access', *Inquiry* 12: pp. 420–26.

Barnes, J. A. (1963) 'Some ethical problems in modern field work', *British Journal of Sociology* 14: pp. 118–34.

―――― (1979) *Who should know what?: Social Science, privacy, and ethics*. Harmondsworth: Penguin.

Becker, H. S. (1958) 'Problems of inference and proof in participant observation', *American Sociological Review* 23: pp. 652–60.

―――― (1963) *Outsiders: studies in the sociology of deviance*. New York: The Free Press of Glencoe.

British Sociological Association (1992) Statement on Ethical Practice.

Bryman, A. (1988) 'Quantity and quality in social research', *Contemporary Social Research*, No. 18. London: Unwin Hyman.

―――― (1991) 'Street corner society as a model for research into organizational culture', in P.J. Frost, L.F. Moore, M.R. Louis, C.C. Lundberg, and J. Martin (eds) *Reframing organizational culture*. Newbury Park, California: Sage, pp. 205–14.

Bulmer, M. (ed) (1980a) *Social research ethics*. London: Macmillan.

―――― (1980b) 'Comment on "The ethics of covert methods"', *British Journal of Sociology* 31: pp. 59–65.

―――― (1982) 'The research ethics of pseudo-patient studies: A new look at the merits of covert ethnographic methods', *Sociological Review* 30: pp. 627–46.

Burgess, R. G. (1982) 'Elements of sampling in field research', in Burgess, R. G. (ed) *Field research: A sourcebook and field manual*. London: George Allen and Unwin.

Cassell, J. (1977) 'The relationship of observer to observed in peer group research', *Human Organization* 36: pp. 412–16.

Coser, L. A. (1974) *Greedy institutions: Patterns of undivided commitment*. New York: The Free Press.

Curry, D., and Kazi, H. (1987) 'Academic feminism and the process of deradicalisation: Re-examining the issues', *Feminist Review* 25: pp. 77–98.

Dandelion, P. (1991) 'Measuring Quaker belief or do Quakers believe?', *Friends' Quarterly* 26/7: pp. 323–33.

——— (1992) 'Quakers and social justice', *Friends Quarterly* 27/4: pp. 160–70.

——— (1993) A Sociological Analysis of the Theology of Quakers. PhD dissertation, University of Brighton.

Ditton, J. (1977) *Part time crime: An ethnography of fiddling and pilferage*. London: Macmillan.

Erikson, K. T. (1967) 'A comment on disguised observation in sociology', *Social Problems* 14: pp. 366–373.

Fielding, N. G. (1982) 'Observational research on the National Front', in Bulmer, M. (ed) *Social research ethics*. London: Macmillan, pp. 80–104.

Flanagan, K. (1991) *Sociology and liturgy: Re-presentations of the holy*. London: Macmillan.

Frank, L. L., and Hackman, J. R. (1975) 'Effects of interviewer- interviewee similarity on interviewer objectivity in college admissions interviews', *Journal of Applied Psychology* 60: pp. 356–60.

Fraser, M. (1993) 'Researching Quaker spiritual expression: Some problems of participant observation among Friends', paper presented to the Quaker Studies Research Association Conference, Birmingham.

Frielich, M. (1970) 'Toward a formalization of field work', in Frielich, M. (ed) *Marginal natives*. New York: Harper and Row, pp. 485–585.

Godlove, T. F., Jr. (1989) *Interpretation and diversity of belief: The framework model from Kant to Davidson*. Cambridge: Cambridge University Press.

Greeley, A. M. (1989) 'Sociology and the Catholic Church: Four decades of bitter memories', *Sociological Analysis* 50: pp. 393–97.

Griffin, J. H. (1977) *Black like me*. 2nd edn. Boston: Houghton Mifflin.

Hayano, D. M. (1979) 'Auto-ethnography: paradigms, problems, and prospects', *Human Organization* 38: pp. 99–104.

Heilman, S. C. (1976) *Synagogue life*. Chicago: University of Chicago Press.

——— (1980) 'Jewish Sociologist: Native As Stranger', *American Sociologist* 15: pp. 100–08.

Hobbs, D. (1989) *Doing the business: Entrepreneurship, the working class and detectives in the East End of London.* Oxford: Oxford University Press.

Holdaway, S. (1982) 'An inside job: A case study of covert research on the police', in Bulmer, M. (ed) *Social Research Ethics.* London: Macmillan, pp. 59–79.

Homan, R. E. (1978) 'A sociological interpretation of the language-behaviour of old-time Pentecostals', Ph. D dissertation, University of Lancaster.

―――― (1980) 'The ethics of covert methods', *British Journal of Sociology* 31: pp. 46–59.

―――― (1991) *The ethics of social research.* London: Longman.

―――― (1992) 'The ethics of open methods', *British Journal of Sociology* 43: pp. 321–32.

Ianni, F. A. J., and Reus-Ianni, E. (1972) *A family business: Kinship and social control in organized crime.* London: Routledge.

Jarvie, I. C. (1982) 'The problem of ethical integrity in participant observation', in Burgess, R. G. (ed) *Field research: A sourcebook and field manual.* London: George Allen and Unwin, pp. 68–72.

Krieger, S. (1985) 'Beyond "subjectivity": The use of self in social science', *Qualitative Sociology* 8: pp. 309–24.

Merton, R. K. (1972) 'Insiders and outsiders: A chapter in the sociology of knowledge', *American Journal of Sociology* 78: pp. 9–47.

Moffett, J. (1988) *Pennterra.* Sevenoaks: Hodder and Stoughton.

Oakley, A. (1981) 'Interviewing women: A contradiction in terms', in Roberts, H. (ed) *Doing feminist research.* London: Routledge and Kegan Paul, pp. 30–61.

Parry, O. (1990) 'Fitting in with the setting: A problem of adjustment for both students and the researcher', *Sociology* 24: pp. 417–30.

Platt, J. (1981) 'On interviewing one's peers', *British Journal of Sociology* 32: pp. 75–91.

Poll, S. (1962) *The Hassidic community of Williamsburg.* Glencoe, Illinois: Free Press.

Polsky, N. (1967) *Hustlers, beats, and others.* New York: Aldine.

Pryce, K. (1979) *Endless pressure: A study of West Indian life-styles in Bristol.* Harmondsworth: Penguin.

Quaker Faith and Practice: The book of Christian discipline of the Yearly Meeting of the Religious Society of Friends (Quakers) in Britain (1995) London: Britain Yearly Meeting.

Robbins, T., Anthony, D., and Curtis, T. E. (1973) 'The limits of symbolic realism: Problems of empathic field observation in a sectarian context', *Journal for the Scientific Study of Religion* 12: pp. 259–72.

Roth, J. A. (1962) 'Comments on "secret observation"', *Social Problems* 9: pp. 283–84.

Sanders, C. R. (1980) 'Rope burns: Impediments to the achievement of basic comfort early in field research experience', in Shaffir, W. B., Stebbins, R. A., and Turowetz, A. (eds) *Fieldwork experience: Qualitative approaches to social research.* New York: St Martin's Press, pp. 158–71.

Schwartz, M. S., and Schwartz, C. G. (1955) 'Problems in participant observation', *American Journal of Sociology* 60: pp. 343–60.

Shaffir, W. (1974) *Life in a religious community: The Lubavitcher Chassidim in Montreal.* Toronto: Holt, Rinehart and Winston of Canada.

Sheeran, M. J. (1983) *Beyond majority rule: Voteless decisions in the Society of Friends.* Philadelphia: Philadelphia Yearly Meeting.

Simons, H. (1984) 'Guidelines for the conduct of an independent evaluation', in Adelman, C. (ed) *The politics and ethics of evaluation.* London: Croom Helm, pp. 87–92.

Smircich, L. (1983) 'Studying organizations as culture', in Morgan, G. (ed) *Beyond method: Social research strategies.* Beverly Hills: Sage, pp. 160–72.

Snow, D. A. (1980) 'The disengagement process: A neglected problem in participant observation', *Qualitative Sociology* 3: pp. 100–22.

Social Research Association (1984) 'Interim Statement on Ethical Issues in Social Research'.

Stanley, L., and Wise, S. (1979) 'Feminist research, feminist consciousness and experiences of sexism', *Women's Studies International Quarterly* 2: pp. 359–79.

Van Zandt, D. E. (1985) 'Ideology and structure in the Children of God: A study of a new sect', Ph.D. dissertation, London School of Economics.

Wallis, R. (1976) *The road to total freedom: A sociological analysis of Scientology.* London: Heinemann.

Wax, R. H. (1971) *Doing fieldwork: Warnings and advice*. Chicago: University of Chicago Press.

Wilkof, M. V. (1989) 'Organisational culture and decision-making: A case of consensus management', *R. and D. Management* 19: pp. 185–99.

Wolf, D. R. (1991) 'High-risk methodology: Reflections on leaving an outlaw society, in Shaffir, W. B. and Stebbins, R. A. (eds) *Experiencing fieldwork: An inside view of qualitative research*. Newbury Park, California: Sage.

QUESTIONNAIRES AS INSTRUMENTS OF INTRUSION

Pauline Cox
University of Brighton

Introduction

In the past much of the literature on social and educational research has focused on technical procedures such as design, collection and analysis of research data. Unlike in medical science, ethics has rarely played a prominent role in social science, apart from research scandals, but now ethical issues are being linked with both the freedom to conduct, and the quality of, social research. Researchers can no longer deny that ethical, moral and political questions embrace their daily experience of social and education research.

Karhausen (1987: p. 25) recognises ethics as a philosophical discipline 'primarily concerned with the evaluation and justification of norms and standards of personal and interpersonal behaviour'. Generally, in an everyday sense ethics is perceived as the science of morality: those involved in it will establish values regulating human behaviour. However, Homan (1991: p. 1) argues that when ethics is applied and developed within a particular professional context such as medicine or social research, it acquires a distinctive form, and general definitions which appear in dictionaries and philosophical literature may be inappropriate. In the case of social research, ethics commonly refers to codes established to regulate the conduct of members of the profession.

Drafting these codes has generated considerable arguments and controversy, as for example, with the codes proposed for the American and British Sociological Associations. Other professional organizations have debated the matter over the years, only to conclude that no code is necessary for them, or that each individual member should work to his or her personal code. The preliminary statement on ethical principles that was published in 1970, revised in 1973, and amended in 1982 (BSA, 1970, 1973, 1982) is still used today, and has been reiterated in the BSA's journal *Sociology* (BSA, 1992). This statement refers to the duties of sociologists to the discipline and to the 'subjects' of their studies and maintains that it is the duty of sociologists:

> ... to maintain the independence and the integrity of sociology to the discipline, the freedom to research and to study, publish and disseminate the results of sociological research, saving that in the pursuit of these ends they should remember at all times their responsibility to safeguard the proper interests of those studied or affected. (BSA, 1982: p. 1)

Open methods of research are advocated and covert research should only be resorted to where it is not possible to employ other methods to collect essential data. However, open procedures are advocated, not only because subjects are entitled to know what is happening, but because future researchers could suffer and receive less co-operation in the long term if covert research leads to negative publicity.

A similar argument for the adherence to ethical principles is expressed in the code of conduct of the Market Research Society (1986: p. 7):

> Research is founded upon the willing cooperation of the public and of business organisations. It depends upon public and business confidence and that it is conducted honestly, objectively, without intrusion and without harm to informants.

Thus, sociologists are urged to avoid intrusive methods, which may be harmful to respondents and cause them to withdraw cooperation in future researches. However, Baumrind (1964: p. 421) points out that where there is conflict between the scientific interests and the interests of his prospective subjects, compromise may have to be reached in order to do 'the best possible job with the least possible harm to his subjects and methodology must be adjusted'. On the other hand, compromise and relaxation of methodological rigour not only affects social researchers' aspirations to disclose and interpret data, but it could threaten rights asserted by other parties involved in social research, such as the public right to know — the pursuit of truth.

Questionnaires

However, Barnes (1979: p. 5) points out that more recently 'citizens' have increasingly begun to question the part they are called upon to play as informants or respondents to questionnaires. Individually or collectively they have begun to ask "What's in it for me? Why should I answer your questions? If you ask me, why shouldn't I ask you?". In some extreme cases there has been a blanket refusal to cooperate in social inquiry, especially when it is a government inquiry such as a census or when individuals suspect that their answers will be filed in some computer data bank, which may be retrieved at some later date and employed against their interests. Thus, sociologists need to focus on how they can achieve their research aims without violating the rights of the subjects they study.

The formal interview and self-completed questionnaire are among the most explicit of all research methods and yet they may be as intrusive as any. Furthermore, it is harder than might be imagined to produce a really good questionnaire. Oppenheim (1966: p. vii), in the preface to his book *Questionnaire Design and Attitude Measurement,* writes that "the world is full of well meaning people who believe that anyone who can write plain English and has a modicum of common sense can produce a good questionnaire". He goes on to demonstrate that though commonsense and the ability to write plain English will help, it will not be sufficient. Extreme care has to be taken in selecting question type, in question writing, in the design, piloting, distribution and return of questionnaire. Careful consideration needs to be given to how responses will be analysed at the time of the design stage, not after the questionnaire has been returned. Cohen and Manion (1980: p. 80) believe that an ideal questionnaire possesses the same properties as a good law:

> It is clear, unambiguous and uniformly workable. Its design must minimize potential errors from respondents ... and coders. And since people's participation in surveys is voluntary, a questionnaire has to help in engaging their interest, encouraging their co-operation, and eliciting answers as close as possible to the truth'.

Again, there is an emphasis on self-interest — how to achieve the closest cooperation in the pursuit of truth. Whilst survey methods using closed questions to gain quantitative data may involve relatively little invasion, in-depth

questionnaires and interviews with extensive supplementary questions may lead
to the pursuit of subjects down whatever escape route they try to take. Although
in theory response is voluntary, in practice measures are often taken to dispose
the respondent favourably to the questioning procedure, and even to lead them
to cooperate with the most impertinent enquiries.

Nevertheless, Carlson (1967: p. 187) argues that interviewing is inevitably, if
justifiably, invasive and recognizes the principle of designing questionnaires to
work from innocuous items towards questions about more sensitive subjects.
However, Bell (1987) stresses that "questions that may cause offence should be
removed". If a researcher really needs information on what might be regarded
by some respondents as sensitive issues, extra care is needed in the wording and
the positioning of the questions. Thus Bell, too, seems to be condoning intrusion
if it is done 'sensitively' and is recognising the principle of placing sensitive
issues in the part of the questionnaire where they are most likely to be answered.

Advice is given to include personal questions in the body of the interview:

> Sticky questions should come in the body of the interview, about or just
> after midway, when rapport is strongest and before boredom or
> impatience sets in. (Gardner, 1978: p. 47)

Some researchers even place sensitive questions at the end of the questionnaire,
the theory being that if the respondent abandons the questionnaire at that point,
at least the answers are available to all earlier questions. This aligns with covert
methodology by leading respondents through innocuous questions until they
reach the important focus of the research, at a point when they feel unable to
withdraw — they are committed to cooperation even with the most impertinent
questions. Thus, refusal may, in theory, be legitimate for voluntary respondents,
but everything possible is done to prevent it.

Informed consent

All codes of ethics and statements of ethical principles (e.g. those of the
American Anthropological Association of 1971; of the BSA of 1982) view
informed consent as central to research. This principle arises out of the Nuremberg war trials in the wake of the Second World War and advocates that
respondents should be informed that research is taking place, what its purpose
is, and what implications it may have for them. The Nuremberg Code prioritises
the rights of the individual:

The voluntary consent of the human subject is absolutely essential. This means that the person involved should have legal capacity to give consent ... without the intervention of any element of force, fraud, deceit, duress, overreaching or any other ulterior form of constraint or coercion; and should have sufficient knowledge and comprehension of the elements of the subject matter involved as to enable him to make an understanding and enlightened decision. (Nuremburg Code, 1949, cited in Homan, 1991: p. 69)

However, problems may still emerge when consent has been obtained. Burgess (1989: p. 19) argues that researchers cannot forecast all such implications at the beginning of a research project for interests and priorities shift as the research proceeds. Furthermore, it is not always possible to specify what data will be collected, or how it may be used, (cf. Jorgenson, 1971). Therefore it can be reasonably argued that subjects are not fully informed, consent has not been obtained and privacy has been therefore violated — intrusion has been effected.

Bulmer (1982: p. 5) argues that although researchers may regard themselves as practising overt research, they are not always open and frank about their purposes and interests. Or they choose to emphasise only the least threatening aspects of the research, justifying this by advocating the importance of keeping the explanation simple so that their respondents understand the nature of the research.

Such was the case in the Brighton Leisure Card Survey, initially conducted to discover the feasibility of a Leisure Card in Brighton (Lawrence and Tomlinson, 1991). Students, having been specifically instructed *not* to reveal that the survey had been initiated by Brighton Council, led the potential respondent to believe that the research, carried out by the Leisure Research Unit of the Brighton Polytechnic, was research for the Polytechnic. Here the Leisure Research Unit is minimizing the risk of refusal which is often associated with Council/ government research.

Gardner (1978) claims that ducking the explanation of the motive and sponsorship of the research is a standard procedure — but does not such a practice undermine the principle of informed consent by failing to honour the ethical principle that participants should be fully informed so that they can protect themselves from unwanted intrusion? Researchers need to consider carefully the cost of such deception, for: 'It may be possible to persuade people to part with information for inadequately explained reasons or to mislead them once, but the respondents may discover they have been duped and will react badly in future to the same and other research workers'. (Stacey, 1959: p. 72). This kind of prior experience may well have been a factor in the high refusal rate experienced by the LRU in their street based research. Furthermore, what often passes for information is often no more than a softening-up of respondents, particularly when they are being urged to participate in the furthering of a good cause or investigators suggest they are doing respondents a favour. Nevertheless, the practice of establishing rapport and credibility in the opening stages of questionnaires and interviews, and hopefully weakening the subject's defences of privacy, is often commended as a fundamental principal in questionnaire design. (Richardson _et al._ 1965: p. 43).

Such an example of inveiglement of respondents is the _Hite Report on Female Sexuality_ (Hite, 1977), where women were urged to participate to further the cause of feminism, "to try to understand ourselves better", to unburden themselves and to accept an invitation to share intimate secrets with other women.

Gatekeepers

In some research settings before negotiations can begin with subjects, the researcher must first gain the permission of, or perhaps surreptitiously by-pass other individuals or organisations who control access to them — the gatekeepers. With gatekeeper support, the question of the volitional status of the respondent is called into question. Dingwall (1980) argues that once consent has been secured from the hierarchy, subordinates may take a risk by declining to participate. Ball points out that research in school usually proceeds after consent by head-teachers, and sometimes class teachers, is gained. "No one consults the pupils" (Ball, 1985: p. 39). Thus, again, the letter of the ethic is satisfied in that the nature and purpose of research are declared, but children would find it extremely difficult to refuse to cooperate in school-based research and could in turn risk incurring official disfavour.

In the case of Urdry and Billy's research, 'Initiation of Coitus in Early Adolescence', (1987: pp. 841–55), interviewers visited the homes of over a thousand pupils in 1980 to explain the study to a parent or guardian, and requested the parent's permission for the adolescent to participate in the study —

thus meticulously following the standard procedure of vicarious consent. Once the signed parental permission was obtained, adolescents were then requested to participate.

An ethical issue which emerges here concerns those teenagers who may have felt obliged to participate in this particularly sensitive research because their parents had already given their consent. Consequently, children aged 11 years upwards filled in self-administered questionnaires and participated in interviews over a period of two years about intimate sexual matters. They were asked how often they had sexual intercourse, thus suggesting to impressionable youngsters that sexual experimentation was normal at their age. Furthermore, the questionnaire encouraged those children who had not experienced sexual intercourse to believe that perhaps they were abnormal, and to indulge in future experimentation, by posing the question: "How much do you think you would like to have sex in the next year?".

As part of the DART research, (Denscombe & Aubrook, 1922: p. 853) pupils were asked to complete a self-report questionnaire in class on their use of alcohol, tobacco and other drugs. Pupil participation was regarded as voluntary and meticulous efforts were made to respect their rights. Consent of Heads, governors and even LEAs was sought. However, subsequent comments about these questionnaires suggested that even these laudable measures may not have provided an adequate ethical basis on which to conduct such research in schools. The fact that pupils were asked to fill in the questionnaires in school time when tasks set are not normally voluntary; that the format of the questionnaire had the connotations of a test; and the nature of the institutional context in which the questionnaires were actually administered, may have led pupils to believe that "It's just another piece of school work".

The researchers, Denscombe and Aubrook, (1992) concluded that this comment more than any other reflected the pupils' attitude to the questionnaire. Thus, it could be argued that this was a form of institutional coercion and that institutionally-based research in itself can be a licence for intrusion with pupils feeling obliged to respond.

Clearly there is an ethical issue here for both sociologists and gatekeepers — the rights of the pupils to refuse to cooperate in research. However, if researchers are to avoid the possibility of institutional coercion, this could lead to the prohibition of questionnaire research in schools, which in turn would restrict the quality and extent of coverage and data — a price which social researchers would not be prepared to pay. Thus, sociologists must strive to ensure that pupils feel free in the institutional context to say 'no'.

Privacy

Closely linked with informed consent is another fundamental ethical issue in social science — 'How much does research in social science threaten to destroy privacy, and how much does the protection of privacy threaten to block research?' (Barnes, 1979: p. 16). This leads on to the vexed question of how to find the appropriate balance in the conduct of research between the public 'right to know' and the individual right to privacy.

Codes and guidelines have little to say about privacy, which is barely mentioned and certainly not elaborated upon. Conceptions of privacy are so complex in social science that they defy simple definitions. The Younger Committee in its search for a workable formula eventually succumbed to defeat. (Younger, 1972: p. 18). One of the most helpful codes — that of Social Research Association — aims not at regulation, but at raising awareness by placing researchers' motivation in the context of other social values and interests. The guidelines place 'avoiding undue intrusion' first amongst obligations of a researcher to his/her subjects. Furthermore, social science literature and codes acknowledge the variable quality of privacy from one place to another and from one person to another. For example, in this country, income, voting and sexual behaviour are regarded as very private matters; therefore interviewers are instructed to deal with these issues in a circumspect manner. However, Homan (1991: p. 41) points out that in Sweden such caution is not adopted since income is a matter for public information. Nevertheless, some people may not want to reveal intimate sexual details, whereas others will readily discuss such private matters with counsellors, doctors, friends or social researchers. Thus, the boundaries of privacy are being controlled, at least in theory, by those whose privacy may be invaded.

Westin's definition of privacy (1970: p. 7) places as central "the claim of individuals, groups or institutions to determine for themselves when, how and to what extent information is communicated to others". However, far from affording respondents greater protection of their privacy, their notional control may weaken their defences. For the researcher has training and practice in extending the boundaries as far as possible in relation to privacy — s/he is the more practised and powerful negotiator. S/he can penetrate private spheres with the subject's consent by employing 'the softening up process'. Thus, the interviewer revokes moral responsibility in endeavouring to procure a favourable response from the subject, and adopts the most intrusive form of questioning which will yield intimate revelations.

However, genuine respect for privacy will recognise that there are no-go areas and the negotiator will accept their refusal to collaborate on sensitive issues, even though such a refusal may have a detrimental effect on the response rate. Lynda Measor condemns what she terms 'poking around the issue'; or the strategy of 'probing':

> If respondents have decided they do not want to tell you why they never married, failed to get promotion, or left their boyfriend last week, they have a right to privacy. It is unethical to poke around the issue, trying to pressure them for the data you want. (Measor, 1985: p. 72)

The Brighton Leisure Card Survey (Lawrence and Tomlinson, 1991) opened with instructions to student interviewers to obtain personal data such as address, including postcode, and telephone number at the end of the interview — thus respondents were led to believe they were giving an anonymous interview and only when they had divulged all their information were they asked for such personal details. The request for these details may be justified by the researchers on the grounds that they need to check the validity of the data; however, the insistence on the postal code is ominous and may indicate that further intrusion may occur, when respondents are inundated with marketing mail. The 'ACORN' possibility — classification of residential neighbourhood — is an analytical justification for seeking such detail, but the very collection of the detail marks out the respondent as vulnerable to further approaches.

According to the Brighton Leisure Survey Report (1991, Phase 2, Appendix 2, Question 3), throughout the Leisure Survey interview students were instructed "to '*PROBE*' in order to acquire details about family situation, income etc." — clear evidence of intrusive methods used in interviewing the more reluctant respondent and contravening the ethical outlines in the Market Research Code which condemns intrusion.

Furthermore, covert methods are adopted by the interviewer in observing and noting ethnic origin — only if there is some doubt is the respondent questioned on this matter. Yet race is such a sensitive issue that, though recently reintroduced, it was withdrawn from the Public Census in 1971! The Leisure Research Unit may have argued that such information was essential to gain a cross section of the Brighton-Hove area, but respondents were unaware that this information was being recorded and may be used later for other more sensitive research.

In view of what has already been said about the placement of 'sticky questions' it is not surprising, perhaps, to discover that questions on political affiliation and private income appear at the very end of the questionnaire. Not only were respondents asked how they had voted in the 1987 General Election, they were also asked how they intended to vote in the May Local Council elections of that year — clearly an unwarranted invasion of privacy! Such questions were apparently asked in order to establish class and later to link statistics with the attraction of Council-run leisure units as opposed to privately-run schemes — thus assessing the feasibility of extending the Leisure Card to private leisure facilities. The validity of evidence may, however, be questioned on the grounds of stereotyping — not all Conservatives may use private leisure facilities, or Labour voters council facilities.

Although political questions were omitted in Phase III of the research, the question about household income was retained and not surprisingly is the last question in the questionnaire. Thus the LRU was following the well-recognised procedure in intrusive questioning referred to by Stacey (1980: p. 81):

> Having already answered so many questions, respondents may well be prepared to answer a final one or two rather personal questions which might have shocked them at the beginning.

Nevertheless, this question resulted in a 27% refusal.

Information divulged in interviews and questionnaires is sometimes infinitely more private than political views and incomes. Sexual behaviour ranks high in the privacy league. Shere Hite's investigation into female sexuality is a prime example of gross invasion of privacy. In the course of her research she asked women in an age range from early teens to the late seventies questions about orgasm, masturbation and intercourse. They were asked: "Could you describe what an orgasm feels like to you". (Hite, 1976: p. 574) and "How do you masturbate? Please explain with a drawing or detailed description" (Hite, 1976: p. 576). Reading through a very long list of what many may regard as grossly offensive questions, it is not unreasonable to wonder why women were prepared to divulge such intimate details even though they were urged to respond to 'a good cause'. However, in examining the Hite Report, it becomes clear that some lonely and vulnerable women have perceived their collaboration as a therapeutic exercise: "There's no one I can talk to that would understand, and now I feel really good, like a burden's been lifted" (Hite, 1976: p. 43).

Informants

The Hite Report also raises another ethical issue in the use of questionnaires — the use of informants. Interviews can be structured in such a way that questions can switch from one type to another, leading to researchers deploying interviewees as informants who are not compelled by the scruples about invasion and consent which are urged on professionals. Thus the responsibility passes from the investigator to the unwitting subject. The private world of the respondent is extended to include other people who have not consented to the research.

Not only does Shere Hite ask women questions about their own sexual behaviour, they are also asked to provide explicit details of the sexual behaviour of their partners: "Did you ever see anyone else masturbating? How did they look?" (Hite, 1977:p. xiv).

Respondents are often regarded as objects of measurement in questionnaires. Following Cassell (1980), the Social Research Association's 'Ethical Guidelines' argued that "people can feel wronged without being harmed by research; they may feel that they have been treated as objects of measurement without respect for their individual values and sense of privacy" (SRA, 1989: p. 97).

A general sense of indignation caused by the perceived 'nosiness' of researchers was voiced by some pupils who were, in turn, offended by such intrusion: "In places I found this questionnaire very personal and offensive which is why I haven't answered all questions" (Denscombe and Aubrook, 1992: p. 119).

Concern expressed by some pupils echoed Burgess' research experience (1989: p. 19): "The questions that do prove sensitive, and are sometimes met with refusals, are those that ask about young people's parents and families". While young people may be happy to answer questions about themselves, they can be more discerning than adults in recognising informant questions, and are less willing to divulge personal information about others.

In the DART Questionnaire (Denscombe & Aubrook, 1992) some pupils refused to answer questions about parental work status and education, arguing that this area was irrelevant to the research topic and/or outside the bounds of what was permissible for them to comment on. Pupils were also very sensitive to being stereotyped: naturally, it was the negative stereotyping which upset respondents, especially when linked with ethnic origin which pupils perceived as a thinly disguised attempt to place respondents in predetermined categories:

"Question 54 seemed to me a racist question because black people are sometimes linked with drugs, but white people are as much, if not more, likely to be linked with drugs." (Denscombe and Aubrook, 1992: p. 120)

These comments confirm that pupils must be recognised as critical consumers and not regarded as 'research dopes' (Denscombe & Aubrook, 1992: p. 121). They are sensitive to intrusive questions and will valiantly defend attempts to invade their highly valued privacy.

The questionnaire also identifies a desperate pregnant girl and establishes those who use illegal drugs, both respondents and 'anyone they know'. Thus those who formulate questionnaires need to ask themselves, before giving assurances of confidentiality, in what circumstances they would divulge sensitive data and what they might divulge, or what they might do in a life or death matter. Such an assurance may prove to be a great burden on the researcher; the fundamental principle though is that such assurances should not be given unless they can be honoured.

Dissemination of data

On the other hand, having acquired such private data on the assurances of anonymity and confidentiality, it could be argued that no direct harm has been caused to respondents; only if subjects discover deception is involved, and they have been betrayed, will problems emerge. The data will then be widely disseminated. But the dissemination of data — a process which includes the communication of research data orally, visually and in writing — is rarely discussed in any detail with respondents. Many of the issues already discussed in the research process itself, again emerge in data dissemination: confidentiality, privacy, deception and harm.

Nevertheless, researchers are encouraged to disseminate their data as extensively and as quickly as possible. While this may be in the interests of sponsors and researchers, individuals who cooperate may want anonymity and confidentiality, especially when such assurances have been given in order to persuade respondents to yield sensitive information. In these terms researchers have to consider what to include and what to exclude in their research findings. Platt (1976) expresses this dilemma well when she remarks:

People often told me things that they would not have been prepared to see published in ways that could identify them, or that could have embarrassed them or other people.

What was the response of some of those women who (perhaps in a moment of weakness) responded to the Hite questionnaire, baring their souls, only to see their own and their partner's intimate behaviour printed for the world to see in a best seller? Irreparable damage may have been caused by feelings of guilt and betrayal.

Even the best attempts to conceal identities may be frustrated in the dissemination of data. The combination of a few statistics may lead to the possible identification of respondents when age, occupation, religion and background details are requested. Not only does the Hite questionnaire require these details, but unknown to respondents postmarks were used to identify the geographic distribution of replies, yet another example of covert methods used in open research. The claim that the respondents will be anonymous would appear to be in further doubt when women were urged to respond using tape cassettes to record their responses!

Finally, in the very complex matter of data dissemination the issues of ownership of data, storing procedures, and secondary analysis are raised by the Brighton Leisure Survey. Those who responded to the LRU research were led to believe they were cooperating with student research and were, therefore, unaware that the sponsors — Brighton Council — would have access to the data. Nor were they given assurances of confidentiality when personal details were sought at the end of the survey. Whilst the Data Protection Act affords protection to data which are stored anonymously in computers, information recorded manually, however private or personal, is not afforded such protection. Therefore whilst subjects may be given a code, the key to such a code may be retained in manual form.

A wealth of data was collected by the LRU and stored in a computer bank for up to two years. Although such data were anonymized, and those handling data were briefed on confidentiality, they were stored over a period of two years on the basis that: "There remains immense potential for further analysis of many aspects of the *extensive* data base" (Lawrence and Tomlinson, 1992: p. 4). Yet the Younger Report (1972) found that the aspect of the protection of privacy which caused the most alarm was computerized storage of personal data such as the Leisure Report collected — family circumstances, financial situations and political views.

The question must be asked here: 'To what future use may such data be used and what are the implications for respondents?' Would their consent be sought for secondary analysis — a process in itself causing further intrusion? And respondents, in turn, may feel that what began as a brief encounter in the street may never end — especially if they are also inundated with market research mail and advertisements.

Only professional scruples and the Data Protection Act can inhibit the trading of private information. Yet whilst the latter regulates the disclosure of personal data, individuals have no general right here. Indeed, one of the disclosure exemptions permits personal data to be revealed for taxation purposes in emergencies.

Conclusions

What has emerged from this discussion is that, although the questionnaire is widely approved for its openness, it can be used as a strategy for the invasion of privacy. The voluntary cooperation of the respondent becomes an opportunity for the practised researcher to probe the most personal aspects of his subject's life.

In spite of current guidelines and codes which focus on the obligations of the researcher to his subject, these may only be adhered to by members of professional organisations for reasons of self-interest. Fortified by such ethical codes and professional expertise, insidious softening-up techniques are practised and informed consent becomes licence for a systematic erosion of the subject's defences. Far from informing subjects of their rights, and the possible hazards they may face in cooperating with research, informed consent is used to allay their fears and suspicions and thus achieve the most favourable response rate which is essential to all research.

In observing the letter of the law, the researcher's conscience is cleared, since theoretically subjects can refuse to yield to such invasion of privacy. Informant interviewing transfers the moral responsibility from the investigator to the unwitting informant and gatekeepers are used to by-pass the rights of subjects. Since investigators can argue that they cannot always know the dissemination of data, again they are relieved of the responsibility to the subject through the principle of informed consent. Yet if the kind of democratic relations which

Simons (1984: p. 91) established with her subjects in SAFARI — allowing them subsequently to screen or even to withdraw data — were adopted universally, this would deny research its essential objectivity and would in turn raise another ethical problem — the control of the researcher by the subject and the questions raised over the validity of the research. On the other hand, researchers have an obligation to their audiences — the public right to know — especially since subjects may be funded from public sources or because lives may be at risk.

It is clear that without the cooperation of subjects the fundamental aim of research — the pursuit of truth — would be impossible. Therefore since covert research is only advocated in special circumstances, the subject in open research is left to the moral scruples of the researcher who in turn is answerable to his professional associates, and in the case of students, to their institutions.

For it is here that the future of research lies — in the professional training of research students — and yet surprisingly there is a notable absence of any systematic lead in institutions. While in some ethical and professional practices have a high profile, others pay little attention to them. Indeed, out of the fifty-eight institutions which responded to Homan's (1990) educational survey, only two polytechnics and three universities had established ethical guidelines. It appears that the majority of institutions rely on supervisors to educate students in professional and ethical standards — a deplorable situation — since many supervisors themselves may have little practical experience of ethical matters in research, whilst others may manifest little explicit concern about ethical issues.

The development of clear ethical guidelines and professional practices by universities and colleges is not only desirable, but essential if our future researchers are to negotiate successfully the ethical minefields of research. And since students embark on research as undergraduates, they should be aware of such important matters then, rather than embrace them for the first time at post-graduate level. In spite of the restrictions on time, it is clearly unsatisfactory to advise those undergraduates involved in research merely about such technical procedures such as design, collection and analysis of research data. Since the questionnaire is a fundamental tool of research, it is surprising that some time is not allocated for examining the ethical implications of questionnaires.

Opportunities should be available to discuss the role of researcher in relation to the subject with the emphasis on valuing subjects as human beings — fellow citizens — and not research objects or dupes. There should be more emphasis on the piloting of questionnaires to iron out any difficulties or misunderstandings.

Furthermore, students need to be aware of the danger of giving assurances of anonymity and confidentiality which they will find impossible to maintain. Making promises that only an examiner or supervisor will have access to their work is clearly untenable when dissertations are distributed to other lecturers and students who may in turn possess enough local knowledge to identify institutions or individuals. In my own case, in spite of adopting careful procedures to ensure both anonymity and confidentiality, such procedures were confounded when the binder of the dissertation turned out to be a parent of a child at the school researched, and on collection of the work remarked cheerfully how she had enjoyed reading about her son's school! So much for anonymity and confidentiality!

Furthermore, students need to be cautioned about the use of gatekeepers and the implications of presenting questionnaires under the guise of school work; while both practices could ensure a high response, they could be perceived as institutional coercion. Research involving children is a high risk area and therefore students need to be aware of the potential damage which could be caused, both short term and long term. Such a dialogue about ethical issues raised by research will, in turn, enable staff, too, to examine their own research practice and perhaps to gain fresh insights on their own research methodology and the possible effects on subjects.

For those subjects who feel that they have been duped or betrayed by researchers will understandably refuse to cooperate in the future, particularly with street-based research. Therefore in order to avoid conflict between the sociologists' interest and those of the subjects, the researcher may have to accept compromise in order to do the best possible job with the least possible harm, since the future of research depends on the voluntary cooperation of subjects. However, whilst training and ethical codes will raise an awareness and understanding of the damage which can be effected by the use of unethical methods in open research, this cannot in itself resolve the problem. For as Bronfehrenner (1952: p. 453) remarked: "There is no easy solution — unless, of course, all research ceased".

Yet there must be trust and confidence between the professional researcher and the subject; between the profession as a whole and the public. Ultimately it is a matter of personal responsibility and morality; researchers need to review regularly their own work and address the extent to which their activities may be unethical. Only then, by constant self-evaluation and reflection on each research

experience, can the proper interests of subjects be safeguarded and the fundamental values which are at the heart of social research be upheld.

References

Ball, S. J. (1985) 'Participation observation with pupils', in Burgess, R. (ed)
Strategies of educational research: Qualitative methods. Lewes: Falmer Press,
pp. 23–53.

Barnes, J. A. (1977) *The ethics of inquiry in social science.* Delhi: Oxford.

———(1979) *Who should know what? Social science, privacy and ethics.*
Harmondsworth: Penguin.

Baumrind, D. (1964) 'Some thoughts on ethics of research: After reading Milgrim's
Behavioural Study of obedience', *American Psychologist*, pp. 421-3.

Bell, J. (1987) *Doing your research project: A guide for the first time researcher in
education and social science.* Milton Keynes: Open University.

Bell, C. and Roberts, H. (eds) (1984) *Social researching: Politics, problems,
practice.* London: Routledge and Kegan Paul.

British Sociological Association (1992) 'Statement of ethical practice', *Sociology*,
Vol. 26, pp. 703–707.

Bronfehrenner, U. (1952) 'Principles of professional ethics: Cornell Studies in social
growth', *American Psychologist*, Vol. 7, No. 2: pp. 452–5.

Bulmer, M. (ed) (1979) *Censuses, surveys and privacy.* London: Macmillan.

Bulmer, M. (ed) (1982a) *Social research ethics.* London: Macmillan.

Burgess, R. (ed) (1984) *The research process in educational settings: Ten case
studies.* Lewes: Falmer Press.

———(1984) *In the field.* London: Routledge.

———(ed) (1989) *The ethics of educational research.* Lewes: Falmer Press.

Carlson, E. O. (1967) 'The issue of privacy in public opinion research', *Public
Opinion Quarterly*, pp. 1-8.

Cassell, J. and Wax, M. L. (eds) (1980) 'Ethical problems of fieldwork, *Social
problems* (Special Issue), Vol. 27: pp. 259–378.

Cohen, L. and Manion, L. (1980) *Research methods in education.* London: Croom
Helm Ltd.

Data Protection Registrar, (1989) *Data Protection Act 1984: Guidelines 1-8*, 2nd
Series.

Denscombe, M. and Aubrook, L. (1992) 'The ethics of questionnaire research', *British Educational Research Journal*, Vol. 18, No. 2.

Dingwall, R. (1980) 'Ethics and ethnography', *Sociological Review*, Vol. 28, No. 4: pp. 871–91.

Gardner, G. (1978) *Social surveys for social planners*. Milton Keynes: Open University.

Hite, S. (1976) *The Hite Report: A nationwide study on female sexuality*. London, Tammy Franklin.

Homan, R. (1978) 'Interpersonal communication in Pentecostal meetings', *Sociological Review*, Vol. 26, No. 3: pp. 499–518.

———(1990) 'Institutional controls and educational research', *British Educational Research Journal*, Vol. 16, No. 3: pp. 237–48.

———(1991) *The ethics of social research*. London: Longman Group UK Limited.

———(1992) 'The ethics of open methods', *British Journal of Sociology*, Vol. 43, No. 3.

Jenkins, D. (1980) 'An adversary's account of SAFARI's ethics of case study', in Simons, H. (ed) *Towards a science of the singular: essays about case study in educational research and evaluation*. University of East Anglia: CARE Occasional Publications, Vol. 10: pp. 147–59.

Jorgensen, T. G. (1971) 'On ethics and anthropology', *Current Anthropology*, 12 June: pp. 321–34.

Jowell, R. (1982) Ethical concern in data collection', in Raals C. D. (ed) *Data protection and privacy: Proceedings of a conference*. London: Social Research Association, pp. 43–53.

Karhausen, L. (1987) 'From ethics to medical ethics', in Doxiadis, S. (ed) *Ethical dilemmas in health promotion*. London: Wiley, pp. 25–33.

Lawrence, L. and Tomlinson, A. (1991) *Brighton Leisure Survey Report (Phase Two)*. Leisure Research Unit, Brighton Polytechnic.

——— (1992) *Brighton Leisure Card Survey Report (Phase Three)*. Leisure Research Unit, Brighton Polytechnic.

Market Research Society (1986) *Code of conduct*, London.

Measor, L. (1985) 'Interviewing in qualitative research', in Burgess, R. G. (ed) *Strategies of educational research: Qualitative methods*. Lewes: Falmer, pp. 55–57.

Oppenheim, A. N. (1966) *Questionnaire design and attitude measurement*. London: Heinemann.

Platt, J. (1976) *Realities of social research: An empirical study of British sociologists*. London: Chatto and Windus.

Pond, D. (Chair) (1987) *Report of a working party on the teaching of medical ethics*. Institute of Medical Ethics.

Richardson, E. (1973) *The teacher, the school and the task of management*. London: Heinemann.

Richardson, S. A., Dohrenwend, B. S. and Klein, D. (1965) *Interviewing: Its form and functions*. New York: Basic Books.

Simons, H. (1979) 'Suggestions for a school self-evaluation based on democratic principles', *Classroom Action Research, Network Bulletin* 3, pp. 49–55.

—— (1984) 'Guidelines for the conduct of an independent evaluation', in Adelman, C. (ed) *The politics and ethics of evaluation*. London: Croom Helm, pp. 87–92.

Social Research Association (1989) *Ethical guidelines*. London.

Stacey, M. (1959) *Methods of social research*. Oxford: Pergamon (Reprinted 1980).

Urdry, J. R. and Billy, J. O. G. (1987) 'Initiation of coitus in early adolescence', *American Sociological Review*, Vol. 52, pp. 841–55.

Wax, M. L. and Cassell, J. (1981) 'From regulation to reflection: Ethics in social research', *American Sociologist*, 16, 4, pp. 224–9.

Westin, A. F. (1970) *Privacy and freedom*. Oxford: Bodley Head.

Younger, K. (Chair) (1972) *Report of the Committee on Privacy. Cmnd. 5012*. London: Her Majesty's Stationery Office.

Zweig, F. (1948) *Labour, life and poverty*. London: Gollancz.

FIELD WORKERS RUSH IN (WHERE THEORISTS FEAR TO TREAD): THE PERILS OF ETHNOGRAPHY

John Sugden
University Of Ulster

This essay is mostly about the ethical and physical perils associated with doing ethnographic research. As a way into this subject I have chosen to 'tell the story' of how, through a combination of accidents and informed choice, I came to view ethnography as the purest form of sociological inquiry as well as to anticipate some of the pit-falls involved with this style of research.

Most of the sociology which I encountered as an undergraduate at the University of Essex was of a grand theoretical nature. The relative explanatory powers of classical scholars such as Marx, Weber and Durkheim were discussed against a backcloth of multi-national capitalism and international socialism. The final stages of my undergraduate education tended to be dominated by under-standing and refining the competition among a small number of theoretical derivatives of Marxism. This left me well equipped to identify which theory of the state could do most to explain the emergence of and eventual repression of the Tupamaros, Uruguay's urban guerrilla movement, the topic of my final year dissertation. In those days the fact that I had never set foot in Uruguay or, indeed, even met a Uruguayan did not seem to hinder such discourse or stop me becoming a self-proclaimed 'expert' on the subject.

As a final year depth-study option at Essex I elected to take a seminar course on anarchism. For the most part this discussion group was dominated by familiar squabbles between representatives of various factions of the left over the role of the state, ideology and repression in capitalist and communist societies. In the midst of all this, however, there was an interlude wherein we were asked to consider actual examples of societies apparently held together without any central apparatus of authority, i.e. no state. It was at this point that I was introduced to the writings of the social anthropologist, Evans-Pritchard, who, amongst other things, had made a series of studies of stateless primitive societies in Africa, particularly in central and southern Sudan. Having so recently ploughed my way through Habermas, Marcuse, Althusser and the like, I was immediately struck by the sense of local authenticity conveyed by Evans-Pritchard's writings. I admired the way in which he was able to move to theorisations on power and social relations without ever overwhelming his grounded narrative. I remember being particularly impressed by his book on the Nuer, a nomadic tribe of cattle herdsmen, and being mesmerised by his description of the leopard skin chief. I was struck too by his explanation of his role as an arbitrator among the Nuer's kinship networks (Evans-Pritchard, 1951a). I reflected on my own abstracted scribblings on Uruguay and felt embarrassed by their inadequacy.

On graduating from Essex, Evans-Pritchard, classical social theorists and neo-Marxists seemed to be of equally little use to me as dejectedly I looked through the job advertisements. Three months after graduation I found myself working in a pub in North London. (What else did one do with a degree in politics and sociology in the 1970s?) The choice seemed to lie between school teaching and social work, two worthy careers, neither of which I had much interest in. I was on the verge of accepting a job with Tower Hamlets Social Services when I spotted an advertisement in the Guardian for volunteers to work in the Sudan. Within two weeks I was in Khartoum being briefed for my sojourn as a teacher of English in the Southern Sahara (the fact that I had not taught a day in my life and had an accent which would have graced the set of Channel 4's "Brookside" did not seem to put off the Sudanese Ministry of Education).

Ten months spent in the village of Khor Taggat, 10 miles outside of the desert city of El Obeid proved to be a humbling experience as I reflected on the abundance of first world existence in comparison to the pressures of life in one of the world's poorest nations. My interlude in Sudan left me with lots of time for reflection, much of which I expressed in written form, either in letters home or through entries in a daily journal which I kept. I have unearthed these 'memoirs' and patched together a section which illustrates how, even though I did not realise it at the time, ethnography became established as a key element in my own personal and intellectual development.

It was half way through my stay in Africa, during a journey to southern Sudan, that I had one of the more bizarre experiences of my life which, for the first time, had echoes back in my work as an Essex undergraduate. I had travelled with another Englishman, overland from El Obeid to El Muglad, in the most extreme discomfort in the rear of a lorry which was otherwise jammed full of half naked Dinka tribesmen making their way from working in the peanut harvest in the north to their homes in the south.

El Muglad is in mid-west of Sudan and is one of the points where the Arab north meets the black African south. It is also one of the staging posts for the Baggara, a nomadic tribe of Arab descent, who centuries before had abandoned the camel as a means of transport in favour of long-horned cattle which they ride in a manner curiously reminiscent of Peter Fonda on his chopped Harley in the cult film, *Easy Rider*. Because my companion and I were the first whites to visit El Muglad for some time we were objects of great curiosity. We were given shelter by a government official in the only non-mud-and-straw dwelling in the town. For the first time since graduation my university education came in handy as our host proved to be somewhat of an expert on Evans-Pritchard who had lived and worked in the region in the 1950s and who had written books on many of the nomadic tribes who roamed around here. We talked into the small hours about the different peoples who inhabited this part of the world, about the rift between the Arab north and the African south and about the merits and demerits of the military regime which ruled from Khartoum. Before we left the next morning he presented me with a copy of Evans-Pritchard's book on the Nuer.

There was a slight sand-storm blowing just after dawn as we waited at the station for a train to take us further south. Sudan has only one railway line upon which run a handful of ageing diesel engines pulling ancient rolling stock left over from the British Empire. The gauge of the track is narrow and this causes the train to travel quite slowly. I heard the train approaching, but I was not prepared for the sight of it as it emerged from the dawn's almost purple gloom quite close to the station. The labouring engine hauled approximately ten ancient Pullman carriages on the roofs of which were spread what seemed to be a whole tribe of Dinka, sitting cross-legged with clusters of spears waving in the air like bull-rushes on the banks of the Nile. We had government passes which permitted us to travel "first class" below which were three other classes, excluding the roof. I remember thinking, God help classes 2, 3 and 4 as I surveyed the cramped and dusty accommodation which would house me and about 6 other people for the next 72 hours. The first class toilet deserves a special mention. It was the size of a small telephone booth and contained a porcelain W.C. and a tiny wash hand basin to which no water flowed. Tethered to the W.C. was a goat. Given that perpetual diarrhoea is a fact of life for first-world visitors in many third-world countries, for the next two days the goat and I got to be firm friends and I was dismayed when on the third day he was no longer there to share my frequent constitutionals and goat's head soup appeared on the menu handed out by the steward. (Has there ever been a worse venue for death row?) I was beginning to learn the hard way the meaning of cultural relativism. Eventually, I ate the soup.

A further surprise awaited me the following afternoon as I awoke from a nap and peered out of the compartment's slatted windows straight into the eyes of a Nuer leopard skin chief in full regalia, with a leopard's head for a crown and the rest of the pelt hanging as a cloak down the back of his otherwise naked body. It was as if he had stepped straight out of the pages of one of Evans-Pritchard's texts. My travelling companion was taken aback when I was able to explain how this figure fitted into the power structure of Dinka kinship networks. For the first time I began to think that my undergraduate education had not been a total waste of time.

This episode was not without its down side. In the six months prior to these events I had already contracted malaria and somewhere between El Muglad and our destination, Wau, I was bitten by an unidentified insect and became smitten with one of the thousands of tropical diseases they have yet to find a name for. During a delirious ten days I lost more than 20lbs (which in those days, unlike now, I could ill afford) and, according to the emergency medical team when they finally reached me I was almost dead. Luckily the drugs they gave me worked and I survived to tell the tale. While it did not occur to me at the time, the fact that I had nearly died to get the tale was part and parcel of my ethnographer's apprenticeship.

Five years later I was making another journey of discovery in a totally different context in the United States of America. I was on my way to a boxing club in a black and Hispanic ghetto in the self-proclaimed "insurance capital of the world", Hartford, Connecticut. I described the setting for this fieldwork like this:

> Below the horizon, in the shadows of the houses of corporate finance and partly hidden beneath the elevated steel and concrete network of highways, there is a wasteland of urban decomposition and social subsistence...the down town residential showcase of nineteenth century Hartford has gradually deteriorated into its twentieth century ghetto.

In the intervening period I had revisited the theoretical and methodological debates which had informed so much of my undergraduate education, now as a postgraduate at the University of Connecticut. I was particularly fortunate to have taken a course under the guidance of Albert Cohen who was somewhat of a guru on delinquent subcultures. He and other colleagues who were likewise devotees of the Chicago School of urban sociology/ethnography, provided me with an informed and analytical framework within which to embed the self-taught social observation and recording skills picked up in sub-Saharan Africa.

At the same time, largely inspired by work of Raymond Williams (1977) and E. P. Thompson (1968), critical theorists and researchers were beginning to turn their attention to areas of cultural production which hitherto had fallen outside of the embrace of serious academic scholarship. In terms of additional empirical research the CCCS (Centre for Contemporary Cultural Studies) at the University of Birmingham took a lead in this area and much of the work it produced was at least quasi-ethnographic in style and interpretation. While in terms of clarity of prose and richness of interpretation none of this work seriously challenged the supremacy of the early Chicago School [classics such as Wirth's *The ghetto* (1928) or Whyte's *Street corner society* (1955)], texts such as *Resistance through rituals* (Hall and Jeffferson, 1975) and Paul Willis's excellent *Learning to labour* (1977) by placing an emphasis on the social-structural and power related elements which frame the subcultural experience, provided me with another piece of the jigsaw which would comprise the epistemological foundation for the research style which has tended to characterise my work ever since. Ironically, the final piece of this puzzle was provided by a detached theoriser, Anthony Giddens who, in *New rules of sociological method* (1976), spelled out in theoretical terms justification for the methods of the CCCS and fellow travellers. Summarising a long and complex journey through the sociology of knowledge, Giddens argued that the critical point of social reproduction is at the moment where human agency interacts with institutional determination and that this is precisely the site where the development of social theory should begin and end. Because of the highly complex and subliminal nature of this process of social reproduction, Durkheim's 'old rules of sociological method' (1964), that is principles which cast the researcher at a detatched vantage point from those to be studied [in their most modern guise accurately characterised by C. Wright Mills (1970) as 'abstracted empiricism'] are inadequate for accessing and making sense of the lived experience of cultural transformation. Thus, Giddens makes a strong case for hermeneutics as a philosophical foundation for empirical research in sociology, arguing that "immersion" in structurally bounded spheres of social interaction — points of praxis once power relationships are introduced into the equation — is the most appropriate method for sociological analyses and — presumably — theoretical construction and theoretical transformation:

> The production and constitution of society is a skilled accomplishment of its members, but one that does not take place under conditions that are wholly intended or wholly comprehended by its members. The key to understanding social order — is not the 'internalisation of values', but the shifting relations between the production and representation of social life by its constituent actors. (Giddens, 1976: p. 102)

With Gidden's benediction I was finally ready to set out for the field. Evans-Pritchard finally met Marx (albeit through Gramsci), and my epistemological learning curve, at least in theory, was complete.

However, what Giddens and many others who have written on the theory of qualitative methodology fail to point out is that done properly, the practice of ethnography is very time-consuming, emotionally draining, extremely unpredictable and, from time to time, ethically problematic and personally dangerous. For the remainder of this short paper I intend to draw upon personal experiences encountererd in formal ethnographic research settings to focus on the latter of these impediments: the ethical dilemmas and physical perils of ethnography.

Of course it is totally acceptable to undertake qualitative research in relatively non-threatening settings. For instance, participant observation in a physiotherapist's clinic or interviewing retired professional soccer players in their homes. However, ethnography has a long tradition of engaging the researcher in subterranean aspects of social life which, trading upon their invisibility from the public gaze, either border on or are smack in the centre of that area of social life designated as deviant by the guardians of social order. Becker's (1963) and Polsky's (1971) work with drug users and other social misfits and various scholars' work with delinquent gangs (Cohen, 1955; Robins and Cohen, 1978), would be fairly typical of this genre. In the sociology of sport there have been several excellent studies which have required the researcher to spend long periods of time in the company of often quite violent football hooligans (Marsh, 1978; Williams, *et al., 1984)*. The title of Bill Buford's book *Among the thugs* (1991) eloquently captures the location of this particular research role (although it can be argued that Buford's ethnography was, at best, incomplete). This title does raise some interesting ethical questions, not the least of which is '*how much* of the guise of a thug, delinquent, sexual deviant, drug user and so on does a researcher adopt in order to get at authentic information?'.

The main problem here is that real life has an often unpredictable flow which, as we shall see, the field worker cannot turn his or her back on as dangers and ethical problems drift along. If, for instance, you happen to be a participant observer in the midst of West Ham's Inner City Firm (élite hooligan gang) when there is a spontaneous movement to charge the rival Chelsea Head Hunters, even if you should so desire, it would be both difficult and dangerous to "manage your marginality" (Hammersley and Atkinson, 1983: p. 97) and beam yourself back to the library (see, too, Giulanotti, 1995).

In terms of my own focus, for more than a decade I have been interested in the subculture which surrounds amateur and professional boxing in various cultural settings. While boxing itself has a tenuous degree of social legitimacy, the social space which the boxing subculture traditionally occupies is usually the poorest areas of the inner city where deprivation, crime, delinquency and violence are common bedfellows. The poorer and more degenerate a neighbourhood is, the more likely it is to sustain a strong boxing tradition. In addition, in the United States in particular, it is not unusual for criminal elements to take an active interest in the goings on of the boxing fraternity. Thus, at a time when urban crime is reaching epidemic proportions on both sides of the Atlantic, if a researcher really wants to get to know the inner workings of the boxing subculture he or she has to be prepared to spend extended periods in some of the

most dangerous neighbourhoods in some of the world's meanest cities, sometimes rubbing shoulders with people who regularly operate outside of the law.
In reality the danger is partially real and partially a socially constructed
fiction. On the separate occasions that I announced that I was considering
spending extended time in a black ghetto in Hartford Connecticut and in the New
Lodge estate of north Belfast I was strongly advised not to by friends and
colleagues who had absolutely no practical knowledge of these neighbourhoods.
In the first case it was the fact that I was white which, according to concerned
associates, would make me stand out in a neighbourhood which had the highest
murder rate in the city and where the only whites were usually armed police in
squad cars. In the second case I was English, which, different but equally
concerned, acquaintances assured me would make me a target in one of Belfast's
most nationalist enclaves in the proximity of which more than a quarter of those
civilians killed in the Troubles had perished.

The views of these largely middle class and detached audiences augmented
the feelings of apprehension I had when I first entered the field on both
occasions. Partially as a result of listening to relatives and friends and partly
because of a prepossession of my own cultural biases, I felt as if I did not belong
in the location, that my incongruity was obvious to the locals and that I was sure
to be attacked at any moment. Of course the neighbourhoods in question turned
out to be far less threatening than the boundaries of my imagination suggested.
The more often I visited the boxing clubs and the longer I spent in the field, the
more familiar the terrain became and the less scared I was.

However, while overcoming fear is an important step towards doing good
ethnography in potentially dangerous locations, fearlessness is not to be
recommended. I can honestly state that from the day I began up to the day I
finished each investigation my spine would tingle each time I entered the field
and my pulse would not return to its normal pattern until I had a few miles
between myself and the boxing club's doors. On reflection I consider this to have
been a good thing because, accounting for the inflated sense of risk experienced
in my earliest days and despite the protective embrace of those about whom I
was researching, these areas were dangerous places. It was vitally important to
keep this in mind and be aware of the dangers at all times, otherwise the doom-
filled predictions of some colleagues may well have come true.

My experience suggests that it is usually not those in whom you are interested
who pose the greatest direct threat. On the contrary, in the case of my boxing

studies, their managers and trainers and most of the others who drift in and out of boxing clubs have been extremely friendly and helpful. What is more, once they accept your research role they are very protective because they above anybody else understand the many dangers which come with hanging around ghetto environments. Ethical considerations notwithstanding, this is an important reason why being 'up front' about one's research role, particularly in potentially dangerous settings, is a cardinal principle of good ethnography. I learned that your presence as a researcher can soon be forgotten so long as you adopt a participant role (for instance, sparring, helping with equipment, cleaning mouth guards, sweeping the floor and so forth). To be accepted as 'one of them' came to be very important not just in terms of access to information but also in terms of self-preservation. Along with the status of 'boxer' — or someone with a role in the boxing fraternity — comes an unofficial immunity from the vicissitudes which tend to be routine in the ghetto experience (such as gang fighting; drug dealing; car theft and, in the case of north Belfast, involvement or confrontation with the paramilitary gangs). Thus, the closer I got to key figures in the boxing subculture and the more public these relationships became, the safer I felt.

I have three boxing related episodes — from the USA, Northern Ireland and Cuba — which should illustrate how simply being in settings such as these can be dangerous and can raise certain ethical issues. Ironically, the first story which is based on experiences in the United States, relates to an event which took place in an affluent part of Rhode Island 100 miles away from the north Hartford ghetto gym where I spent most of my time while in the field:

> Late one night I had arranged to meet a boxing promoter (let's call him Cavanagh) in a restaurant on Route 1 close to the Atlantic coast in the small state of Rhode Island. He came straight from the airport having spent the day in Washington D.C. negotiating a contract for one of the Sugar Ray Leonard — Roberto Duran fights. He had the contract and who knows what else in the dark brown leather briefcase which he held tightly in his hand as he stepped out of his Lincoln Continental. We sat down to eat at about 10pm along with one of Cavanagh's associates and chatted about the wheeling and dealing that goes on between promoters, managers and match makers in the fight game.

After the meal Cavanagh invited me to travel with him in his car so we could carry on the conversation which had been going on over dinner. It was about midnight when we left the restaurant. Cavanagh stopped at the doorway and announced that he was going back inside to use the rest rooms. I continued to the car park with the other dinner guest who got into his car and drove off. On the way out we passed two heavy set men on their way into the restaurant from the car park. Before Cavanagh arrived back the two men returned to separate cars and drove out of the car park at speed. When Cavanagh did appear he was in a state of panic. He asked me had I seen his briefcase which he said he had left by the entrance thinking I was waiting for him there. It was then that I remembered that the two strangers had not had anything with them when they went into the restaurant, but that one of them was carrying a briefcase when they came out. The chase was on!

Cavanagh jumped into his car and urged me to get in with him. We sped off down the highway in hot pursuit of the suspected thieves. I dreaded to think what we were going to do if we caught up with them and I was rather hoping we wouldn't. However, Cavanagh, who must have valued the contents of his briefcase more than his life (not to mention mine) had other ideas and he floored the Continental. Eventually the two suspect cars, a Mercedes and a Camero, came into view and as Cavanagh drew level with them he told me to lean out of the window and tell them to pull over. The famous defence at the Nuremberg trials, "I was only obeying orders" springs to mind at this point as almost without thinking I found myself hanging out of the window of a car doing in excess of 100 miles per hour screaming to a rather sinister looking stranger in a Mercedes to "Pull over!". What else was I to do? It was too late to run for cover behind my academic persona. "Fuck you" the Mercedes driver roared back in reply. With Cavanagh urging me on I persisted in my overtures until eventually, filling me with even more trepidation, the suspect yelled, "Okay, you fucking arse hole I'll pull over and then you'll get yours buddy!".

At the next exit both of the suspect cars peeled off the highway and we followed them into the deserted parking lot of a closed shopping mall. By now my palms were sweating. Cavanagh, who is by no means a big man, got out of the car and walked towards the strangers who likewise stepped out of their vehicles. Both were big men. One in particular I remember being very broad and weighing about 200 pounds with longish black hair and black designer stubble. He walked towards Cavanagh who was trying to be diplomatic by saying, "Hey guys, sorry to trouble you, but I guess none of you picked up my brief case by mistake back at that restaurant?" To which the stranger shouted back less than diplomatically, "You calling me a thief, you fucking arse hole, I'm not a thief I'm a fucking business man!". He then lifted Cavanagh off the ground by the lapels of his expensive suit, slapped him across the face a few times and stuck him face forward into the trunk of his Camero which his friend had opened, banging his head repeatedly on the inside of the boot and shouting, "Go on, see if you can find your briefcase in there you fucking arse hole!".

At this point I was glad I had Cavanagh's car between me and the two thugs who I was sure I could not out fight, but was equally certain I could out run, assuming my legs, which seemed to have gone to jelly, would carry me. At any moment I was expecting one of them to produce a fire arm. However, by now the disturbance had attracted the attention of a group of teenagers who had been hanging out in the shelter of the distant mall and who were now approaching to see what all the excitement was about. Our two assailants exchanged glances before pushing Cavanagh to the ground and jumping in their cars to speed back onto the highway.

I picked Cavanagh up, feeling slightly embarrassed that I had not come to his assistance. Even if I thought we could have out fought them, would this have been a legitimate course of action? How far can a researcher take his participant observer's role? As it happened, both he and I knew that we were out of our depth and that it was time to call in the cavalry. With the assistance of the police we tracked down the thugs, whose cars I spotted at the back of another restaurant in the next town. The police waited outside and when our suspects went to drive off pulled them over to search their cars. Cavanagh and I observed from the shadows but one of them spotted us and, despite the attentions of the police, began shouting life threatening insults which, after what had just happened, seemed quite plausible to me. Although the police found nothing in the thugs' cars they believed our story. Why? Because when they called in the names of our suspects they discovered that the heavy set one had recently completed a seven year prison term for armed robbery and malicious wounding and that his colleague had no convictions but was the nephew of the local Mafia boss. I knew then that up to this point this was the closest I have ever come to being killed and that if I stuck around much longer that this event may indeed come to pass!. The cop asked Cavanagh did he want to press charges for the assault and I breathed a very heavy sigh of relief when he said that he did not, obviating my responsibility to stay around for the court case.

Laughably the briefcase did turn up much later that night when Cavanagh and I conducted a search outside the restaurant where the suspected theft had taken place. I found it hidden in a low hedge near to where the thugs had parked their cars. Obviously they had stolen it in the doorway and stashed it in the hedge when they saw me still in the car park, hoping to come back for it some time later when the coast was clear. I thought Cavanagh was going to cry when he saw it and to this day I would dearly like to know what was in that bag for which he was prepared to risk our lives.

An accidental encounter likewise had a lot to do with the next life-threatening research experience I was to have. While I was once more engaged in research on boxing this, in itself, had nothing directly to do with the fact that I came face to face with an IRA gun man. I was carrying out fieldwork for the BBC who had hired me as a consultant to a production team which was making a documentary about a boxing club in north Belfast. I was also using this as an opportunity to gather information for a book about boxing in diverse cultural settings:

It was Halloween and we were filming a bonfire scene in the middle of the New Lodge housing estate because some of the young boys who boxed at the local club were having some fun with other children around a bonfire while watching a fireworks display. The New Lodge is a stronghold of Irish nationalism and is controlled by various factions of Irish Republican paramilitaries. The strongest of these groups is the Provisional IRA and we had to seek permission from them in order to be allowed in the area, particularly for filming. Unbeknown to us, throughout Belfast the Provos were using the cover of Halloween to assert their authority over another Republican faction, the INLA (Irish National Liberation Army) who they had accused of being too closely involved with drug dealing.

We were filming about 50 yards back from the group around the bonfire when two hooded men stepped out of the shadows and grabbed another man who was standing watching the fire, dragging him off through our camera angle back into the shadows before disappearing around the back of a block of flats. The camera man cast a concerned look towards the young producer who passed it onto me. I went off to find what was happening only to see a group of men frog marching their victim down a back alley. "If he's lucky he'll only lose his knee caps" I said to the producer when I came back. Just when I was beginning to think that we had not been noticed the two original hooded captors returned and came over to us. I had been living in Northern Ireland for more than ten years but this was the first time I had come face to face (or at least half face) with a terrorist.

The ring leader walked straight up to the camera man and with no emotion in his voice commanded, "Provisional IRA, give us the film". Immediately the producer interceded, "Look I'm sorry we caught you on shot, but it's not that kind of film, there's no way you could be identified, besides, we've got permission to film here". The IRA man stared straight through her and repeated his order, this time with a little more sternness in his voice at which the producer turned to me and pleaded, "John, can't you do something?".

"Like what" I thought, "take notes, wet myself, run?" Instead I heard myself restating her own position, while trying to sound as friendly and 'in the know' as possible, "Listen pal we've no interest in you, we're just filming those kids over there and as she says the film's...". Before I could finish the sentence a rather large looking revolver was being pointed at my head, "Provisional IRA give us the fucking film!" shouted the hooded figure at the other end of the gun. "Andy" I said quietly to the camera man, trying to keep the tremble out of my voice, "give him the fucking film, now".

We explained that this was a technical task which would have to be done back at the van which was parked around the other side of the flats. The terrorists reluctantly agreed and we were marched to the van seated behind the wheel of which was Stan, a local hard man whom we had hired as a minder. "Stan, can't you do something about this?" implored the producer. Stan looked uncomfortable. Nevertheless he turned to the gunman and said, "Come on Badger, give them a break, they're not doing any harm". "No names Stanley!" yelled Badger, obviously displeased that our minder had given away the fact that he had recognised him. I was none too pleased myself: the last thing I needed in this situation was for one of them to think that I could identify him to the RUC [police]!

Meanwhile at the back of the van the camera man and his assistant were making heavy weather of getting the film out of the camera. It was not like an ordinary video cassette and it was highly unlikely that the IRA brigade who were taking it had the technology on hand to view it. It was never disclosed to me but I am almost certain that a switch was worked and they gave the Provos a blank tape. Anyway, cassette in hand they melted away into the darkness. Once they had gone, Andy, the camera man, veteran of many minor war fronts, passed around with a shaking hand the half bottle of dark rum which he kept in his inside pocket for such occasions. As I took a mouthful it occurred to me that even though in this case a gun had been pointed at me and I was pretty scared, I did not feel I was in mortal danger, unlike when Cavanagh was being shoved into the boot of the gangster's Camero in New England.

Two nights later I was ringside in a local hotel not far away from where this incident had taken place checking on an unlicensed night of boxing to see if it would be worth filming at a later date. To my horror I recognised the man sitting at the table in front of me (an anorak hood can only conceal so much). My worst fears were confirmed when a passer by called out, "hey Badger, what about ye?". Now not only did I know the identity of an IRA gun man, but I also knew where he drank.

Once I got safely away from the place it did cross my mind whether or not I should use the confidential phone line and pass this information to the RUC. That I did not continues to bother me and I only hope that nobody has suffered because of my decision. It had to be a matter of judgement. If I had passed information to the security forces, for reasons of personal safety, there is no way that I could have continued my field work. Moreover, one of the unwritten rules of the boxing fraternity in Belfast is that politics and related events are kept outside of the gymnasium. If it became known (and in north Belfast secrets are as rare as snakes) that I had used my position as a researcher under the protection of the Holy Family Boxing Club to inform on a local IRA operative, it is highly unlikely that I would have been allowed to continue my research there. The ethical rule of thumb I obeyed here is that although I witnessed an illegal event, I did not take part in it and as such, my presence in the field did not make a contribution to that act.

The final scenario relates to field work which I recently carried out in Cuba. When this particular event took place I was hanging around the back streets of Havana trying to get a feel for the social milieu which produces some of the world's best amateur boxers. There are some who would think that even going to Cuba at a time when many Cubans were trying to escape from Castro's crumbling socialist experiment was in and of itself a perilous undertaking, particularly if one was determined to live outside of the tourist's cocoon. For the most part my experiences suggested that this view was mistaken. However, once in a while I did find myself in situations which could have got me into serious trouble with the Cuban authorities. The following extract, which is taken unedited from my field notes, should illustrate what I mean:

> Social life in old Havana is three dimensional. In the first place there are those Cubans who live in the slums all year round and who stoically persevere with their poverty. The problem for them is that their poverty is picturesque. Falling down, 200 years old, Spanish colonial apartments with dejected, but white teethed Cubans at the open doors and windows offer great photo opportunities for tourists (and photo-journalists). The presence of ancient buildings such as San Cristobol Cathedral, *el Palicio de los Capitanos Generales* and *el Castilllo de la Real Fuerza* likewise has the tourists flooding in as do more recent additions such as the Revolution Museum and *El Bodigito de Medio*, a bar famously frequented by Ernest Hemingway when he lived and wrote in Cuba. Thus shoulder-to-shoulder with Cubans who can expect to earn no more than the equivalent of $5 per week are flocks of tourists, many of whom are spending more than $100 per day (20 times the average local weekly income).

Under these circumstances it is not surprising that the third dimension of old Havana exists somewhere in between the stoic locals and the influx of tourists. These are Cuba's underworld: the black marketeers, *jiniteros* and varieties of prostitutes whose main aim in life is to gain access to the multi-million dollar tourist economy and profit from it.

Undoubtedly the best place to dwell within this nether region of old Havana is in the Paris Cafe which is in the heart of old Havana on the corner of *Calle Obispo* and *Calle San Ignacio*. This is a place where old Havana's underworld goes when it's not working. It is no more than 200 metres from *El Bodigito de Medio*, one of the city's biggest tourist attractions, but it is rare to see foreigners inside the Paris Cafe. Because it is a dollar only establishment it is equally rare to see "ordinary" Cubans there. It is open for 24 hours a day, but the best time to go is between 12 midnight and 6 am during which period many of old Havana's characters and their entourages will pass through.

Initially, the Paris Cafe can feel intimidating to non Cubans. There is always a heavy police presence outside the large arched entrance and an even larger crowd of locals milling around outside, either waiting for a table or simply interested in watching the social interaction taking place within. The cafe is dominated by a large hardwood bar behind which Cuba's equivalent to Bet Lynch serves small draughts of cheap German larger and cans of Hatuey, the almost undrinkable local beer. A small army of waiters scurry about, ferrying drinks and plates of over-done chicken and *patatas fritas* (thin fried potatoes) to customers at the 10 or so small tables which take up the rest of the Cafe.

The intimidating atmosphere of the place fades as I realise that I am far less accessible here than in other, more tourist oriented bars and that most of the clientele are here for their own good time and are not, at this stage of the evening, interested in hustling foreigners. The best place to be is at the bar, especially if you can get the bar stool close to criss-cross wooded screen which divides the cafe from *Calle Obispo*. From this vantage point it is possible to watch the comings and goings of the bar as well as keep and eye on the chaotic street life of old Havana. It is hard to avoid the impression of stepping out of one zoo and into another, however, as passers by regularly pause at the screen to stare at the people inside the bar.

The next time I am in the Paris Cafe I am invited to join a table of young Cubans who are obviously in the midst of a good night out. One is wearing a 1994 USA soccer World Cup t-shirt and we immediately have a point of common interest. His bad English and my bad Spanish dove-tail perfectly and we manage to have a decent conversation. He tells me proudly that his name is Laredo and that he is named after a town in Texas in the United States. With his mop of curly brown hair and pale olive-brown complexion, Laredo looks more Greek than Cuban. He would like to visit the town which is named after him one day, he informs me with a laugh. Laredo's voice drops to a whisper as he admits that he has been in prison for two years after having been caught trying to escape to Florida. (Is there a young Cuban who has not done time in the pursuit of freedom I wonder?)

Laredo is 26, handsome, intelligent and very dissatisfied with his life in Cuba. The fact that he has been in prison for trying to flee the country means that he is unable to get a decent job — not that this would be worth much in terms of salary, but at least he would have some self respect. He complains about being constantly harassed by the police and produces a piece of paper which tells me that he has had his car confiscated because he acquired it through improper channels — that is, without seeking the permission of the state which would have been denied because of his 'criminal' record. He believes that 30 years ago the revolution was good for Cuba because it got rid of much of the corruption and injustice which had become institutionalised under successive dictatorships. However, he thinks that the revolution has now become stagnant and has failed the people, largely because Castro has stubbornly refused to adapt his view of political economy, despite radical changes in the rest of the world. Even worse, he believes that Castro's Cuba has become as corrupt and dictatorial as the Cuba of Batista. Ché Guevara could see this happening, he tells me, which is why he left to fight and die in Bolivia.

The more beer Laredo drinks the more vociferous he becomes. He insists on an anti-Castro toast and I find myself spontaneously joining him. I am uncomfortable about this in more ways than one. In my days as an Essex undergraduate I held Castro and his revolution in high esteem. While I have come to recognise the many failings of his regime I feel vaguely treacherous cheering for his downfall. Of more pressing concern is the close proximity of armed, paramilitary police who are beginning to pay undue attention to the goings on at our table.

Laredo finishes his anti-Castro polemic and begins to entertain us with a series of conjuring tricks which he learned in prison. Salsa is blaring from the cafe's hi-fi and some people begin to dance in the aisles between the tables. A young black man approaches our table to whisper with Laredo before leaving. Five minutes later he returns and, with a policeman standing no further than three yards away surreptitiously slips Laredo a small silver paper package of what I assume to be drugs of some description. It is an ingenious pass. The dealer has the package concealed beneath his watch strap. He shakes hands with Laredo and as he does so Laredo's middle finger dislodges the drugs from behind the watch strap and flicks them into the palm of his hand. The policeman is looking, but he sees nothing.... Nevertheless I think it is time for me to leave.

This final episode was in no way life-threatening, but I could have easily ended up being arrested, locked up and even deported for seditious behaviour and/or drug dealing. Apart from anything else this would have seriously undermined my capacity to carry out any further research in the country and it is certain that I would have been barred by the Cuban authorities from having any kind of access to the country's elite athletes, including the boxers. However, if I wanted to get deeper insights into the general lived experience of being young in Havana I felt that it was necessary to get close to people like Laredo and his friends.

The researcher cannot suddenly back-off from the reality which he or she needs to grasp the moment that the situation becomes threatening. As Evans-Pritchard argued in his classic series of lectures on social anthropology in exotic locations, the field worker "has no choice but to follow the cultural grain" and must "abandon himself without reserve" to the events he is immersed within (Evans-Pritchard, 1951b: pp. 82–83). In other words, when the sheep's eyes are passed around, you eat one. Equally, without similar guiding principles it is hard to imagine that the Chicago School and those who followed them would have learned much in the mean streets of Los Angeles — or the back streets of old Havana. In this case the anti-Castro toast was a spontaneous gesture which enabled me to win respect among a group who would later provide me with valuable information. Had I refused to participate, in the words of Fetterman, I would have risked committing "methodological suicide" (Fetterman, 1989: p. 136). As such I felt that the risks involved were worth taking, but only up to a point. Like many other people, I have seen *Midnight Express* and did not relish the prospect of comparing a few years in a Cuban prison with its Turkish counterpart.

Conclusion

Even the everyday lives which we know so well are fraught with risks. Indeed the routines which we establish to get ourselves through the day are, at least in part, designed to minimise these risks. We cross roads in safe places, buy houses in crime free neighbourhoods, stay out of areas with bad reputations, associate with people we know, like and trust and so forth. Even so, from time to time we have accidents, have our cars stolen and some of us even get mugged (recently on my way through London to do some field work in the United States my luggage was stolen). For the most part, however, the routines which structure our day-to-day lives are constructed in ways which minimise risks — as a result of which our lives are often boring, but relatively safe. When we take the decision to undertake ethnographic research we are electing to step outside of these familiar and relatively secure routines and once we take to the field the chances of encountering threatening situations are increased.

What I have presented are a few relatively extreme examples of the kind of trouble which a researcher can encounter while engaged in ethnographic research. Of course it is not absolutely necessary to select 'darkest' Africa, American ghettos, Irish nationalist and Republican housing estates and besieged communist dictatorships as venues for this kind of work. Nevertheless, I would argue that there are elements of risk in all forms of ethnography if only because by definition, when we are engaged in ethnographic research we are working within social and political contexts with which we do not have, at least at the outset, intimate familiarity. This initial lack of familiarity renders the ethnographer vulnerable.

Furthermore, unlike as is generally the case with positivistic research designs, we cannot control the research environment. When out in the field things will happen which we cannot prevent (and neither should we seek to) and which will face us with ethical dilemmas and/or place us in physical jeopardy. When this happens, the extent to which we 'stay with the action' then becomes a question of professional judgement balanced with considerations of personal safety. Should I have refused to "follow that car" and lose a valuable contact in the murky world of American professional boxing? Should I have 'turned in' the IRA operative and exiled myself from research in north Belfast? Was it necessary to share anti-Castro toasts with shady characters in old Havana to illicit the truth about what it is like to be young in contemporary Cuba? The answer to all of these questions could have been yes or no. That, in the heat of the ethnographic moment, I chose to answer yes, undoubtedly enhanced my credentials with those upon whom I was dependent for authentic information. I would argue that two out of three of these decisions could be justified on ethical grounds because I was involved in events which would have happened irrespective of my presence in the field, and because I did not take a significant role in them. On reflection I now have a few reservations about my performance in the Rhode Island car chase, primarily because I was a key actor in an affair which probably would not have happened in the first place if I had not set up the meeting with Cavanagh. Also, it now strikes me that taking a proactive role in the car chase went beyond the call of an ethnographer's duty.

Giddens (1976) points out — albeit from his armchair — that while in order to get close to authentic social data we must 'immerse' ourselves in a chosen milieu, there must be limits to how much we become like the people whom we are seeking to understand. We need to develop empathy with our subjects without getting emotionally tied to them. Easier said than done. As the experiences outlined herein illustrate, there can be a grey area between understanding natives and going native. A few of my own simple 'rules' might help:

— Be up front about the research role; remember, we are not secret agents and neither are we investigative journalists, although occasionally we may borrow information-gathering techniques from either camp.
— Neither are we *agent provocateurs* — we should not set in motion procedures which otherwise would not have happened in order to unearth interesting material.

— We are interested in naturally emergent (or concealed) social truths, not good stories.

— Under (almost) all circumstances we should stay within the laws which govern the land within which we are operating.

We may follow all of these 'rules' and still get caught in a flow of interaction which leads us into trouble or reveals to us information about criminal or other forms of anti-social activity. This leads me to the hardest rule of all:

— Never "tell".

That is, never reveal your sources, because — irrespective of the nature of the event witnessed — by reporting it and those involved to a higher authority you not only violate your own research role, but you also endanger the ethnographer as a species. And there are few enough of us as it is. If we choose to work at the coal face or the cutting edge of social construction, we should not be too surprised if, from time to time, we get a little dirty or a little bloody.

References

Becker, H. (1963) *Outsiders: Studies in the sociology of deviance.* New York: Free Press.

Buford, W. (1991) *Among the thugs.* London: Secker and Warburg.

Cohen. A. K. (1955) *Delinquent boys — the subculture of the gang.* London: Collier-MacMillan.

Durkheim, E. (1964) *The rules of sociological method.* New York: Free Press.

Evans-Pritchard, E. (1951a) *Kinship and marriage among the Nuer.* Oxford: Clarendon Press.

———— (1951b) *Social anthropology.* London: Cohen and West.

Fetterman, D. (1989) *Ethnography step by step.* London: Sage.

Giddens, A. (1976) *New rules of sociological method.* London: Hutchinson.

Giulanotti, R. (1995) 'Participant observation and research into football hooliganism: Reflections on the problems of entrée and everyday risks', *Sociology of Sport Journal*, Vol. 12, No. 1: pp. 1-20.

Hall, S. and Jefferson, T. (eds) (1975) *Resistance through rituals.* London: Hutchinson.

Hammersley, M. and Atkinson, P. (1983) *Ethnography, principles and practice.* London: Tavistock.

Marsh, P. (1978) *The rules of disorder.* London: Routledge.

Mills, C. Wright (1970) *The sociological imagination.* Harmondsworth: Penguin.

Polsky, N. (1971) *Hustlers, beats and others.* Harmondsworth: Penguin.

Robins, D. and Cohen, P. (1978) *Knuckle sandwich.* Harmondsworth: Penguin.

Thompson, E.P. (1968) *The making of the English working class.* Harmondsworth: Penguin.

Whyte, W. (1955) *Street corner society.* Chicago: University of Chicago Press.

Williams, J., Dunning, E. and Murphy, P. (1984) *Hooligans abroad.* London: Routledge.

Williams, R. (1977) *Marxism and literature.* Oxford: Oxford University Press.

Willis, P. (1977) *Learning to labour — how working-class kids get working-class jobs.* Farnborough: Saxon House.

Wirth, L. (1928) *The ghetto.* Chicago: University of Chicago Press.

FLATTERY AND BETRAYAL: OBSERVATIONS ON QUALITATIVE AND ORAL SOURCES

Alan Tomlinson
University of Brighton

Opening comments

Much qualitative research is premised on gaining access to particular types of sources, and making connections between different exemplars of a source, or between different types of source. This is true of both social historical research and research into contemporary society and culture. But securing access is itself an entry into a relationship — imagined, but empathetically framed, in historical work on dead individuals and events; more directly rooted and tangible in research involving living individuals and more recent or current events. And the quality of the research outcome could well be dependent upon the way in which such a relationship is established, directed, sustained and continued or terminated. In this sense qualitative research is itself a complex social dynamic. It can change lives, of subjects and of researchers. It can be intrusive, disrupting established views of things, with unpredictable effects.

At times the subject in the qualitative research dynamic is exploited in ways comparable to how the media might seduce and then abandon subjects. The critical sociologist's task can have much in common with that of the investigative journalist or reporter, and effective research and scholarship in the field can be a form of investigative sociology (Douglas, 1976: Polsky, 1971). In this context, to engage in research is to form relationships, but of a quite complex — and sometimes disingenuous — kind.

Getting close to subjects, establishing a relationship and then moving back to the territories and priorities of the researcher is often a retreat from the personal

— in some circumstances the pseudo-personal — to the professional. It can be felt as a betrayal by the subject, after the relationship had been constructed on the basis of flattery. The qualitative research process can in these senses be akin to a soaring and then soured love affair, with both accounts and outcomes open to interpretation and dispute. In reflecting on such research processes and relationships, both researcher and researched can experience a sense of false promises, guilt and regret.

In this article I reflect upon these themes, with particular emphasis upon their ethical implications. In the penultimate section, I draw upon one particular example from my own fieldwork, social historical and sociological enquiry into the working-class sport of knur-and-spell in the North West of England. First, though, to demonstrate the pervasiveness of such issues, examples of ethical reflection, or its absence, are considered in four non-academic examples — a recent debate within the print journalism profession in the USA; an adult's autobiographical account of a parent-child relationship in North-West England; a dramatic narrative of the lived culture of Savannah, Georgia, USA; and a specific piece of broadcasting on the mid-twentieth century North-East England football star Wilf Mannion, premised on oral historical sources. What binds these disparate cases together is the question of trust, in a double sense. Have the writers betrayed the trust of their subjects? And how far can we trust the sorts of data and evidence generated by what in a research sense we know as qualitative and oral historical approaches to data-gathering? Following this, some principles underlying the oral historical method are discussed, and then the elements of flattery and betrayal characteristic of my own oral historical fieldwork are considered. I conclude with not so much a manifesto for the ethics of oral historical fieldwork in sports and leisure cultures, rather a checklist for the realistic and unpretentious investigator.

Writing and power

In ethical terms, the researcher must be prepared to cope with a condition of what the North American journalist Janet Malcolm has identified as the "moral ambiguity of journalism" which "lies not in its texts but in the relationships out of which they arise — relationships that are invariably and inescapably lopsided" (cited in Wood, 1994: p.42). For Malcolm, the journalist-subject dynamic routinely exemplifies a *Promethean theft* practised by all journalists on their victims; the relationship has, inherently as far as Malcolm is concerned, an *authoritarian structure.* The upshot of Malcolm's position is that, as she puts it herself, journalism is "morally indefensible".

Malcolm examines — as an example of what (from the point of view of social science methodology) is an interpretive dilemma — the work by the erstwhile New Journalist writer, Joe McGinniss, on the murderer Jeffrey MacDonald, entitling her book *The Journalist and the Murderer.* McGinnis had spent several years collaborating with a convicted murderer on a book of the latter's life, agreeing to share royalties on the basis of privileged access to material. But during the course of the process McGinnis, who had initially believed in Mac-Donald's innocence, came to believe that the 'murderer' was in fact guilty, and "turned the book into the biography of a monster" (Wood, 1994: p.42). Regardless of this change of mind, McGinnis continued to act out with MacDonald the role of privileged and empathetic insider. On publication, the murderer took the journalist to court, successfully suing for fraud and breach of contract.

Research based on privileged access is inherently caught up in this dynamic of moral ambiguity, and the tensions arising out of the unequal power relationship between the writer and the subject. Issues that arise include: the openness of the investigator *vis-à-vis* his/her motive; the integrity of the investigative project, so justifying pragmatic methodological decisions; and the dynamic of dissemination in which whatever is proposed as reciprocal becomes dominated by the investigator's professional needs and interests.

Publicising the private

In his moving account of his relationship with his father, Blake Morrison points to some important ethical issues. The book, *And when did you last see your father?* (Morrison, 1994), is a reminiscence upon the highs and lows of Morrison's relationship with his family, focusing particularly upon his father. The book is anchored in the process of his father's dying, and the memories that the knowledge of this imminent death provoke in the early middle-aged son. With his poet's and reporter's eye, Morrison captures the intimate dialogues and dynamics of imminent death in the family. These exchanges are reported in speech marks, authenticating the reportage. This also sets a convention, a trust and expectation between writer and reader, that is then used in the relating of some episodes of family and childhood life when, presumably, Morrison did not take notes. The presumed authenticity of the contemporary validates in format what is reported from the long-distant past. There is no need for Morrison, the poet, literary and feature journalist and now autobiographer, to justify the strategy or method employed in the documentation of his father's dying days, or the literary cum journalistic devices employed in reporting those days. We know that in a way Morrison is writing literature as a creative writer. But we know too that this is true to life. It is a beautifully accomplished and artfully crafted text, capturing the essence of the relationships within the middle-class professional family in the not-quite-rural, certainly not urban, setting of North East Lancashire's Pendle country. We feel for the young primary schoolboy Morrison stuck in the weekend traffic snarl-up waiting to get into the motor-racing event. We understand the binding ties of the father-son trips to Turf Moor, Burnley Football Club's ground, during the days when Burnley battled with Tottenham Hotspur for the status of England's top football team. Yet we know that Morrison must have embellished some of the memories, must have sculpted some of the reported dialogue as if scripting a play or a movie. We trust his accounts for their feel, and not for their factuality.

Morrison has written a painfully intimate account, implicating not just himself but also those close to him. The young woman who lived for a while in the household to help run things whilst the dual-doctor parents medicated to the surrounding community also initiated the young Blake into sex. And the family outings often included a friend of the family, "Auntie" Beaty, Arthur Morrison's special friend. Morrison imagines his father talking to him about the developing book:

> "'Let's hear about some of the good times, the holidays, the golf and tennis. What's the big deal about death? No, tell them how good with my hands I could be, all the fun we had and things we built, how I loved you and Gill and Mummy, how I tried to leave the world a better place. And leave Auntie Beaty out of it; it was a phase, no more. There are people who have to be protected here. What else is there to say?'
>
> Yes, Dad, I know I should leave Beaty out, but she is part of your story, and of mine. 'Auntie Beaty', rather: you always called her that, as if the name could give her status as one of the family, as a relation or godparent, one of us, or perhaps because it seemed natural to a man who called his wife 'Mummy' to call the other woman he loved 'Auntie'."
> (Morrison, 1994: pp. 210-211)

After Arthur Morrison's death Beaty became very friendly with his widow, and Blake himself pursued her for detail of her relationship with his father — with "kind, forgiving words ... there in part to draw her out, to snare her like a robin in the snow" (p. 212). Beaty's letter to Blake Morrison is reproduced in its entirety, simultaneously an admission of her affair with his father, and a refusal to go into detail on it: "'Dear Blake, Arthur always said never to put anything in writing" is followed by a moving tribute to the importance of Blake's father in her life, and a recognition of how much Arthur loved his family:

> "I know he loved your mother more than anybody on earth ... Please leave me one last small piece — it's mine. Whatever sadness I am sorry for. Your loving Beaty." (p. 213)

Blake Morrison showed his mother and sister the typescript, removing all references to which there were objections. This process was a form of corroboration: "there's some consensus on how we see my father — mine wasn't a wilful or eccentric version they seem to think" (Morrison, 1995). But the place of Beaty in the book was not corroborated in this way. Morrison's mother did not want her to know of the book, and Morrison changed the name and, slightly, "all the details of her life". I asked Blake Morrison whether he saw any problems in using a private source — the Beaty letter — in such a public way: " ... my solution to the ethical dilemma about using the letter was to change it slightly ... Now, after an awkward patch when she'd first read the book, we talk on the phone occasionally. Everyone's been very brave, or liberal, or forgiving, I'm not sure which" (Morrison, 1995).

No researcher's ethical code constrained Morrison's creative urges, and his book threatens the sanctity of the private and the interpersonal. But as everyone in his book was already enmeshed in the same interpersonal networks, he could negotiate his relationships with his subjects in a genuine and continuing relationship. Any apparent betrayal of confidence in this case could be construed as a shared revelation. Not all writers have, inbuilt, such a degree of accountability.

Beyond the brochures

John Berendt's book *Midnight in the Garden of Good and Evil — A Savannah Story* is a gripping account of the culture of Savannah, Georgia, in the 1980s. The narrative revolves around a controversial murder case, in which a wealthy but nouveau riche individual, Jim Williams, is tried for the murder, in May 1981, of a young man, Danny Hansford (a "walking streak of sex", as one Savannah College of Art and Design student put it [Berendt, 1994: p.130]). Williams lived in the fashionable Monterey Square, one of the town's 21 famous squares. His wealth is founded on antique-dealing and house-restoring in an Old South town which is seeking its salvation or at least recovery by forms of urban redevelopment. Berendt lived in Savannah (on and off) for eight years, and enters the public culture of Savannah and reveals its volatile underbelly: its bohemian art-college elements; the social and cultural ossification of its established elite; and the sexual worlds of transsexuality and gay culture. One black transsexual, Chablis (aka The Lady or the bitch) becomes a key gatekeeper for Berendt. A world of cultural jealousies and betrayals emerges, presented as existing on the margins of the town yet central to it: "But the Savannahians rarely went anywhere at all. They could not be bothered. They were content to remain in their isolated city under self-imposed house arrest. There were exceptions, of course, and Chablis was one of them" (p. 168). The book also documents a world of voodoo and superstition, interlinked with the apparently sophisticated world of institutional justice.

Berendt's reconstruction of this notorious case, and of the cultural dynamics of the changing urban landscape of Savannah, is based upon observation, use of appropriate documents, encounters, interviews and (for the purposes of effect, authenticity and immediacy), a sense of authorial interaction with the characters in the narrative, conveyed through reported dialogue. It is a widely-hailed feat of reportage and writing, and any visitor to Savannah would do well to become acquainted with Berendt's book as well as any tourist paraphernalia that is offered to the arriving visitor. For with a book like Berendt's more sense can be made of the avant-garde, hedonistic, sexually varied semi-public cultures of the city — none of which are featured in the official brochures, or, in one of the town's most famous recent representations, the simpleton's smile on the face of Tom Hanks sitting on his bench in the 1993 film *Forrest Gump*.

Jim Williams died in 1990 soon after finally being acquitted of the murder after trial after trial and retrial, almost nine years after the death of Danny Hansford. Two days after Williams' funeral, Berendt watched and eavesdropped on a tour guide in a horse and carriage which pulled up outside Williams' Monterey Square home, Mercer House. She was:

"... telling her three passengers that General Hugh Mercer had built the house during the Civil war, that the songwriter Johnny Mercer had grown up in it, and that Jacqueline Onassis had once offered to buy it for $2 million. To this by-now familiar routine, the tour guide added that film-makers had used the house the previous spring to shoot scenes for the movie *Glory*. But she said nothing about Jim Williams or Danny Hansford or the sensational murder case that had captivated the city for so long. The tourists would leave Savannah in a few hours, enchanted by the elegance of this romantic garden city but none the wiser about the secrets that lay within the innermost glades of its secluded bower". (p. 387)

Secrets, then, ignored in the marketing of a heritage-led tourist image of the town, but explicitly told in Berendt's evocative, often comic depiction of the town's personalities, private idiosyncrasies and public obsessions.

For Berendt, too, much of this was revealed to him because he had penetrated the perimeter fence of Savannah's jealously guarded identity. He reports how superstar entertainers such as Eric Clapton and Sting could only attract half a capacity crowd to Savannah's auditoriums; how "Savannah was invariably gracious to strangers, but it was immune to their charms. It wanted nothing so much as to be left alone" (p. 387). In the end, for Berendt, it is this "resistance to change" that was the "saving grace" of the place, paradoxically allowing the place to *grow inward* as he calls it, its people flourishing in ways so that: "The ordinary became extraordinary. Eccentrics thrived. Every nuance and quirk of personality achieved greater brilliance in that lush enclosure than would have been possible anywhere else in the world" (p. 388).

To gain access to this world Berendt had to mix with a range of residents, gain the confidence of potential gatekeepers, sustain social relationships and, presumably, manipulate those relationships in the sense that he could rarely tell all that he began to know of the social and cultural dynamics of the Savannah community — that is, until publication. He flattered his subjects and respondents, as in any developing passionate relationship, before gradually withdrawing to construct fully his version of that world. He sought not to betray those subjects, calling upon the principle of anonymisation in appropriate cases, but the version, with its nuances and inflections, is his, not theirs. There is always the lurking possibility of betrayal in such work, because there is interpretation, and the writer's hermeneutic will not necessarily match the lived hermeneutic of all of his/her subjects. Berendt is responsible on this, and his author's note is worth citing fully:

"The characters in this book are real, but it bears mentioning that I have used pseudonyms for a number of them in order to protect their privacy, and in a few cases I have gone a step further by altering their descriptions. Though this is a work of non-fiction, I have taken certain story-telling liberties, particularly having to do with the timing of events. Where the narrative strays from strict non-fiction, my intention has been to remain faithful to the characters and to the essential drift of events as they really happened." (unpaginated *Author's Note*, following p. 388)

Berendt's book has had an effect. It changes the boundaries of possibility in the town's image, and, potentially, in the perceptions of visitors to the town. Certainly to explore the town with Berendt as a guide[1] rather than the official tourist brochures is to make fuller sense of the place of SCAD (the Savannah College of Art and Design), the bohemian art-school bars, and the immigrant cultures of the town. The key ethical questions which can be raised here are whether Berendt has created a faithful image of the town, and whether the "actuality" principle which he has adopted is in the interests of his subjects, his confidantes and his work. A purist ethical line in some areas of social sciences would always argue that the researcher should anonymise the sources and contexts reported in the research — classically, in say the sociology of education, a case-study school is given a fictitious name; or names of subjects are changed in participation-observation studies. Researchers may have guaranteed anonymity to those subjects who knew what they were up to, but such anonymising strategies are often ineffective: the network of scholarly gossip being what it is, the location of the study is exposed; or the veiling process is a relatively superficial one, such as, to contrive an hypothetical but illustrative example, "a prominent elite football club with Protestant sympathies in one of Scotland's two major cities". It would not take demanding detective work to identify the source in a description of this kind. Berendt, of course, had similar professional scruples, as the *Author's Note* reveals — but it is the integrity of his project that guides him: faithfulness to character and "the essential drift of events". Berendt controls the narrative in his work, selects the juxtapositions in the telling of the tale — on this telling there will inevitably be a distanciation from the sources. Subjects will feel misrepresented, respondents betrayed. Some social scientific researchers would do well to recognise as honestly the problems in such work, and to relate with real probity the actual devices employed in moving from the field to the account/interpretive text.

Corroborating memories

Wilf Mannion played professional football for the football club Middlesbrough, in the North-East of England, peaking in the years immediately after the Second World War. He is remembered as, at his prime, one of the greatest players of all-time in his home region, and, more widely, as one of the greatest players of his era. Capturing, in documentary form, the essence of a physical culture and the prowess of a sports performer within a physical culture is problematic, particularly in a relatively early if not primitive phase of the moving-image industry's technological development. Oral accounts of Mannion's impact as a player evoke an image of a magician with a football, a man whose dazzling talent at football transformed him from a shy, inarticulate man off the field to an extrovert maestro on it. A television documentary (BBC Television [North-East], 1978) sought to capture the repute in which Mannion was held, and it is the filmed oral account of a fan — not the newsreel of a performance, not the press report, not Mannion's own modest memories — which captures the impact of the player. Here is a quote from the commentary, in that clipped upper-class tone of the Pathé newsreel announcer, of one of the most famous of Mannion's performances, playing for Great Britain against the Rest of Europe, at Hampden Park, Glasgow in May 1947. After Mannion's goal making and goal taking skills are commended in the match report, it is observed that Mannion must be, without doubt, "One of the most notable discoveries in modern football".

In the television feature Mannion himself faithfully recalled that game and his contribution to it, his recollection consistent with an earlier publicised account in which he modestly acknowledged the "team spirit, and nothing else, which gained that very convincing victory" (Kelly, 1993: p. 160). Mannion reiterates here a written version from close to twenty years previously, almost certainly ghosted in origin. And he also recalls, in the documentary, "the match which provided me with my greatest thrill" (Kelly, 1993: p.160), a game against Blackpool in November 1947. Mannion on video confirms the earlier accounts of Mannion in print — he had become engaged to be married earlier that day, and indulged himself in the game to show off his skills to his fiancée Bernadette, attending her first football match. But the power and the impact of such performances is conveyed most effectively by the fan interviewed in the documentary. Tom, a stalwart Ayresome Park 'Bob Ender', recalls:

"He was magic, he 'ad everything. He was just like a ballerina ... always three yards ahead of everybody else .... Radar was invented long before the last war — Wilfie 'ad it. When 'e spread 'is 'ands like that ... he 'ad the radar in his fingertips. He'd dip ... I've seen 'im beat men, two men behind 'im from a throw in ... never touch the ball ..... When you mention South Bank you're talking about the Enchanted City as far as we're concerned, anybody born in South Bank, he's gifted."

And in the Blackpool game:

"What Wilf did, when 'e 'ad the ball on 'is 'ead one moment and ran fifteen, twenty yards with the ball balanced on 'is 'ead...the owd wings flying there.... I'm not sure whether 'e let it roll down 'is back and brought it over with a back kick and then knocked it in with 'is shoulder.... It was magical."

It is the poetic licence, the passionate expressivity of this account that renders it of such value. The point is not so much what Mannion did or did not do on that particular Saturday at Ayresome Park thirty years previously; rather, it is the fact of the persisting resonances of Mannion's contribution to local sports cultures and folklore, what Mannion is remembered as being capable of. Oral accounts of the extra-ordinary may fluctuate from any faithfully realistic narrative. But that is their very value. They express the depth of feeling, and the power of popular memory in perpetuating that feeling, that contribute towards the buoyancy of a local culture. We do not need to trust such accounts as literal, for that is not the point. Rather, they are *trustworthy* as embodiments of cultural values. Glossed, perhaps, by the haze of (sometimes alcoholically stimulated) reminiscence and nostalgia, they nevertheless provide corroboration of the less tangible but often remarkably durable dimensions of a culture; to distrust their authenticity is a potential cultural betrayal.

Oral sources: a proven need

The contribution of oral evidence to the development of a fuller social history and sociology of sport and leisure has become increasingly widely recognised, particularly for popular cultural and working-class leisure forms. As Paul

Thompson notes:

> Since such leisure activities rarely leave many records, they cannot be seriously examined without oral evidence. There have been recent oral history studies of particular leisure forms such as jazz bands, kazoo bands, fairs, and baseball, and also of the role, more extensive in its social historical ramifications, of the role of the public house. (Thompson, 1988: p.94)

Elite cultures often documented their own practices, in meetings, minutes, or memoirs for instance. Popular cultural practices, equally important to a wider social and cultural context, have often gone un-documented. The oral source is often the only entry point to the recovering of such experience, and has the capacity to stimulate what has been evocatively described by Yeo and Yeo (1981) as a form of discovery: "History in this sense is a matter of arousing sleeping forms..." (pp. 141-142).

Such sources obviously have to be treated with caution, as the cases so far considered demonstrate: "'oral evidence', just as with any other sort of evidence, has to be carefully collected and painstakingly analysed" (Lummis, 1987: p.155). Lummis champions the cause of oral evidence, whose "value ... as a historical source must ultimately be established within its own authenticity" (*ibid.*), and points out — importantly — that if the oral source is authenticated only by confirmation through documentary sources, then it is undervalued and marginalised, and the researcher might as well use just the documents.

For Thompson, oral history is not merely an investigative method; it is a humanistic project with radical and transformative possibilities, making contact and understanding between social classes and generations, challenging "the accepted myths of history". It is a "history built around people. It thrusts life into history itself and it widens its scope. It allows heroes not just from the leaders, but from the unknown majority of the people" (Thompson, 1988: p. 21).

But what if the account is dubious? Or if the same source renders inconsistent accounts? Or if some respondents feel tempted to render heroic accounts of themselves at the expense of others? Interesting ethical questions are raised in reflecting upon the status of the oral evidence, the authenticity of the oral account, and the nature of the researcher-researched relationship — questions which touch upon the flattery-betrayal dynamic as much as upon the empowerment/liberation model that characterises much of the work on oral historical method.

Laikers remember — Ernest, Sam and Herbert

Drawing upon my own oral historical work on the nature and context of the sport knur-and-spell (Tomlinson, 1992)[2], this section draws upon interviews and discussions with three of my key respondents and reflects upon the themes of flattery, betrayal and trust.

My fieldwork on knur-and-spell was carried out in the early 1980s, and an initial search for sources was through the letter column of the local newspaper in Colne, North-East Lancashire. I had been intrigued to read in the *Oxford Companion to Sports and Games* (Arlott, 1975, pp.578-581) of the history of knur-and-spell, often called "poor man's golf" or "tipping". It had thrived particularly in the cotton towns of North-East Lancashire and the factory towns of North-West Yorkshire, yet I had not heard of it, even though I was raised in the area, had always been and still was active in sports and had gone on to teach the social history and sociology of sport at degree level. What was the substance to the entry in the *Oxford Companion*? I determined to follow this up, and was afforded the resources for this by the British Academy, which awarded me a Small Grant for Research in the Humanities to go beyond the initial enquiries that I had set up from a distance.

Researching knur-and-spell meant gaining the confidence of a number of former players or 'laikers', usually elderly people, who were interested in a young researcher's interest in them and their sporting biographies, but in some cases simultaneously cautious about the motives of an outsider. Too many media people, potential sponsors, outsiders had rampaged through the history of this activity for them to be welcomed and trusted on the spot. Also, different individuals had varying stakes in the history of the game, and in the networks implicated in the protection of the game's place in history. A look at three interviewees shows the complexities involved in researching lived cultures and retrieving cultural histories and traditions.

Ernest Thornton

Ernest Thornton (83 years old, born 1894) answered my initial letter to the local press. Fortuitously, he now lived in the same conurbation as I did, and we were able to talk and set up a full interview, which was conducted on 15 October 1978 in Brighton.

As a young unemployed man in the inter-war period Ernest was one of the players competing in handicap matches on Bank Holiday weekends, for instance, which drew crowds of up to 7, 000 to the grounds of pubs such as the Alma Inn, on the hills overlooking Colne. The crowds were, Ernest recalled, particularly large during the periods of higher unemployment, and when the local professional football club, Burnley, was playing its fixture away from home.

Ernest gave me a sense of the culture of the game, its rhythms and its nature, and recollected some of the characters in the game. He also let me have a photo-graph of prominent players, which I copied with a mind to using to stimulate the memories of future respondents.

For Ernest the recollections of his commitment to knur-and-spell were very personal ones, evoking a world of self-organised cultural life, outdoor, patriarchal and highly localised, and at times fiercely competitive: "...they were interested in both the tipping and the betting, and a bit of drinking afterwards".

The interview with Ernest convinced me that there was more work to be done on the sport, and led me to make the successful application to the British Academy.

Sam Ansell

The study as funded by the British Academy was to concentrate on four main sources: the oral historical evidence of past and present participants; local newspaper archives of the 1920s and the 1930s; the records of local clubs, associations and pubs; and contemporary forms of participation, including if possible any current World Championships. Most of the data generated was of the first two types, and in expanding my network of informants at the beginning of the funded study a prominent figure to emerge was Sam Ansell, at the time a sauna-bath attendant at the local municipal baths. It was clear that I had to interview Sam.

Sam Ansell (Walter Ansell, born in 1907 or 1908) spoke to me on 15 December 1980, about knur-and-spell, and again on 20 February 1981, about his own biography in more detail. Once located, it was not difficult to generate detailed responses from him; in fact, Sam's local persona had been self-cultivated by the presentation of himself as the all-round local expert:

Sam: "Mi name's Walter Ansell, but I allus get Sam ... they say that's mi nom-de-plume for TV and all that business .... I'm 73 years of age ... I've been in this game oh 50 years but I've always been interested like before 50

years … about 60 years ago I were interested but I were only a boy ….
(It's) allus bin there ever since I could walk about I think … we allus
played on a big field and it weren't allus easy to get a big field".

AT: "Did a lot of people used to play it?"

Sam: "Oh nearly everybody round here, round Colne. There was more players
in Colne and t'district than there were in t'world … 'ere, oh, nearly
everybody played knur and spell …"

AT: "Did they play it through Summer and Winter?"

Sam: "Oh, they didn't bother about weather, no, weather didn't come into it
only when snow came and then they were beat until I took 'old o't game
and he said well we can't play today cos there's snow on t' ground … I
said 'Why', 'Well' he said, 'we won't be able to find the knurs'. I said
'Well, red knurs will be used'. He says 'Are you paintin' them?'. I said
'Does it matter?'.

AT: "When did you first start playin'?"

Sam: "Misself? … Well I didn't start until I were 50 because I'd five and a half
years in the airforce and then I were self-employed and I'd a big family
and I couldn't do wi missin' workin' … but as soon as mi family were
growin' up a bit I took over … well it 'ad dropped yer see when Second
World War started, it dropped off yer see and when the war was finished
there were nobody right eager at gettin' it goin' again yer see."

AT: "Did it get most popular in the 30s?"

Sam: "When the Depression was on in 1921, that's when it were most popular,
when they'd no money and they 'ad to entertain themselves. There were
only little wireless sets and there were no television so they 'ad to make
their own 'obbies and that's one of the Lancashire 'obbies, but they didn't
play it any farther than Burnley … they 'ad to do somethin' to occupy their
minds."

AT: "When you had the big matches in the thirties were they on Saturdays?"

Sam: "Well it varied, sometimes on a Sunday. No it 'ud be in the 40s. There
were no really big matches in the 30s. It were when I took over that big
matches started to come along. People used to come like, yer know…. But
previous to that there weren't a right lot just a gang of 'em, yer know. One
gang played another gang, yer know."

The interview with Sam convinced me that further sources — key actors who had been playing long before he was involved, and who had first-hand knowledge of the scale of tipping activity — must be found, for their accounts to be lined up alongside Sam's.

Herbert Bateson

Herbert Bateson (interviewed 23 February 1981, two months or so after the interview with Sam Ansell) did not at all corroborate Sam's version of the post-Second World War phase in the game's history. After describing the inter-war game very much as Ernest Thornton had done, and with a more detailed version of the rhythms of practice, challenge and encounter (along the way, disputing Sam's seasonal analysis), Herbert related his role in the revival of the game in 1957. After an interlude in which there was no challenge between Good Friday 1943 and 1957, what became known as the "barrel of ale" match marked the game's re-emergence:

Herbert: "It were no good practisin' in winter, like this [AT — thick snow carpeted the Pennine ground during the interview], if nobody wanted to, if there were nothin' doin' like, yer waited until Spring when there were somethin' doing...."

Herbert recalled the entry of the 1970s champion Stuart Greenfield into the sport in 1957, and I asked him what role Sam had played in the revival:

Herbert: "Later that year we started one at Laneshawbridge. Now he knew there were a shortage of knurs so he 'ung one up in 'is winder — 'e owned a clogger's shop — and it said 'Wanted — these'. Well, 'e gorra big bagful and 'e tried to make money out of it, to cash in on t' knurs, an' 'e gradually got goin' but 'e couldn't do 'owt, only they let 'im in ... well, I let 'im referee wi mi a time or two and showed 'im all 'e knew about the job or else 'e didn't know anything about it ... an' 'e refereed in one or two jobs but 'e weren't fair, they wouldn't 'ave 'im at last one at all, they wouldn't tolerate 'im at all like. He'll do anything will Sam like, yer know, 'e don't just wave a bit to one side, 'e leans to one side like, if 'e's chance".

AT: "Why do you think he does that? Just 'cos he doesn't understand the game?"

Herbert (becoming increasingly agitated as if there had been a distraction):

"No, if there were two appearin' from Colne, and the others out o' Yorkshire, e'd favour Colners if 'e could. E'd give 'im a wrong ... 'e wouldn't pull tape tight enough or owt like, an then 'e did it glarin' like. He didn't just give 'em an advantage, 'e really showed 'imself up wi' t' job. They naturally learnt a bit about it, an' they eventually ran it themselves yer know. Sam, 'e used to go but 'e didn't run owt, 'e couldn't run a raffle couldn't Sam".

When the BBC's long-running Radio 4 feature *Down Your Way* had visited Colne, cricket commentator and broadcaster Brian Johnstone had interviewed Sam Ansell on knur-and-spell. Herbert's assessment on Sam's lack of significance in the annals of the game's history shows how selectively misleading the documentary radio archive might be; or is Herbert not to be trusted, his recollections warped by his envy of the Colne clogger's profile in the post-war phases of the sport's revival(s) ?

Everyday life is itself a cultural feat involving regular acts of interpretation, a lived and living hermeneutic[3] of the mundane (at the same time, nevertheless, a "depth hermeneutic" [Thompson, 1989]). But to the analyst all accounts are not equal. Both Sam's and Herbert's are products of a social relationship that has been established by the researcher, and that relationship involves researcher knowledge which, at certain points, I chose to reveal.

Sam's self-publicizing tendencies glossed some issues, and convinced me that some of his claims might well be disputed by some tipping cognoscenti. Here, I flattered Sam, and betrayed his trust. Was this unethical? Ernest Thornton had been my initial introduction to the knur-and spell-playing world of the earlier and mid-twentieth century. I was honest in my approaches to the people in that script, yet I felt guilty about my use of their stories and accounts, about the metamorphosis of personal interactionally-generated detail into reportable data. It would be naive in the extreme, though, to think that such sources can be used in uncomplicated and uncontroversial ways. As documents feed the appetite for more documents through which to build the fuller and confirmed picture, so with oral accounts and sources. And whatever the feeling of betrayal, it would be dishonest not to report the oral sources in the light of the interpretive work that has gone on in the mind and the ongoing analyses of the researcher. Not to run the risk of betraying or upsetting a source may be a sign of blandness; and when (playing tapes of or reading transcripts of one's dialogue with deceased subjects who sound like old friends) a feeling of guilt approaches, the researcher should recognise the act of cultural survival that is achieved by reporting real passions, authentically disputational cultures, and doing so by reporting the real names of the real people for whom such cultures were so important.

Ernest, Sam and Herbert do not need silly pseudonyms provided, and would probably have resented it if they were. At points in the research local Colne men would tell me: "yer different to t'others, yer really interested in t'game". Well, I certainly wasn't there for a media soundbite, and I was not slow to establish some credentials over a few pints of the local ale in the British Legion. But in many ways I wasn't so different; I knew that I would evaluate and selectively edit the accounts. I knew that this could lead to some respondents feeling misused or exploited. Perhaps I just had more time to reflect on the whole process, to contextualise the laikers' stories and to allow them to make sense alongside the ripples and waves of change in twentieth-century sport and leisure cultures in Britain.

Using oral sources: a checklist

Pragmatism rather than purist ethics is the guiding principle of this checklist, but the following points derive from the consideration of autobiographical, journalistic, sociological, and socio-historical sources:

- be honest to your subject on your motive, but do not hand over rights of veto;

- seek permission to tape accounts;

- do not try to replicate accounts, as pseudo-interviews, from subject to subject;

- do not mislead subjects on the outcome;

- co-produce accounts as dialogues;

- be ready to question the credibility of an account;

- recognise the qualitative research dynamic as a relationship.

And however much the researcher subscribes to the ethical principles of a research discipline, in the messy world of social research at least, the integrity of the project should be at the forefront of the researcher's consideration. The social researcher, despite an argot of methodological reflexivity behind which moral issues might be veiled, faces the same moral issues as the investigative reporter, the journalist or the broadcaster; to sense that the subject or respondent has been flattered and betrayed is to sensitively recognise the essence and strengths of oral sources, and to use them critically. Merely to reproduce an oral account, or to over-anonymise it, would be the greater betrayal, a betrayal of the very task of interpretation.

Notes

[1] As I, and other sociologists of sport, had the opportunity to do in November, 1994, when the North American Society for the Sociology of Sport held its annual conference in Savannah, at the Hyatt Regency, from which some of us ventured into the infinitely more interesting subcultures of bars with live pet snakes accompanying the punters, Lady Chablis look-alikes and embryonic auteurs of Savannah's continuing narrative. Thanks to all those in the Velvet Elvis Bar, Club One, 606, and the Korean Karaoke for such an open-minded welcome to those of us on the trail of Berendt's Savannah rather than Hollywood's or the local tourist board's.

The tourist trails were soon to wind their ways to Monterey Square, to the cemetery where Danny Hansford was buried, and to other sites featuring prominently in Berendt's book.

"Tragedy tours", as Ed Marriott reported it, were up and running in the Summer of 1995, with "true crime" enthusiasts "standing mouths agape" outside Jim Williams' infamous house (BBC Radio 4, 1995). The post-Berendt tourist trail now included chances to meet protagonists in 'Hard-Hearted Hannah's', with tour guides such as Lisa who recalled how Jim was "dressed like Marlene Dietrich", was quick to show off his legs, was gorgeous, with perhaps his only flaw the enjoyment of "the company of young men". Hammersley & Atkinson (aka Mandy) was hostess for the cemetery tour (transportation, naturally, via hearse) when Marriott visited. She was keen to catch the eye, or the ear, of any Warner Brothers executives (recently in town, planning the movie of the book of the murder, rumoured to have Tommy Lee Jones ['Jim'] and Brad Pitt ['Danny'] in mind for the main roles), and treated Marriott to a rousing version of a 'Hard-Hearted Hannah' chorus.

Interestingly, the 'tragedy tours' as reported by Marriott evoked little of the vibrant, hedonistic dynamics of Savannah's subterranean culture. Perhaps Lady Chablis was resisting, to some degree, commodification by the heritage industry.

2   There is no need, for the purposes of this article, to describe in detail the nature of the sport. But because knowledge of and accessibility to appropriate equipment was critical to the history of the sport, and feature in the accounts cited here, clarification of the basic terms is useful:

Knur — small round, hard ball, usually made of 'pot' and acquired from the factories of the Potteries in Stafford-shire.

Spell — contraption rather like a mini-gallows from which the knur is suspended by a 'tape'.

Stick — rather like a golf driver, with a head at the end which is used to strike the knur.

Two versions of the game predominated. In one, the winner was the player who made the longest single strike or hit (a 'long knock'). In the other, it was the player to cover a prescribed distance with the lowest total of strikes or hits.

3   'Hermeneutics' is the science of interpretation, and by the phrase "lived and living hermeneutic" I seek to convey the point that meanings in everyday life are not merely given: they are also made within processes of interpretation. On the pedigree of the term see Bleicher (1993).

Acknowledgements

I would like to thank the British Academy for supporting the fieldwork on the sport of knur-and-spell which is featured in this article; and the players in Colne who were so willing to talk to me.

Many thanks to John Sugden for redirecting me to some of our methodological mentors, and for discussions on our joint experience of Savannah; and to Graham McFee for reading through the draft of this piece as well as for many discussions on the ethics of the research dynamic.

References

Arlott, J. (ed) (1975) *The Oxford Companion to Sports and Games*. London: Oxford University Press.

BBC Radio 4 (1995) *The Afternoon Shift*, August 22: report by Ed Marriott.

BBC Television [North-East] (1978) *Wilf Mannion*. Written and produced by John Mappledeck.

Berendt, J. (1994) *Midnight in the Garden of Good and Evil — A Savannah story.* London: Chatto & Windus.

Bleicher, J. (1993) 'Hermeneutics', in Outhwaite, W and Bottomore, T. (eds) *The Blackwell Dictionary of Twentieth-century Social Thought.* Oxford: Blackwell, pp. 256-259.

Douglas, J. D. (1976) *Investigative social research: Individual and team social research.* London: Sage Publications.

Kelly, S. F. (ed) (1993) *A game of two halves.* London: Mandarin.

Lummis, T. (1987) *Listening to history: The authenticity of oral evidence.* London: Hutchinson.

Morrison, B. (1994) *And when did you last see your father?* London: Granta Books (in association with Penguin Books).

Morrison, B. (1995) Personal communication.

Polsky, N. (1971) *Hustlers, beats and others.* Harmondsworth: Penguin.

Thompson, J. B. (1989) *Ideology and modern culture.* Cambridge: Polity Press.

Thompson, P. (1988) *The voice of the past — oral history* [Second Edition]. Oxford: Oxford University Press.

Tomlinson, A. (1992) 'Shifting patterns of working-class leisure — the case of knur-and-spell', *Sociology of Sport Journal,* Vol. 9, No. 2: pp. 192–206.

Wood, J. (1994) 'A woman of letters' (interview with Janet Malcolm), *The Guardian Weekend,* October 15, pp. 34-42.

Yeo, E. and Yeo. S. [eds] (1981) *Popular culture and class conflict 1590–1914: Explorations in the history of labour and leisure.* Sussex: The Harvester Press.

Index

This is a selective index of themes and topics covered in the volume. It is not an exhaustive index of all the terms and themes that are featured in the text. The index is thematic and does not include the names of authors of work cited, except in a few instances where an author is covered as an important topic, rather than merely cited. Readers are referred to the **References** section at the end of each contribution for a guide to work cited in the volume. The Harvard style of referencing, for all its shortcomings and ambiguities, can then be used as a convenient means of locating the specific points of reference for particular authors.

A

abseiling 86
academic/intellectual freedom 112
access 184
   physical and data, ... 186
   to data and sources, ... 245
aesthetic discussions xvii
American Anthropological Association 178
American College of Sports Medicine 103
American Football players 20
anabolic steroids 43
anonymity for respondents, impossibility of 166, 218
applied sport psychology services 127
armed forces 31, 53
athletes
   lack of control, ... 10
   responsibility training, ... 12
   view of outsiders, ... 19
athletics, purpose of 57
attitudes 60, 64
audiences of sport, naive expectations of 12

B

Barcelona Olympics, cycling team coach at 40
BBC Television Horizon programme "Bitter Cold" .... 111 *passim*
behavioural approach in describing moral judgements, weaknesses of 59-60
behaviour of athletes, morality of 6
behaviour, in sports
   instrumental, ... 35
   expressive, ... 35
behaviour in response to dilemmas in sport, three types of 66
Belfast 230
Berendt, J., author of *Midnight in the Garden of Good and Evil* 249-252

betrayal

in qualitative research relationships 245*passim*

in interpretation 260

blood-doping 46

Boardman, C., cyclist 38

British Academy 256

British Amateur Athletic Federation 55

British Association for Sport and Exercise Sciences (BASES, formerly,

British Association for Sport Sciences [BASS]) 37, 96, 101, 128, 133

British Educational Research Association (BERA) 178

British Institute of Sports Coaching (BISC) 37, 38

British Legion 261

British Lions Rugby Team, in New Zealand in 1971 60

British Olympic Association 133

British Sociological Association, its guidelines for

researchers 152, 154-157

Burnley Football Club 248

C

cardiac death in athletes 103

certification/accreditation of sport psychologists 129, 130

Chicago School, of urban sociology 227

children in sport, see *"young people in sport"*

Chinese women runners 44

coach

as humanist, ... 39

romantic view of, ... 39

coaching

autocratic style of, ... 53

as cooperation, education, facilitation, ... 47

as interactive method, ... 53

as partnership/cooperation, ... 51

as pragmatism, not science, ... 38

inappropriateness of autocratic style of, ...·.............. 48

poor coaching, consequences of 54

code of conduct, of BASES physiology section 108-110

code of ethics, for ethnography 145

code of practice for investigators 96, 128, 210

college athletes, their valuing of competence values 65

Colne, Lancashire town 256-258

commercialization 13

competitive sport, inherently self-interested nature of 57

compromise in research, between purist ethics and

pragmatic judgement 169-170

confidentiality 96, 100, 101, 110, 218

conflict creation, from findings of insider-researcher 192
conformity, as expressed value in young people's sport 68
continuum of sport and athletic commitment.. 58
contracts, lack of in coach-athlete relationship 43
corruption, in the administration of dope-control 44
counselling psychology technique 128
counselling style 129, 130
covert investigation/methods 121
covert role of researcher...151, 153, 163, 176, 182
crisis intervention and referral 127
Cuba... 231, 237

D

Danto, A. .... xviii, xxi
Data, dissemination of 214
Data Protection Act 215
data protection and publication 110
deception
    in teaching, ... 88
    in the field, ... 147
    in research of covert kind, ... 155-156, 163, 178
deductive science 39
democratic relations with subjects 217
dependency in sport 18
developmental age, sensitivities of physiological testing 104
deviance in sport
    cricket as example of,.. 26
    delinquency among high-school students,.. 10
    explanatory models, ... 4
    off-the-field, ... 10
    over-conformity to sports ethic's contribution to, ... 14
    positive nature of,.. 17
    sport organizations' contribution to,... 33
deviant behaviour.. 25
    three types of, ... 26
deviant behaviour, types of 27
    male prominence in, ... 27
Dinka, tribe in Sudan 225
Down Your Way, BBC Radio programme 260

E

East German sports, sports science support for 43, 48
East Europe, sports system of 30, 49, 51, 101
eating disorders 99
economic system, effects on sport 4

educative code, for research morality 179
empathy, with subjects 242
enjoyment, as expressed value in young people's sport 68
environmental issues, in outdoor education 89-90
environmental physiology 111
erosion of values in sport 4
essentialist views of sport as character building 5
ethics
    ethical basis for sport behaviour, ... 56
    ethical issues, practitioner challenges, ... 90
    ethical issues, practical value for teachers, ... 79
    ethical issues, in dangerous research settings, ... 231
    ethical judgements, objectivity and nature of, ... xvii
    ethical/moral tools, individual formulation of, ... 45
    ethical objectivism, ... 82
    ethical practices, ... 118
    ethical questions as moral questions, ... xviii
    ethical questions, abstract, ... xiv
    ethical questions, analytical 56
    ethical questions, descriptive, ... xvi, 56
    ethical questions, normative, ... 56
    ethical questions, philosophical approaches to, ... 81
    ethical subjectivism, ... 82
ethics, consequentialist and non-consequentialist theories of 82-83
ethics, human experimental issues, ... 115
ethics, pragmatism in research, ... 196
ethics, professional conduct codes and, ... 203
ethics, sport-related research and, ... xx
ethnographically-rooted fieldwork 163
ethnographic research 137
ethnography, and subterranean aspects of life 229
ethos of sport 33
Evans-Pritchard, E. 224, 228, 240

F

fair play .... xvi, xvii, 11, 57, 60, 64, 69, 70
familiarity, in research relation 185
fear, need to overcome it in ethnography 230
feminist research 158, 169
field testing, at athlete's venue 97-99
figure skaters 20
flattery, in qualitative research relationship 245
functionalism, and deviance 28

G

gatekeepers, in research process and
relationship 138, 194, 208, 218
Giddens, A. 227-228, 242
guidelines for good practice in qualitative research, limits of 146
guilt in the dynamic of the research relationship 261
guilty knowledge.. 144

H

Hartford, Connecticut 227, 230
Hawthorne effect.. 152
health and fitness, as.expressed value in young people's sport........................... 68
Hendry, S., snooker player 57
hermeneutics 228, 260
Hite report, questionnaires used in... 212-213

I

identity,
of athletes 17
of subjects, the concealing of 215
true athlete's identity and feelings 19
informants 213
informed consent......................... 80, 86-88, 96, 100, 109, 111*passim*, 164, 206-208
INLA (Irish National Liberation Army) 235
insider identity, stages of... 183
insider research .... 181 *passim*
advantages of,... 184-187
constraints of, ... 187-192
four types of, ... 181
integrity of investigative project 247, 261
integrity, impossibility of as both researcher and friend 194
interaction between individual and sport/societal
structures, in physiology... 105
International Olympic Committee (IOC) 6, 41
interviews.. 157
as intrusive technique 205
intrusion 166, 211
invasion of privacy... 212
see too "intrusion" and "privacy"
investigative sociology 245
IRA (Irish Republican Army)... 234, 235, 236
isolation, in insider research role 190

J

journalism
attraction to clinical/scientific view of coaching, ... 38, 39

moral indefensibility of, ... 247
tabloids' invasion of privacy, ... 112
researcher-journalist dual role, complexity of, ... 168
Johnson, B., Olympic sprinter 55, 101
Johnstone, B., broadcaster 260

K
Kerrigan, N., ice-skater 20
knur-and-spell 246, 256, 260-263

L
labelling theory 29
laikers (knur-and-spell players) 256
leisure, study of through oral sources 254-255
Lyme Bay, tragic accident at 83, 124

M
manipulation, of group in insider research 192
Mannion, W., footballer 253-254
Market Research Society 204
Marx, K. 155, 228
McManus, M., wrestler 174
media (see, too, "Journalism")
  hero-building in sport, ... 7
  hype on spectator expectation, ... 13
  private life of athlete, and media, ... 7
Milgram, S. 179
men, and their power/influence in sport 3
men, as hypocrites 33
moral dilemmas in the research setting
  of women interviewing women, ... 158
  lack of moral obligation of researcher 153
moralising, its necessity to the researcher in some
  circumstances 155
morals and sport
  moral behaviour in children's sport, ... 55
  moral corruption of sport, agencies' collusion in, ... 30
  moral decisions in sport, behavioural and cognitive
    perspectives of, ... 58
  moral evaluation and basis of sport, ... xix
  moral problems faced by competitive athletes
    and youngsters, ... 72
  moral state of sport today, views of, ... 21
Morrison, B., author of *When Did You Last See Your Father?* 247-249
Mountain Leadership training 87

N

National Coaching Foundation 37
negotiation of results, in insider research 190-192
nicknames and jokes, at expense of researcher 143
norms, in social life 27
Nuremberg Code 112, 179, 206-207

O

obligation to continue, of subject within experimental process 116
Obree, G,. cyclist 39
observation, of wrestling 173
Official Secrets Act 124
Olympic motto 14
opening up, of informants 141
open methods of research 204
oral historical method 246, 254-256
oral sources
    authenticity of, ... 255
    checklist, ... 261
order in sport, its threatened disintegration 35
outdoor centres 83
outdoor education
    areas of learning in, ... 84
    objectives in, ... 79
    rapidity and gravity of decisions in, ... 80
    risk-benefit questions in, ... 80
ownership of data 191

P

Pallo, J., wrestler 174
participant observation
    advantages of, ... 151
    complete participant role, ... 164
    difficulties of, ... 138
    effect on others, ... 139
    expected behaviours in, ... 167
    managing marginality in, ... 229
participation in sports
    access, ... 8
    disruptive nature of, ... 16
    personal pleasure in, ... 71
Pendle Country 248
perils, ethical and physical, in ethnographic fieldwork 223*passim*
performance-enhancing drugs .... xviii, 14, 20, 43, 45

Physical Education Association 105
physical education, response of young people to 137
physiological assessment/exercise testing 95*passim*
physiological intervention.. 41
placebo and placebo effect in research................................. 44, 120, 164
poor man's golf, see "knur-and-spell"
practical ethics 80. 195
precision of measurement, in laboratory 97
premature saturation, in insider research 189
prisons.. 31, 53
privacy, of subjects 166, 173*passim*, 210-213
private face of researcher 144
professional relationships.. 109
psychological skills, and the organisation of athletic performance...... 127
psychotherapy 129
public right to know 217
pupils, as critical consumers 214

Q

Quaker meetings 184
questionnaires
    deceitfulness of,... 206
    ethical principles of, ... 156
    intrusive nature of, ... 205

R

race, as sensitive issue... 211
racism in sport... 3
radical criminology 30
real life, unpredictable flow of 229
repugnant views of interviewee 159
research environment, uncontrollability of 241
research relationship 245
responsibility, of researcher to theory 155
reward structure in professional sport, consequences of.................... 35
rhetoric, of sacrifice in sport 42
rights of subjects 112, 122
risk
    ethnographic research, risks to researched, ... 145
    ethnographic research, risks to researcher, ... 241
    exercise testing, risks in, ... 101
    pain in sport, as norm guideline, ... 15
    subjective-objective nature of, ... 85
rituals, in society and sport 32-33, 35
rock climbing 86

role-conflict, in ethnographic research... 137
role-identity of insider researcher 189
Royal Ulster Constabulary (RUC) 236
rules
    contravention of, ... xix
    ethnography, rules of, ... 242-243
    proliferation of by sports policy makers,.. 6
    rule-breaking in sport, ... 5
    social life, rules in, ... 27

S

Savannah... 246, 249-252
SCUBA and saturation diving research 111
secrecy, as withholding of information in outdoor education 89
sexual harassment and sport, problems in
    researching it 151*passim*
sexual intercourse, as topic for questionnaire research 209
shame, lack of in sports practice 32
showing skills, as expressed value in young people's sport................................... 68
situational research ethic.. 178
smoking at school, as researcher knowledge 144
social control.. 31
social distance between researcher and researched... 141
socialisation 31
social order... 25
Social Research Association 210
spirit of the game 34
sport activity holidays 124
sport(s)
    corruption of,.. 18
    lack of understanding of human performance in, ... 39
    moral and ethical purity of, ... 3
    racism and sexism in, ... 3, 7, 8
    social organization and normative structure of,.. 21
    sponsors of, ... 8
    thrilling and exhilarating nature of, ... 17
sport ethic
    discomfort of and hurt in,.. 52
    moral guidelines of, 14 *passim*
    openness of possibility in, ... 15
sportsmanship
    and motivational priorities, ...58, 70, 71
    and cognitive representations, ... 60
    as expressed value in young people's sport, ... 68

softening-up techniques, as insidious strategy 216
sport psychologist as therapist rather than scientist 40
sport psychologist, need to adopt flexible style 133
sports science and technology, need for new norms from 22
sports scientist
    as technician, ... 37
    awareness of boundaries of competence, ... 99
    duty to fulfil legal demands, ... 104
stage theories, their determinist view of moral judgements 70
status, in windsurfing culture 165
subjective risk, novice's high experience of 86
subjects
    effects of experimentation on, ... 120
    told half-truths, to satisfy researcher's moral obligation, ... 165
    use of students as, ... 119
    right to be informed, ... 195
    right to refuse, ... 209
Sudan 224-226

T
teacher-pupil relation, in ethnographic research 140
tension, in research setting 147
tension, extreme states of in sport 31
time allocation, underlying principles for sport psychologist
    egalitarianism, ... 132
    investment, ... 132
    "means test", ... 131
    winning, ... 131
tipping, see "knur-and-spell"
tolerance, as expressed value in young people's sport 68
Tottenham Hotspur 248
trading of private information 216
trust, of motives 186
trust, regarding the researcher relationship and the nature
    of sources 246
trust, regarding the researcher/researched 117, 218
trust, betrayal of in research relationship 140, 156, 246, 260, 261
trusting relationship between athlete and consultant 129
Turf Moor, ground of Burnley Football Club 248
Tupumaros, Uruguayan urban guerrilla movement 223

U
United States Olympic Training Centre (USOC) 6

V

values 64
   attitudes, behaviour and values, model of relationships
     between, ... 63
   domains, and motivational types in children's sport, ... 72
   expressed values, from young football/tennis players, ... 67
   model of structural relationships among motivational
     types of, ... 62
   recognition of validity of, ... 178
   Schwarz's five characteristics of, ... 61
   structure of values, sustaining independent
     participation in sport, ... 69
   values in society, ... 27
   values in sport, ... 61
   Victorian values, ... 34
voyeur, perceived identity of in covert observation 176

W

White, J., snooker player 57
windsurfing and surfing subcultures 163
winning, as expressed value in young people's sport 68
withdrawal, terms of for sports coach 42
women in sport
   empowerment of windsurfers, ... 168
   females more conventional than men, ... 34
   females more cooperative than men for coach, ... 49
wrestling
   amateurist/domesticated nature of, ... 176
   ambiguity of, ... 177
   spectatorship of, ... 178

Y

young people
   high risk area for researchers, ... 218
   as informants on others, ... 213
young people in sport
   children and coaching, 47
   cycling/gymnastics, 48
   formalised physical education and, ... 137
   investment for future, 132
   socialisation into sport, 31